THE

RED THREAD
ACADEMY

SCHOOL OF AMERICAN FOLKLORIC
WITCHCRAFT

YEAR 3: MASTERY

Course Manual

THE

RED THREAD ACADEMY

SCHOOL OF AMERICAN FOLKLORIC
WITCHCRAFT

YEAR 3: MASTERY

Course Manual

Laurelei Black

ASTERIA BOOKS

Red Thread Academy Year 3: Mastery Course Manual
By Laurelei Black
Cover Design by Laurelei Black

ISBN-13: 978-1-956765-07-6 (digital/e-book)

ISBN-13: 978-1-956765-06-9 (paperback)

ISBN-13: 978-1-956765-12-0 (hardback)

"I am the womb: of every holt,
I am the blaze: on every hill,
I am the queen: of every hive,
I am the shield: for every head,
I am the tomb: of every hope."

from "The Song of Amergin" translated
by Robert Graves in *The White Goddess*

For YOU.

Thank you.

Table of Contents

The Study Guide

Unit 1: Explore the Mysteries of the Craft and lay the foundation for further exploration.

Unit 2: Perform Witch Flight safely and regularly.

Unit 3: Create experiences to honor the Sabbats in a ritual setting.

Unit 4: Understand the process of Blasting and have a personal understanding of when and how to use it.

Unit 5: Honor the Spirits/Deities of your personal Covenant(s) through developing an understanding of their needs, preferences & lore.

Unit 6: Develop an understanding of some ministerial aspects of being a Queen/Devil within the Craft.

Unit 7: Create a plan for managing a coven.

Unit 8: Make preparations for teaching the Craft to others.

Unit 9: Gather or make the remaining altar and personal tools.

Unit 10: Understand the role, uses, and advised precautions within SCT for performing sex magick.

Unit 11: Be knowledgeable in Craft lore and history.

Unit 12: Prepare for 3rd Level Self-Initiation.

Table of Contents, pt 2

Coven Leadership

CCS Guidance (Norms & Expectations, Leadership, Schedule & Membership)
SCT Titles and Offices
Subrosa
Laurelei's Lineage Letter

Regalia and Gifts

SCT Regalia & Gifts   Garter
Cords   Crown
Jewels   Robe, Cloak & Hood
Amber and Jet and Bone

Practical Craft

Entheogens in Witchcraft
Sabbat Wine
Non-Tox Flying Ointment

Tools

SCT Personal & Coven Tools List   Glass Orb
Skull & Bones   Stone Bowl
Sword   Golden Lantern
Helm & Mask   Silver Cup
Staff   Broom
Shield   The Gandreid

Mysteries

Energy & Using Power

3rd Degree Self-Initiation

How to Use The Course Guide

This course is designed to follow the Red Thread Academy's second year course (Practicum). If you completed all of the course work, reached a level of proficiency with the concepts and skills introduced there, and underwent the 2nd Degree Self-Initiation, you are ready for the challenges and deepening of the Work that awaits you here in Year 3.

This is the final level of study required within the Spiral Castle Tradition before a Witch of our Family is considered trained and qualified to lead their own Coven. Please note two points (both of which will be covered in more depth later in this section):

1) No requirement is laid upon 3rd Degree SCT Witches to "hive off" and start a Coven. If that is not your calling, you are supported to pursue those callings that are yours.
2) SCT Witches who plan to establish a SCT Coven need to receive a Charter, which is available after the conclusion of the 3rd Degree initiation.

Checklist

I've included a checklist that notates all of the lessons and their corresponding assignments. You can find it at the beginning of these materials, before the actual lessons start. I offer this to you as a tool for your personal tracking and accountability of your own work.

Order of the Lessons

There is a sheet (located just behind the checklist) that provides a rough schedule for students to use, if they are so inclined. This schedule is only a suggestion, and it is open to lots of wiggle room. In fact, this year's units are more self-contained than previous years. You can probably tackle whole units without needed to jump around to other lessons to get the needed background. By this stage, you already have most of the background you need!

As in the previous two courses, you might need to tweak the schedule a little, depending on when you launch this course for yourself. The only lessons that should be done exactly where they are indicated in the schedule are the last three (Planning for the Future, Final Exam, and Initiation).

Everything else is very negotiable. If you want to do all four book analyses in the same month, do it. Go for it! I spread them out to make it a little easier on you, but you are the ultimate arbiter of what makes sense in your life and your practice.

Planning Ahead
Some assignments are not conquerable in a single week. These include the 4 book analyses you will write, the collection/creation of tools, and possibly others.

In order to best address these more involved assignments, I recommend taking some time here at the beginning of this course to familiarize yourself with the work ahead and make your own plan for addressing these projects.

The Nature of THE WORK
Now more than ever, I will be acting in the role of the "Guide on the Side" instead of the "Sage on the Stage," as your teacher and mentor. This "year's" work is deeply practical in some ways, and notably esoteric in others — all toward the goal of bringing you to a place of independence and true mastery.

This course will only reward you in a way that is proportionate to the effort you give it. It requires that you THINK. It demands that you DO. It relies on you to REFLECT.

Sensitivity, Privacy, and "Redacted" Assignments
This year's work can be of a highly personal, intimate, and sensitive nature. When you are writing the reflections for this year, please explore the concepts as fully as possible, for your own benefit. If you are sharing assignments with an RTA Mentor, we will understand if you redact — basically, delete or mark through — areas that you are not comfortable sharing. Contact me or your Mentor about that, if you have concerns or other questions.

Sharing Assignments
The work continues to be for your benefit, not mine. I do not require anyone to share their work with me personally or with their peers. However, you probably know by now that I see value in making those opportunities available.

If you want to be initiated within the Spiral Castle Tradition, as part of my lineage (which can only happen via in-person initiation), then I need to see your work and we need to build a connection. The same is true if you want to Charter an SCT Coven. (Note: You can apply for a Charter even without the in-person initiation. Please see the application in the Appendix for more details.)

Scoring of Assignments
The scoring of assignments is carried out along the same rubric as in previous years and only applies to Red Thread Academy students who are sharing assignments for me to see. But I thought it would be helpful for everyone to know the scoring rubric, for visibility.

There are only 3 scores for all assignments in this course:

Mastery (3) = The work covers a depth or breadth beyond the requirement, shows great insight, is reflective of profound talent or skill, or is in some other way remarkable. This is the rarest of scores, reserved for work that wows me.

Proficiency (2) = The work meets the requirements, shows solid progression toward lesson objectives, is complete and has no major flaws. There may still be some areas of the work that could use some polishing or deeper thought, but it is understood that this will come in time. This is the most common passing score.

Developing (1) = The work does not meet the requirements, shows some confusion or misunderstanding, isn't complete, or needs to be reapproached. This is the only non-passing score. Use the feedback provided to try again.

You will ultimately achieve Mastery (3) or Proficiency (2) in every lesson. If you get a Developing (1) score on any assignment, you will need to finish/redo it until you have reached Proficiency (2).

Supplies and Materials

To get started in Year 3, you just need the Course Guide (this book), the tools you made and gathered in the Foundations and Practicum courses, and the skills you have been building. You're ready to start!

There will be other materials, tools, and supplies that you will buy as you work through the course. Each lesson provides a list of needed or suggested materials. As you plan ahead, you might take note of what you will need in the future. There are books, altar/personal tools, and other projects that will require that you make or buy some supplies.

Additional Resources

There are **Book of Shadows pages** included within this Course Guide. They are taken from the growing library of pages I make available in my Etsy shop. They are here for you to print and use within your own BoS, and they are intended as supplemental reading materials for your studies; but you may not reproduce them for others — no, not even for members of your Coven. (They are all available for sale in the shop, if you would like to recommend them to friends.)

I have plans to create more **YouTube videos** to act as supplemental resources (there are a few already). As those are posted, they will be available on the RedThreadAcademy channel. Check there (and favorite it) for updates. (They will also be accessible in The Thread app — which is free.)

The **BladeAndBroom channel on YouTube** also has lots of videos that can act as resources. You'll see where I link to a few of those videos in this Course Guide, but a lot of the material there can be a great supplement to what you are studying here.

The **blog entries** at http://afwcraft.blogspot.com were all created by me and my ex-wife, "Glaux." We are the founders of American Folkloric Witchcraft and the first (to my knowledge) to use that term. All of the work there is foundational material for this course. It is an archive now.

New content for the **Spiral Castle Tradition** (which is now the oldest and one of several expressions of American Folkloric Witchcraft) is being posted at http://spiralcastletrad.wordpress.com. (Initiated Witches of the Spiral Castle are encouraged to contribute their insights and experiences to this blog.)

Private coaching with me is also a resource available to you. This would involve a monthly Zoom (or other VOIP) session in which we talk about your studies, your challenges, your goals, etc. Psychic readings can be part of these sessions, if you like, to help shed light on situations/questions. This is a great way to deepen your studies and to connect with me as your mentor, but you can also utilize our coaching sessions to work on goals unrelated to your Witchcraft studies. Coaching is 100% optional, of course. You can find more details at the end of the Course Guide.

The **Amazon links for books** and other tools at the back of this book are made available via affiliate links. I won't have my feelings hurt if you don't use the affiliate links, but using them helps me a little and doesn't hurt you, if you're buying the book/tool/product anyway. (I do like to be up-front about it, though.)

Final Exam, Initiation, and Certificate

The final exam and self-initiation for 3rd Degree are both included as part of the course materials. Sure, you can skip to the end and read the ritual, but Knowledge is not the same as Understanding. And Understanding is not the same as Wisdom. Engage sincerely with the Work and the Rite, and it will have the impact it is meant to have. I trust that.

For 3rd Degree, in-person initiation is available, as an alternative to the Self-Initiation contained in this book. (Please don't do both.) You can schedule a weekend-long initiation experience with me for the culmination of the entire program -- but only if I've had the opportunity to see your work and get to know you during (most of) Years 1-3. This is a different ritual than the one provided as self-initiation. It would be undertaken in a cabin in either Southern Indiana or Central Kentucky with a small but trusted team. Information about this option is available at the back of this book. Reach out to me AFTER you have read that info.)

At the end of the course, if you're interested in receiving a certificate to commemorate your achievement, please write to me at the address below. I'll ask a small task of you (sending me a couple of specific assignments) if you haven't been my private student throughout your studies, but I would love to honor your hard work!

What Comes Next?

You are under no obligation to form a Coven after you have completed this course. You will have laid the groundwork to teach others and to act in the capacity of a Coven leader, but some students will inherently feel more drawn to serving as a "Master Healer" or "Master Seer" (etc) — either within the local community or in a Coven established by another Spiral Castle Witch. These are choices for you to make individually.

As I have reminded you in every course manual, this program of study has been designed to bring you to a place of adeptness. What you do with your skill and power are your choices to make.

Foundations -- akin to a Bachelor's Degree in Witchcraft. You have studied hard, sharpened your critical thinking skills, practiced and perfected the Craft basics, and you are fully qualified to practice your Craft. You have entered the Gates. You are an initiated Witch!

Practicum -- akin to a Master's Degree in a specific area of Witchcraft. You have dedicated yourself to a particular skill set and have honed your understanding and ability within that area. You have continued to deepen your practice of the Craft, and are proficient enough to serve in the ways you have been called. You have been to the Castles. You are a Healer (or Seer, or Artisan, or Warden, or Bard, Conjurer, or a Votary)!

Mastery -- akin to a Doctorate Degree in Witchcraft. You have learned just about everything you can learn from another person, and you are devoted to learning directly from the Godds and Spirits after this point. You are open to the Mysteries of the Craft and have spent some time pondering those things that can't be spoken. You are ordained to initiate others into the Craft. You travel all the Realms. You are a Queen/Devil!

How far you go with your studies is entirely in your own hands. There is no "must" in this choice. There will be no pressure from me. I will fully support you in your choice, whatever you decide.

Weekend Retreat & Initiation Ritual (optional)

For your final initiation within the Spiral Castle Tradition, you have the option to undergo initiation in-person with Laurelei. This is designed as a weekend-long, retreat-style experience. More details about this option are located in the Appendix of this book (after the BoS pages).

Coven Charter

Any RTA student who wishes to form their own Coven within the Spiral Castle Tradition must submit a portfolio of their work for review in order to receive an official Charter. If you have already been submitting your work for review throughout the first two courses, then you can simply continue the same process throughout the Mastery Course. If, however, you haven't submitted your work prior to this point (AND you wish to form an SCT Coven), you will need to follow the instructions (found in the Appendix, after the BoS pages) in order to create a portfolio that will accompany your application. The application packet can be submitted after your 3rd Degree Initiation.

Student Discounts at Blade & Broom

Blade & Broom is a two-pronged online shop run by Laurelei. The Etsy shop houses all of our digital and physical products (like Book of Shadows pages, course guides, witchy novels, etc.). The independent shop at www.bladeandbroom.com features readings, coaching, and other ritual services. It also offers product and book recommendations through affiliate links.

As a student of mine, you can use the code RTASTUDENT25 for 25% products and services in both shops.

Blade & Broom on Etsy -- www.bladeandbroom.etsy.com -- physical & digital products

Blade & Broom website -- www.bladeandbroom.com -- psychic & spiritual services

The Thread App

You can access the app by scanning the following QR code, or by going to thethread1.goodbarber.app. Android users can choose to download from the Play Store. If you're using an iPhone or connecting from a PC, get the web app. BOTH have the same great features — videos, audios (meditations), blog content, all the lessons, pics, shared work from other students, comments, and chat.

NOTE: Once you've created a user account, contact me (through Chat or Contact in the app) so I can unlock the Year 1 sections for you! This doesn't happen automatically, since some app users will be enrolled in other courses.

Questions

If you have questions related to the course-work (or the resources/discounts mentioned above) that can't be answered with the Course Guide alone, please email me at laurelei@asteriabooks.com — or via Chat in The Thread!

Year 3: Mastery
Student Progress Checklist

		Before beginning, the student should have completed the Self-Initiation Ritual at the end of Year 2: Practicum.			
Unit	Objective	Lesson	Assignments/Projects	Completion Date	Score
1	Explore the Mysteries of the Craft and lay the foundation for further exploration.				
		Seeking the Mysteries	Reflection		
		Clan of Tubal Cain & 1734	Reflection		
		Mythopoesis, Folklore & Balladry	Reflection		
		A Few of Our SCT Waypoints	Reflection		
2	Perform Witch flight safely and regularly.				
		Witch flight	Flight Log — 3 flights		
		Meeting at the Sabbat	Description of "Dancing Place"		
		Writing/Leading Hedge Crossings	Write 1 guided meditation		
		Gandreid	Reflection		
3	Create experiences to honor the Sabbats in a ritual setting.				
		Samhain	Write/perform ritual/hedge-cross		
		Yule	Write/perform ritual/hedge-cross		
		Imbolc	Write/perform ritual/hedge-cross		
		Spring Equinox	Write/perform ritual/hedge-cross		
		Beltaine	Write/perform ritual/hedge-cross		
		Midsummer	Write/perform ritual/hedge-cross		
		Lammas	Write/perform ritual/hedge-cross		
		Fall Equinox	Write/perform ritual/hedge-cross		
4	Understand the process of Blasting and have a personal understanding of when to use it.				
		Ethics, Revisited	Revisit personal ethics statement		
		Cautions	Reflection		
		Banishing	Banish spell (perform if needed)		
		Hexing & Cursing	Curse spell (perform if needed)		

Year 3: Mastery

Student Progress Checklist, cont.

5	Honor the Spirits/Deities of your personal Covenant(s) through developing an understanding of their needs, preferences & lore				
		Historical research	Historical worship/work essay		
		Associations & Areas of Influence	Associations/Influence essay		
		Personal Relationship	Personal work with Deity essay		
		Representing Deity	Teaching, ministering, etc. essay		
6	Develop an understanding of some ministerial aspects of being a Queen/Devil within the Craft.				
		Rites of Passage	Questions		
		Pastoral Care	Questions		
		Weddings & Ordination	Planning worksheet		
		Children	Questions		
7	Create a plan for managing a coven.				
		Roles & Rules	Draft of Group Norms		
		Meeting Structures & Schedules	Draft of Proposed Schedule		
		Interpersonal Dynamics	Reflection		
		Puppy Papers, Lineage & "Authority"	Create your lineage letter; reflection		
8	Make preparations for teaching the Craft to others.				
		Study Group & Chartered Coven	Reflection		
		Mentorship	Reflection		
		Initiations	Reflection		
		Secrecy, Ethics, Mysteries	Reflection		

9		Gather or make the remaining altar and personal tools.			
		Skull & Bones	Reflection and pics		
		Weapons & Treasures	Reflection and pics		
		Dolly	Reflection and pics		
		7 Circles of Personal Power (Cords, Garter, Necklace, Ring, Bracelet)	Reflection and pics		
10		Understand the role, uses, and advised precautions within SCT for performing sex magick.			
		Consent Culture in SCT	Reflection		
		Sex Magick in Trad Craft	Reflection		
		Spirit Spouse/Lover	Reflection		
		Hieros Gamos	Reflection		
11		Be knowledgeable in Craft lore and history.			
		Craft Mysteries reading list	Book analysis of one title		
		Coven Leadership reading list	Book analysis of one title		
		Historical/Anthropological reading list	Book analysis of one title		
		Ministerial reading list	Book analysis of one title		
12		Prepare for 3rd Level Self-Initiation.			
		Planning for the future	Answer planning questions		
		Final Exam	Complete final exam		
		Self-Initiation Ritual ~OR~ In-Person Lineaged Initiation Ritual	Essay following Initiation		

Suggested Weekly Lesson Progression

Wk	Lesson Topic	Unit/Section	Lesson #
1	Seeking the Mysteries	Mysteries	01-01
2	Clan of Tubal Cain & 1734 Mysteries	Mysteries	01-02
3	Witch Flight	Witch Flight	02-01
4	Sabbat	Sabbats	03-0*
5	Meeting at the Sabbat	Witch Flight	02-02
6	Historical Research	Godd/Spirit Work	05-01
7	Mythopoesis, Balladry & Folklore	Mysteries	01-03
8	A Few SCT Waypoints	Mysteries	01-04
9	Writing/Leading Hedge-Crossings	Witch Flight	02-03
10	Sabbat	Sabbats	03-0*
11	Gandreid	Witch Flight	02-04
12	Craft Mysteries reading list	History and Lore	11-01
13	Ethics, Revisited	Blasting Magick	04-01
14	Cautions	Blasting Magick	04-02
15	Associations & Areas of Influence	Godd/Spirit Work	05-02
16	Sabbat	Sabbats	03-0*
17	Banishing	Blasting Magick	04-03
18	Hexing & Cursing	Blasting Magick	04-04
19	Personal Relationship w/Spirit/Deity	Godd/Spirit Work	05-03
20	Representing Deity/Spirit	Godd/Spirit Work	05-04
21	Rites of Passage	Ministerial Work	06-01
22	Sabbat	Sabbats	03-0*
23	Pastoral Care	Ministerial Work	06-02
24	Weddings & Ordination	Ministerial Work	06-03
25	Children	Ministerial Work	06-04
26	Roles & Rules	Coven Management	07-01
27	Skull & Bones	Tools	09-01
28	Sabbat	Sabbats	03-0*
29	Meeting Structures & Schedules	Coven Management	07-02
30	Coven Leadership reading list	History and Lore	11-02
31	Interpersonal Dynamics	Coven Management	07-03
32	Puppy Papers, Lineage & "Authority"	Coven Management	07-04
33	Study Group & Chartered Coven	Teaching the Craft	08-01
34	Sabbat	Sabbats	03-0*

35	Weapons & Treasures	Tools	09-02
36	Mentorship	Teaching the Craft	08-02
37	Initiations	Teaching the Craft	08-03
38	Historical/Anthropological reading list	History and Lore	11-03
39	Dolly	Tools	09-03
40	Sabbat	Sabbats	03-0*
41	Secrecy, Ethics, Mysteries	Teaching the Craft	08-04
42	Consent Culture in SCT	Sex Magick	10-01
43	Sex Magick in Trad Craft	Sex Magick	10-02
44	5 Circles of Personal Power	Tools	09-04
42	Spirit Spouse/Lover	Sex Magick	10-03
46	Sabbat	Sabbats	03-0*
47	Hieros Gamos	Sex Magick	10-04
48	Ministerial reading list	History and Lore	1104
49	Planning for the Future	Initiation Prep	12-01
50	Final Exam	Initiation Prep	12-02
51	1st Level Self-Initiation Ritual	Initiation Prep	12-03

Seeking the Mysteries

<u>Prerequisite Lesson</u>   None specified

<u>Objective</u>

To discuss the nature of the Mysteries

To establish SCT as a "Mystery School"

To propose methods and techniques for approaching the Mysteries

---

<u>Materials Needed</u>   Journaling materials

<u>Study Notes</u>

I would describe the Spiral Castle Tradition of Witchcraft, at its core, as a Mystery School. Our purpose is to uncover the Truth of our own nature and to gain gnosis regarding those ineffable Truths to which we are witness in the Universe.

Our Mystery School is built upon the folk magick and folk ways of our forebears, and so to the casual observer, it might look very "Pagan" (in the sense of being rustic, agricultural, or tied to earthly cycles of fertility and fallowness). Indeed, those elements of our practice are present and undeniable. We celebrate the turn of the seasons. We practice laying charms and enchantments.

But running throughout all we do is the Red Thread of fire and blood — of enlightenment, power, life, and death. It is always with us, and we are always spiraling through the layers of meaning and magick to come face to face with ourselves as both the Sacred One and Profane Seeker in the heart of the shrine.

Oral Traditions and Secret Rituals

There's a very good reason that the Mysteries are not generally spoken. Good reason as to why they are shared through storytelling and initiatory rituals.

The reason is: It can be very tricky to put into adequate prosaic words the Truth that is cloaked in the Mysteries. Such straightforward language often falls far short of the poetic, symbolic, and experiential methods of transmitting the Mysteries that are typically employed within initiations — or the symbol-rich experiences of visionary work.

Think of it this way: when you awaken from a profound and moving dream, and you try to share it with a friend or family member, words often fail to convey what you actually found impactful. The person listening to your dream-story almost never "gets it." And it's not just a failing of your word choice that is to blame. They weren't there, immersed in the sensations, symbols, ambience, etc. They weren't primed to have the experience/understanding you are trying to describe for them.

It is the same with the Mysteries. You can do your best to describe the powerful piece of wisdom you have received, but only a person who is primed and ready to receive it will "have eyes to see and ears to hear" — as the saying goes.

For these reasons (and others, I'm sure), the Mysteries tend to be talked about in metaphor, poetry, song, and art — and actively shared only in "sooper seekrit" rituals.

How to Approach the Mysteries

Initiations are one vehicle for transmitting the Mysteries. Secret societies like the Order of the Golden Dawn, Freemasons, Ordo Templi Orientis, and others have systems of ritual initiations designed to impart a great many esoteric Truths. (In fact, these systems all tend to share a great deal of overlap in their methods/messages, and the Eastern/Muslim/Templar thread runs very heavily through the practice of European Witch cults, as well.) Our own initiations, while drawing on different symbol sets, progressions, and patterns than the ceremonial fraternal Orders mentioned here, are very much a place where the Mysteries are revealed, experienced, and explored. In fact, initiations are the ONLY rituals that Witches in our Tradition are guaranteed to experience in common (since lunar and solar rituals tend to be more experimental). It is important, then, that we all have access to the same initiations (ie, that the initiations aren't radically altered), so that we all have access to the Mysteries that are embedded within them.

Guided meditations, seething, possessory work, Spirit communication, and Witch Flight are also important techniques within this Tradition for individuals and groups to explore the Mysteries. We have a series of guided meditations related to some of the Mysteries uncovered at the Sabbats — all of which were made available to you in Year 2: Practicum. I make it a practice to listen to these every year. (Either a Coven member reads them, or I'll listen to the recordings I've made of them.)

The other techniques (seething, possessory work, Spirit communication, and Flight) are more free-form, but you may notice that there is a lot of opportunity and encouragement in this course (and indeed through the whole training process) to really dig into these.

Finally, I feel like it is worth talking about entheogens again as we approach this work. Entheogens are those "drugs" or "poisons" that help us to "generate the Godd within." They can be milder — like wine or mugwort tea (or the mugwort-infused wine that you may have used at both of your previous initiations). Or they can be stronger — like cannabis, belladonna, datura, and psylocibin. They are absolutely not required, and nobody should ever feel any pressured to use any entheogen within the Spiral Castle Trad. (In fact, I hope you will have discovered already that you have access to breathwork, movement, fasting, and Mazey Stone techniques that can alter your perception just as effectively.) But entheogens are also not prohibited within our rites — as long as a few precautions are in place:

1. Only use our Sabbat Wine and "Non-Toxic" Flying Ointment recipes for initiations. With the fasting and other preparations that are in place, stronger entheogens will interfere with the process and could even result in a physical or mental health crisis.

2. If you are working with a Coven/group, the person leading the ritual should know what entheogens you are using.

3. In a group ritual setting, at least one person should be set in the role of Warden — and should not partake in any entheogens. This will allow them to monitor and react to both physical and energetic crisis, should a problem arise.

4. If you are working alone, take/use less of the entheogen than you think you need. (Use a LOT less if you are unable to have someone act as a "safety" for you.)

5. Only try a new entheogen in the presence of a "safety" — a person you trust who can hold safe space for you and who can help you in the event of a problem.

Assignment

Write a brief reflection in which you address the following:

- Do you feel as though you have stood in the light of a deep Mystery already?
- If so, was it one that you uncovered via the Craft, or elsewhere?
- If not, journal a bit about your relationship with the more esoteric aspects of the Craft.

Additional Resources

Oates, Shani and Robert Cochrane. *The Taper that Lights the Way: Robert Cochrane's Letters Revealed*. — https://amzn.to/3FTpA3O

Oates, Shani. *Tubelo's Green Fire*. — https://amzn.to/3WmutJE

Graves, Robert. *The White Goddess: An Historical Grammar of Poetic Myth*. — https://amzn.to/3BUplnF

Howard, Michael. *The Book of Fallen Angels*.

Jackson, Nigel Aldcraft. *Call of the Horned Piper*.

Jackson, Nigel. *Masks of Misrule: The Horned God & His Cult in Europe*.

Jackson, Nigel and Michael Howard. *Pillars of Tubal Cain*.

Faerywolf, Storm. *Forbidden Mysteries of Faery Witchcraft*. — https://amzn.to/3hRUtNZ

Grimassi, Raven. *Wiccan Mysteries: Ancient Origins and Teachings*. —https://amzn.to/3POhPR8

Farrar, Janet and Gavin Bone. *The Inner Mysteries: Progressive Witchcraft and Connection to the Divine*. —https://amzn.to/3WAHzTc

Mankey, Jason. *Transformative Witchcraft: The Greater Mysteries*. — https://amzn.to/3jfH2rp

---

BoS Pages Included

Entheogens in Witchcraft

From CTC & 1734

Prerequisite Lesson

01-01 Seeking the Mysteries

Objective

To establish Clan of Tubal Cain and 1734 as "parent" Traditions

To point to Mysteries within these Traditions , which we share

Materials Needed

Journaling materials

Printed or digital copies of writings by Roy Bowers (aka Robert Cochrane), Joe Wilson, Evan John Jones, and Shani Oates

Study Notes

If you have been avoiding the foundational writings of the Clan of Tubal Cain and of 1734 to this point, let me fervently encourage you to start taking the plunge now. As someone who has walked this crooked path for better than two decades, I find myself returning to the hints and riddles hidden within them for inspiration, enlightenment, and wisdom. And I find new meaning with every pass.

Robert Cochrane and Evan John Jones have been two of the Magisters of the Clan of Tubal Cain in the United Kingdom — with Shani Oates being its most well-known Maid, chronicler, and exegete. All three have written and published about the CTC, and their collective work is a treasure trove for any who come to the Spiral Castle in search of the Mysteries.

Cochrane (whose legal name was Roy Bowers) wrote publicly in esoteric magazines like *Pentagram* and *New Dimensions*, and he also maintained correspondence with three other keepers of the Old Faith for which we have records. His correspondence with Joe Wilson (from the US — who founded 1734), Norman Gilles, and Bill Gray constitute a large portion of the corpus of CTC foundational material. Indeed, his correspondence with Joe Wilson, along with Wilson's own essays and articles on the Craft, are the foundation of the 1734 Tradition and are often referred to as the "1734 Papers."

My own training and initiating Dame (she used the term High Priestess) had been a student in a 1734-style coven in Southern California (one of the Roebuck covens under the guidance of Ann and Dave Finnin). The Craft that I learned (and which I subsequently teach) was very heavily influenced by Roebuck, 1734, and CTC, therefore.

Joe Wilson felt strongly that the foundational writings of 1734 should be made publicly available. During his lifetime, he maintained a website to that end. (I downloaded and printed my own copies of the "papers" from that site in 1999. I scan and post one occasionally to a blog, and you can see the many years of highlighting, different colors of ink underlines and notes, and the intermittent dribble — which happens on a 23-year-old computer print-out.) Sometime after his death, members of the 1734 Tradition came together to act as stewards of this information, and they now maintain www.1734-witchcraft.org as well as a 1734 Witchcraft group on Facebook. I highly recommend securing copies of this material for your own on-going study.

Similarly, first Evan John Jones and later Shani Oates (and the Magister with whom she partnered, Robin the Dart) have done an amazing job of providing Cochrane's original writings as well as their own commentary and explorations to interested practitioners. Perusing the library, links, and blog at http://www.clanoftubalcain.org.uk/ is a great way to dive deeper into the Mysteries that underlie our work. Shani has also written several books which are very thought-provoking and illuminating, and which I whole-heartedly recommend.

Which Mysteries?

There are too many to simply list, but I'll point out a few of the "glyphs" or riddles that are associated with them. Some of these have exegesis (critical explanation and interpretation, especially of religious material) already provided by Bowers/Cochrane, Wilson, Jones, and Oates (or even the Finnins in their book *Forge of Tubal Cain*). For others, we just have the waypoints — the riddles, symbols, or glyphs that tickle our psyches and let us know to keep digging.

The following are all alluded to (or openly discussed) in the letters exchanged between Cochrane and Wilson.

- Two Words Not Spoken from the Cauldron
- Whirling Without Motion Between Three Elements
- The Order of 1734
- Where the Evening Star and Dark of Night Meet
- The Rose Beyond the Grave
- One Become Seven, and Seven Become One

Shani Oates specifically writes about the Masculine Mysteries, Feminine Mysteries, and Priestly Mysteries of CTC in her excellent book *Tubelo's Green Fire*. She names (or rather "points to") them thusly:

Masculine Mysteries
- Abbots Bromley, the Wild Hunt and Saint Nick
- Summer and Winter Solstice Customs
- The Wild Hunt
- Green Knight—Dark God of Light

Feminine Mysteries
- Hekate—Dark Mistress of the Soul
- The Wisdom of Courtly Love
- The Dance of the Seven Veils
- The Hand of Fatima
- Sila na Gigh

- Dia de los Muertos

Priestly Mysteries
- The Fisher King—Gnostic Priest of the High Mysteries of the Grail
- The Divine Duellists
- Why Cranes? An Exploration into their Mythic Significance in Legend and Lore
- The Fruit of Wisom—Genesis: Myth of the Fall

There are others to discover, unfold, and examine. These are just a few to ponder.

Assignment

Write a brief reflection regarding one of the Mysteries that you have approached or pondered from the Clan of Tubal Cain or 1734.

Additional Resources

1734 website — www.1734-witchcraft.org

CTC website — http://www.clanoftubalcain.org.uk/

Oates, Shani and Robert Cochrane. *The Taper that Lights the Way: Robert Cochrane's Letters Revealed*. — https://amzn.to/36Lezni

Oates, Shani. *Tubelo's Green Fire*. — https://amzn.to/3qtZ0aE

Finnin, Ann. *The Forge of Tubal Cain*. — https://amzn.to/3j7n5jb

---

BoS Pages Included

None

Mythopoesis, Folklore & Balladry

Prerequisite Lesson   01-01 Seeking the Mysteries

Objective   To embrace mythopoesis as a tool of the Wise

To explore traditional folkloric literature and balladry as sources of Craft wisdom

Materials Needed   Journaling materials

Texts of ballads, poems, myths, folk tales, nursery rhymes, etc

Study Notes   Mythopoeia or mythopoesis means "myth-making." In literature, it is generally defined as a narrative genre in modern/contemporary fiction in which a fictional mythology is created.

Folkloric Witches (like us) are often said to engage in mythopoeia — or, more accurately, in Mythopoetic Inquiry. Susanna Ruebsaat, in her abstract to "What does a Mythopoetic Inquiry look like?" for the *SFU Educational Review* described it this way:

> *A Mythopoetic Inquiry is a narrative of the imagination which creates an alternate story to the dominant story (individually or collectively). We create the story as we are living it; writing the narrative at the same time as we are reading it to ourselves and the world. Creating a vision while seeing; an imaginative vision about what is and what can be. A mythopoetic inquiry has its own logic but also needs to connect to reality. Art making (and other creative activities), can be a bridge between imagination and reality; letting the art tell the story from that liminal place between the conscious and unconscious. It is important to consider that there are practical aspects of this imagining. As humans we have a shared imagination (myths and archetypes) that is the common ground of this imagining.*

Robert Graves subtitled his formative work (*The White Goddess*) as "A Historical Grammar of Poetic Myth," and it deals very heavily with the nature of mythopoeia — and of reading deeply into the myths to suck out the meaning. Indeed, we find ourselves reading beyond the myths, beyond the poetry, beyond the folklore as we connect our own experiences, our understanding of deep symbols, and cultural understandings to the exploration.

We tend, therefore, to take a fluid approach to our reading and study of the source materials — the myths, ballads, legends, and poems. We know that interpretation plays a role. We understand that *fact* is not equivalent to Truth, and we are much more interested in the latter.

This is not a straightforward process, and students who have been taught that there is a "correct" answer to most questions will find themselves frustrated. A lot. Maybe even angry. ("Just tell me what it means!") To be fair, I think all of us hit brick walls at times when we're dealing with allegory, metaphor, and other "riddling" language — even if we generally enjoy this type of analysis and inquiry.

To that end, I have some advice as you engage in mythopoetic inquiry:

- Be gentle with yourself. Don't try to force the light bulb to click on. Sometimes you need to walk away from a text or a concept and let it brew. It's too wrapped up in symbol to be graspable — until you've done some sorting of the symbols. Sometimes the lesson buried in the text isn't available to you right now because you aren't ready for it yet. It will click and connect when the time is right.
- There is almost never a clear-cut "correct" analysis, but some are more/less relatable or universal than others. Look for layers of meaning in the material, not just the piece that applies directly to you and your experience. The most meaningful symbols are rich and complex, and myths are nothing if not a story told using symbols and symbolic language.
- Really engage with the text/material. This is a "full contact" process. Give yourself permission to feel powerful emotions, bring the myth into your body, explore it through art/dance/writing or some other creative process.
- Explore lots of myth, legend, folklore, balladry, etc in your quest. By doing so, you are adding to your symbolic lexicon and giving yourself more data to be able to make connections.

Where to Start?

There are more sources than could possibly be listed here, but I'll give you some ideas for places to start your journey (if you feel at a loss). Googling any of these will potentially lead you down a rabbit hole of great material. (Try searching for "Collections of X.")

The Child Ballads

The Roud Folk Song Index

Other folk song collections

Nursery Rhymes

Fairy Tales

Fables

Mythology

Folk Tales

Arthurian Legends

Suggestion: look at European folklore and folk songs, as well as Classical mythology, the myths and legends of indigenous folk, as well as that of enslaved peoples, along with the myths and folklore related to your own cultural heritage. Look for connections as well as points of difference and diversity. All of these point to great wisdom and enlightenment.

Assignment

Write a reflection on your engagement in the mythopoetic inquiry process. You can cover how you have engaged so far, what materials you've engaged with, and/or how you hope to engage in the future. Has an area of folk-literature or mythology been of special interest to you lately (or at some point in the past?) Feel free to share insights you have already had from fairy tales, nursery rhymes, ballads or other folk-literature.

Additional Resources

Ruebsaat, S. (2013). What Does a Mythopoetic Inquiry Look Like?. *SFU Educational Review, 6.* https://doi.org/10.21810/sfuer.v6i.372

Some examples from within SCT/AFW writings:

"Familiars and Familiar Spirits" — http://afwcraft.blogspot.com/2011/08/familiars-and-familiar-spirits.html — (At the end of the article, where Glaux wrote about the "Crooked Man" chant/poem as a guidemap to acquiring a familiar.)

"Counting Out Chants" — http://afwcraft.blogspot.com/2011/07/counting-out-chant.html

"The Lame Step" — http://afwcraft.blogspot.com/2011/06/lame-step.html — (In the middle, where I write about the Lame Step in nursery rhymes)

"Thomas the Rhymer" — http://afwcraft.blogspot.com/2011/08/thomas-rhymer.html

BoS Pages Included

None

SCT Waypoints

Prerequisite Lesson

01-03 — Mythopoesis, Folklore & Balladry

Objective

To get a glimpse of the Mysteries within the Spiral Castle Tradition

To begin unpacking the Mysteries that have already been experienced (if applicable)

Materials Needed

Journaling materials

Study Notes

Within Spiral Castle Trad, there has been a general understanding about the Mysteries that probably has never been openly stated by us until now:

Nobody owns the Mysteries.

Not us. Not Clan of Tubal Cain. Not 1734 or Roebuck. Not the ancient mystery schools of Egypt, Greece, or Rome. Nobody.

The Mysteries make themselves known to people who are ready to experience and grapple with understanding them — wherever, whenever, and whoever those people may be. This is why we see the Great Truths expressed in varying ways by artists, poets, and mystics across cultural and temporal boundaries.

The sources and "waypoints" of the Mysteries that we have discussed from other groups are very much a part of what we explore and experience within SCT. They are "ours" as much as they are anyone's.

We also have a few that we feel have sort of "bubbled up" from the cauldron of our own collective working and symbol set. Again, it is sometimes difficult to put into clear language, so we tend to talk about them in glyphs or phrases. (Perhaps I — or one of you — will someday take on the task that Shani Oates did for CTC in trying to verbalize and lay bare the full spectrum of what is contained in these waypoints. But we're not there yet.)

I invite you to begin spending time with these to see what is available to you within them. Use all of the tools and techniques at your disposal — entheogens (to your comfort level), flight, trance, Spirit work, meditation, journaling, dramatic ritual, etc. Be open to going beyond the surface understanding of these things. Many of the waypoints (as I call them — since they only point toward the Mystery but don't explain it in any way) are concepts, tools, and phrases you encountered in your first year of study. (Some are not.)

The Red Thread — umbilicus, lifeline, life-blood, blood bonds, line of Qayin, the East-West line of the sun, red thread of fate, Ariadne's thread, rogue's yarn, throughline, sacred string

Light in Darkness; Dark in Light (also Life in Death; Death in Life)

The Compass as the Year Wheel (ideas of sacred space-time) — and connections to the Nail Star and the Cosmic Mill

Starfire above; Forge-fire below (above and below the Spiral Castle)

That which is below (and fuels) the Forge

The Stang — World Tree and "hobby horse"; distaff and fork

Red, Black, and White

I don't want to overwhelm and inundate you with Mysteries to ponder. This is plenty to start with and provides a good jumping off point for further study and contemplation.

Assignment

Write a brief reflection regarding your experience and understanding of one of these Mysteries. Be sure to include the following:

- When and how you first remember encountering it
- Initial impressions and thoughts that you remember
- Insights and understandings that you have gained over time
- Questions or points of interest that you wish to explore within or related to this Mystery

---

Additional Resources

Liber Qayin (included in Year 1 BOS)

BoS Pages Included

The Mysteries (set)

Witch Flight

Prerequisite Lesson

None

Objective

To gain a better/deeper understanding of Witch Flight

To explore areas of concern or question

Materials Needed

Journaling materials

Drumming track

Study Notes

By this point in your studies, you have experienced (or attempted) Witch Flight. I know this because in Year 1, you celebrated Beltaine (or, more accurately in this case, Walpurgisnacht) by flying to the Brocken to join in the Sabbat.

We didn't really talk about Witch Flight a whole lot at the time, so I'd like to take a little time to talk about it now. Why? Because as a Witch of the 3rd Degree in this Trad, you are likely to engage in more flight than you did earlier on, and you may also be preparing to lead and teach others — which will undoubtedly mean leading some guided meditations and soul flights.

What is Witch Flight?

At its most basic level, Witch Flight is the same as astral projection or soul journey-ing. (We sometimes call it "hedge-crossing" since we are crossing the boundaries between the worlds.) Studying materials produced by other metaphysicists and sha-manic practitioners can give a lot of insight on this process, if you find that you are struggling with it or need more guidance following our lessons.

But Witch Flight differs a bit in execution from what is usually called astral travel, etc. We have seen and discussed some aspects of those differences already. Namely, folkloric Witches often make use of a Fetch and a Gandreid (or Gandreigh) when flying.

You created your Fetch in Year 1, as well as at least one Gandreid (or riding pole — which you either made or bought in the form of a Stang).

The Fetch is an etheric "body" that the Black Soul inhabits while traveling in the Unseen Realms. It is anchored to the physical realm through the use of a "fetish" or "fetich" that houses the Fetch when not in use.

The Gandreid is a riding pole that is (in its most essential form) a representation of the World Tree and acts as your "steed" while you travel. It can be a stang, a staff, or a broom. And it is the Witch's hobby horse. Our own Sleipnir with his 8 legs in each of the worlds hung within Yggdrasil. It is the Spiral Castle, with its 8 arms reaching to the Castles and Gates. (We'll be talking more about this important tool in Lesson 02-04.)

How to Fly

There is no single way to fly. (By the way, we use the term "flight" to encompass any soul journey, even when we don't necessarily picture ourselves flying across the skies.)

We can follow a guided meditation with the aid of flying ointment or sabbat tea — perhaps with our Gandreid under or between our knees or held lengthwise across our bodies.

We can dance with staff or stang in hand, falling to the ground in a trance, and let our Spirits wander free.

We can tap out a rhythm with our Stang on the ground and/or tap an arrow against the shaft of the Stang while chanting or intoning the runes (performing galdr).

We can seethe while sitting, as we learned in Year 1, swaying and rocking to loosen our Spirits.

It's a great idea to explore all of these methods and to spend some time working with each to get a feel for its use in your practice. I would encourage you to use some of the moons and Sabbats this year to explore and engage in this work.

The Purpose of Witch Flight

There are many, many reasons to cross the hedge. At first, our motivations are usually experiential. We want to see and discover what is there. Meet the inhabitants of the Unseen. Encounter the places and objects that are there.

Eventually, though, we go "out and about" in search of information, as a way to performhealings (or blastings), or to engage with the Powers or other Witches. All of the reasons that are common to shamanic practitioners for soul journeying apply to us, as well.

Flying as a Group

If you are working with a study group or if you plan to start a coven later, it is worth thinking about how the dynamics change a little when there are multiple people to consider and account for. Just as you may have a preference for one of the above methods, so too will the other group members have their preferences. In some cases, each person can "do their own thing" without causing a disturbance or distraction for the others. For instance, one or two people could be "playing" the Stang while one person seethes in a sitting position and two others seethe by dancing. As long as the dancers don't trip over the seated one, this could work quite well for everyone.

Another possibility for including multiple modalities is to let one or two folks "play" the Stang while another leads the guided meditation and everyone else follows.

For the most part, though, the guided mediation method doesn't really lend itself to other noise and activity. So, although it is effective for many, it doesn't have quite the same level of flexibility.

Aphantasia

Aphantasia is the more-common-than-you'd-think condition that results in partial to total lack of visual imagery for a person. Witch Flight doesn't HAVE to be a visual experience, despite the overwhelming visual descriptions that people associate with it. If you have this condition, allow yourself to approach flight from the perspective of some other inner sense (or a combination thereof). What do you feel, hear, smell, taste?

Still struggling? Allow yourself to experience the journey as a story or narrative that is being spoken (one that is told to your Black Soul by your White Soul — or perhaps by the Godds). Allow your sense of knowing, of understanding, to take the lead.

Folks with aphantasia don't lack creativity or imagination, per se. But it presents in a different way.

Precautions & Safeguards

Newer practitioners to the art of hedge-riding are often thrilled by tales of danger and the prospect of catastrophe. Online sources and unethical guides are all-too-willing to share these stories, which bolster the need for charms and specialized guidance (which, of course, they can sell at a price).

The truth is that jumping the hedge is a reasonably safe practice with very few catastrophic results. The most common unexpected or mildly unpleasant results include a jarring return to the physical body, a brief period of disorientation upon return, and a sense of homesickness or longing to return to the Other Worlds. The worst thing I have ever witnessed (or heard tell of happening from a trusted source) is what my High Priestess referred to as "cauldron-diving." (Our coven was engaged in Witch Flight, which we began from a scrying activity using personal cauldrons. One of my coven brothers struggled to return. If he had been operating alone, I have every confidence that he would have returned without our intervention. He would have eventually drifted into sleep, and when he awoke, his Black Soul would have been comfortably reincorporated into his body and operating in harmony with his Red and White Souls. As it was, we **called** him back — because we couldn't leave him unconscious outdoors alone.)

There may come a time when you, too, need to help a covenmate or student to return. Ultimately, the choice to "call the Black Soul home" is more a matter of convenience than it is saving someone from disaster. If you're doing group ritual, there is only so long you can allot for folks to be "gone." If you're working outside, particularly in the cold or chill, there are practical considerations that have to do with physical well-being.

It is important, I think to teach your students or other new Witches not to fear these techniques of Soul journey. What we do is mysterious and frightening to the masses because they don't understand it, and because they have chosen to believe that there is danger. That choice absolves them of the need to do the work themselves. We are Witches, though, and we are both capable and responsible — for our own growth, healing, and gnosis.

If you are working alone, and you fear "getting lost" during your travels, remember that your initiation cords are an umbilicus that tethers you to the other members of this Tradition and to our Great Powers (Kolyo, Goda, Qayin). Use the Red Thread to trace your way back out of the labyrinth. And embrace sleep and the Dreaming as doorways through which your Black Soul can pass freely. You can use it to travel Out, and also to return.

When working in a group setting, if you need to bring someone back, remind yourself that this is not a search and rescue mission. There's no "saving" them that's needed, which means there is no need to panic. Try first to speak them back, using your voice to remind them of the Red Thread that they wear. Speak words that help them connect to their body again. (Instruct them to change their breathing pattern, to feel their limbs, wiggle their toes, be aware of the temperature on their skin, etc.) If you've been chanting or singing, change the chant or drumbeat. Make it something more lively. Strong. Florida Water and other perfumes are fantastic for bringing a person back. Place some on the back of their neck, the front of the chest, the palms of the hands, and the soles of the feet.

I've never known those methods not to work. However, you can also utilize other techniques if the person's Fylgjia requires more vigorous coaxing to return. Three Soul Alignment and Witches' LBRP would be super-effective.

Assignment

Engage in flight. Cross the hedge. Perform 3 flights to the same place (on different occasions — perhaps as a series of lunar or Sabbat workings) and document your experiences. Places might include the Hexentanzenplatz where the Great Sabbats are held (and which we visited in the Walpurgis/Beltaine ritual in Year 1 and is discussed again in 02-02 here), Tubelo's Forge below the Spiral Castle, or any of the Castles/Gates/Realms. Share what you experience there, and what you discover about your flying techniques.

Additional Resources

"Aphantasia and Astral Travel" — https://www.thedragonslibrary.net/blog/aphantasia-and-astral-travel

Shamanic Drumming track — https://www.youtube.com/watch?v=ivCOrc1HWxI

"Was the Eko Eko Chant Originally an Arabic Chant to the Devil?" — https://witchesandpagans.com/pagan-culture-blogs/paganistan/was-eko-eko-azarak-originally-an-arabic-chant-to-the-devil.html — This article is included here because one of the versions of the Eko Eko Chant is often used within our Trad when seething.

BoS Pages Included

Witch Flight
Eko Eko Chants

Meeting at the Sabbat

Prerequisite Lesson 02-01 Witch Flight

Objective To describe and explore our Hexentanzenplatz

Materials Needed Journaling materials

Study Notes One of the "known secrets" of folkloric Witchcraft is that Witches travel to meet each other using Soul journey techniques, and these meetings happen in what some might call "astral temples." That is a very New Age sounding term for what some of our European Craft ancestors would have called the Brocken (or Blocksburg — the highest mountain peak in Northern Germany) or the Hexentanzenplatz (hexen = witches', tanzen = dancing, platz = place).

The Brocken was a specific place that was associated with Witchcraft rituals in the pre-modern era in Europe. Other mountains had similar honors and associations. There are peaks and groves, caves and heaths on every inhabited continent that have come to be known as gathering places for Witches.

When we fly to the Witches' Sabbat (usually at Beltaine or Samhain, though we can technically access this place anytime of year), it is part of the Spiral Castle lore that we are flying to the same Witches' Dance Floor as other members of this Tradition. Maybe it is the same place where all Witches gather. Maybe it is unique to us — and to our shared spiritual Ancestors.

I know when I go there, I have encountered a mighty throng of Witches — many of whom I have never met in waking life. Many of whom aren't part of the waking, living world in this time that you and I share. The Meeting Place exists outside of time and space, so it is just accessible to Witches from 1324 as is it us now. I have danced there with Alice and Petronila, just as I have with covenmates who flew there next to me (starting from the Compass we laid in my parlor).

Here is what I know of the place: I cross water and fields and stars during my flight.

It is in a high place, with a grove of sacred trees encircling it. We know these Tree Allies. It is a broad, open place. Hard-packed earth on a table of rock. Flat. A bonfire is usually set in the center, and stars swim in the dark sky overhead. Witches and Familiars of every ilk revel together here. A huge banquet is laid on a table. The WitchFather and Witch-Mother preside over the scene — though I can only ever approach one of them at a time. (If I see Him, she is unavailable to me on that flight — and vice versa.)

What do we do there? All manner of magic can be undertaken from here. All manner of journeys can lead out from here. At its most basic level, we can allow our Souls to play, revel, heal, and be inspired here.

One of my hopes for RTA/SCT members is that we learn to recognize and interact with each other in this place. But regardless of whether we actively engage in "astral workings" together, I feel it is important for each of us to develop a relationship and familiarity with our Dancing Place — our Mill Grounds.

The act of meeting in this place is often called "Meeting at the Sabbat." Walpurgis/Beltaine is the Sabbat most strongly associated with this gathering, but since this "astral temple" exists outside of time, we are in the "eternal now" when we arrive there. That means we can access that otherworldly Witches' Sabbat from whatever date and time we find ourselves within the physical world. In other words, you don't have to wait until the first of May to go.

Assignment

Write a brief reflection regarding the Witches' Dance Floor (Hexentanzenplatz). Be sure to include the following:

- The journey(s) you take to reach it
- How it looks to you
- Who you find there
- What you have done there

Additional Resources

None

BoS Pages Included

The Witches' Dance Floor

Writing/Leading Hedge Crossings

Prerequisite Lesson

02-02 Meeting at the Sabbat

Objective

To begin writing your own hedge-crossings for use by yourself or others

To consider effective principles of guided meditation

To understand others' reactions and experiences within hedge-crossing

Materials Needed

Journaling or writing materials

Study Notes

Hedge-crossing is not exactly the same as guided meditation, in a strict sense. I sometimes use the terms a bit interchangeably because guided meditation can be a step in the training of Soul Flight. I know the distinction between the two can be confusing, and the lines can easily get blurred.

Hedge-crossing IS synonymous with the terms Soul journeying, Witch Flight, Soul flight, and astral travel.

Guided Meditation is a tool used in this type of journey. It is a way to lead a group in the same flight and to offer exposure and introductions to the figures who inhabit the Otherworlds. It is a method for following on the flight path where others have gone.

In Year 2: Practicum, I offered a guided meditation for every Sabbat. And there is a ninth that was offered in Year 1: Foundations as part of the Beltaine celebration. When you engaged in these guided meditations, you might have flown. They were set up in a way to allow that. When we perform them at Coven Caer Sidhe, we use them as a way to train ourselves to fly.

In all sincerity, I am content for SCT covens and RTA study groups to use these guided meditations verbatim, if they are effective and useful. However, I want our Witches of the 3rd Degree to be able to engage in Flight without being guided there, as well. AND, I also want you to be able to lead others to places that we don't yet have written meditations for.

Considerations for Writing Guided Meditations

As you explore the Sabbats this year, you are going to be engaging in more ritual creation. I'm asking you to design your own rituals, write your own meditations, and do some exploring and experimenting. You won't be writing eight brand new guided meditations, per se. In fact, maybe you only write one, and the rest of your rituals are of a different nature.

I do want you to write at least one, though. It doesn't have to be associated with a Sabbat, but doing so will let you tackle two assignments with the same task, since you are being asked to write a guided meditation in this lesson, and you've got to do something for the Sabbats.

The most effective guided meditations have the following components:

- Induction — that beginning part where you help the Soul Traveler relax and rise out of their body
- Tether — a link between the physical body of the Traveler and their Black Soul; this often happens by reminding the person that their body is safe and guarded, but it can also happen via reminders of the Red Thread
- Map — description of the steps along the journey
- Sensory Details — include references to all the senses; some of us can use all of our inner senses, but many of us are stronger in one or two (and not always with our inner-sight); it is important to provide other descriptions
- Storyline — it's often a "choose your own adventure" sort of story, where the Traveler has some open-ended opportunities to receive messages or experience actions that aren't being described to them; but there is a sense of a story that is playing out, including a climax
- Return/Exit — fully describe the process of returning, using the same path that was traveled into the journey; help the Traveler reconnect with their physical body

---

<u>Assignment</u>

Use the planning worksheet to write a guided meditation that can be used by a group or individual to journey to some place/figure of significance. You might write a guided journey to the Spiral Castle itself, to Tubelo's Forge, to the Witches' Dance Floor, to the Witch Mother's loom, etc. The purpose of the journey might be to speak with one of the Powers, to untangle or read the Threads of Fate, or to meet with a Familiar. Go on the journey you have written, and include a debrief of your experience. (You can record or have someone else read the meditation to you.)

<u>Additional Resources</u>   Planning Worksheet for Guided Journey

---

<u>BoS Pages Included</u>   None

Planning Worksheet for Guided Journeys

Induction :	
Destination:	**Guideposts/** **Guardians:** _____ _____
Visual Elements **(Sight)**	**Auditory Elements** **(Sound)**
Tactile Elements (Feel)	**Olfactory Elements** **(Smell)**
Gustatory Elements **(Taste)**	
Open-Ended Experiences	

Gandreid

Prerequisite Lesson

None

Objective

To form a deeper connection with the Spirit of your Gandreid

Materials Needed

Staff, Broom, or Stang

Study Notes

We've talked about the Gandreid before, both in direct and in oblique ways. We spent a fair amount of time in Year 1: Foundations discussing the Stang, in particular, and you have been encouraged to experience the Stang as a riding pole — a way to cross the hedge.

This lesson isn't necessarily to introduce you to the concept of the Gandreid (or gandr), but rather to deepen your connection to the tool that serves in this capacity for you.

Since we started our exploration of the concept of the "riding pole" with the Stang, and since the Stang was one of your first tools in this Tradition, you may have bonded with it to the point where you are unlikely to consider using any other tool in flight.

Or … you may not resonate with your Stang in quite that way. Perhaps the connection has been lacking. Perhaps you are drawn more to using a Staff, Distaff, or a Broom in this capacity. Which tool you use is a personal choice, and all three are considered valid within this Tradition.

It is also possible that you may enjoy the variety of having more than one, choosing the one that speaks up for specific flights/crossings. Again, this is a matter of personal preference and style.

If you have access to a Broom or a Staff, you might give them a "test drive" to see how you like them in this capacity.

The Spirit of Your Gandreid

If you have more than one riding pole, I invite you to consider this process and reflection regarding each one.

The Gandreid is almost always an enspirited tool. While I feel that all Witch's tools are capable of being en-Souled, it is my experience and observation that not all ARE, for most Witches. The Gandreid, though, is the Steed — a Hob Horse (Hob being a diminutive form of Robin — and therefore pointing to our WitchFather). And as such, we are usually aware of it having a presence and personality of its own.

Spend some time in communion with your Gandreid. Seek to know it on a personal level. If this idea of its Spirit is one you never considered, try to tap into it to see if you feel one already there. If not, invite one — offering this tool as its vessel, and your allyship in the bargain.

Ask its name, and safeguard that knowledge. This is a very personal tool, and nobody else need know its name but you. (Not even me. Not even if you share your work with me. Not even if I am your Initiator or close friend.)

Spend some time sleeping with your Gandreid — in your bed, if you can manage it (or under your bed, if not).

Make offerings to it, and repeat the offerings at regular intervals.

Work with it, talk to it, praise it.

Maintain and care for it.

Assignment

Write a brief reflection regarding your Gandreid. Be sure to include the following:

- The type of tool it is
- Your history with this specific tool
- What you have come to know of its personality, preferences, strength, offerings
- NOT its name

Additional Resources

"Vcror and Gandr: Helping Spirits in Norse Magic" — https://journals.lub.lu.se/anf/article/download/11542/10231/26582 (This is a PDF download)

BoS Pages Included

The Gandreid

Samhain

Prerequisite Lesson

None

Objective

To align with the seasonal energies of the Sabbat

To explore the Mysteries related to the Sabbat

To create a Samhain ritual (or hedge-crossing) for personal and/or group use

To practice and perform ritual

Materials Needed

Stang, candle, lighter

Cauldron, water

Anvil, hammer

Three knives (red, black, white)

Triple Cord

Service Cord

Bread, lipped dish or bowl

Red wine, cup

Incense, holder, charcoal

Other materials, as dictated by the rite

Note: This list represents general ritual materials. Add or subtract whatever is needed for the ritual you choose to experience.

Study Notes

For this and all Sabbats in Year 3, you will be writing your own ritual. This is an opportunity to explore, experiment, and create. The ritual does NOT have to be complicated or include lots of steps. In fact, if your sense of the Magical Artes is more simple, this is a great opportunity to tailor workings to match your proclivities.

If you are working with a group (or plan to do so in the future) this is a chance to experiment with putting things together for more than one person. Group ritual can have some different considerations than solo ritual.

For every Sabbat in this year, we will take the time to talk about some of the Mysteries, themes, taboos, and traditions you might draw from. You are also encouraged to revisit the Sabbats in Years 1 and 2 for inspiration.

Seasonal Themes, Traditions, and Taboos

We view the Samhain season as a whole "month" unto itself — even though we don't necessarily block out 28 calendar days for it. There is a lot of opportunity to dive deeply into the traditions and themes that we have already explored in Years 1 & 2. Perhaps you want to do multiple rituals during Samhaintide — starting on the Dark Moon just before Samhain (which is when we herald this particular season) and/or ending on 15* Scorpio (usually Nov 2-6) which is the astrological cross-quarter point between the Fall Equinox and the Winter Solstice in the Northern Hemisphere. You aren't required to do more than one ritual, but the season lends itself to it nicely, and there is great work to be done then.

Rituals might include Lighting Jack, Enlivening the Skull, a Dumb Supper, a possessory Oracle with Qayin, an Ancestor Séance, a Wild Hunt, the Rose Beyond the Grave, and more.

You can look to the Year 1 and Year 2 rituals, BoS pages, and study notes for inspiration and guidance; but also feel encouraged to do your own digging into the folklore and folk magick surrounding this holiday to see if there are other aspects you would like to explore or incorporate. Maybe something stands out to you from a cultural tradition that we haven't studied as a group, but which nevertheless informs your personal practice.

Mysteries Associated with this Sabbat

Within the framework of the lesson, our goal cannot be to transmit the Mysteries, themselves. We can only hint at them here. These are opportunities to consider the underlying Truths and to allow them to reveal themselves to you.

These are not necessarily the ONLY Mysteries that we could approach or contemplate at this season. I recommend jotting down other big Truths that are very present for you at this time of year.

"Life in Death; Death in Life" — This is a phrase we use to reference something very fundamental to this Tradition. While the WitchMother isn't particular prominent at this Sabbat, this phrase IS. (And this phrase is very much associated with Her.) This Mystery is also very present with us at Beltaine.

"Rose Beyond the Grave" — Writers from within the Clan of Tubal Cain have written about this Mystery. To contemplate the Rose Beyond (or Within) the Grave is to contemplate what happens to the Souls of the Witch after Death.

"What the Mask Reveals" — The Spiral Castle Tradition associates the West with Samhain. The weapon of the West is the Helm (or Mask). We sometimes work with the Mask in order to better understand both ourselves and That which is represented by a specific mask.

| Assignment | Write and perform a Samhain ritual. This can be a group or personal ritual. Debrief the ritual with the other participants (if applicable) and also by writing a reflection of your experience. |

Your debrief should include:
- any impressions you had or challenges you experienced during the set-up
- how you might alter this ritual for solo/group use
- a notation of the date and general time you did the ritual
- who (if anyone) was with you
- impressions, insights, and sensations you had throughout the ritual (during the opening portions, the working, or the meal)
- any challenges you experienced while executing the ritual
- ideas that this ritual sparked for you (either for other rituals or for other creative/philosophical endeavors in your world)
- anything else that you feel should be noted

Additional Resources

"Beyond the Realms of Death" by Robin the Dart — http://www.clanoftubalcain.org.uk/beyond.html

Liber Qayin — http://afwcraft.blogspot.com/2015/03/liber-qayin-complete-text.html

"The Profane Art of Masking" by Shani Oates — http://www.clanoftubalcain.org.uk/masks.html

"The Jaw-Dropping History of Jack O'Lanterns: A Tale of Turnips, Samhain, and Severed Heads" — https://irishmyths.com/2021/09/19/jack-o-lantern-history/

BoS Pages Included

Laying the Compass
Opening the Gates
Raising the Castles
Calling the Realms
The Housle
Samhain Mysteries

Yule

<u>Prerequisite Lesson</u>

None

<u>Objective</u>

To align with the seasonal energies of the Sabbat

To explore the Mysteries related to the Sabbat

To create a Yule ritual (or hedge-crossing) for personal and/or group use

To practice and perform ritual

<u>Materials Needed</u>

Stang, candle, lighter

Cauldron, water, lancet

Anvil, hammer

Three knives (red, black, white)

Triple Cord

Service Cord

Bread, lipped dish or bowl

Red wine, cup

Incense, holder, charcoal

Other materials, as dictated by the rite

Note: This list represents general ritual materials. Add or subtract whatever is needed for the ritual you choose to experience.

<u>Study Notes</u>

For this and all Sabbats in Year 3, you will be writing your own ritual. This is an opportunity to explore, experiment, and create. The ritual does NOT have to be complicated or include lots of steps. In fact, if your sense of the Magical Artes is more simple, this is a great opportunity to tailor workings to match your proclivities.

If you are working with a group (or plan to do so in the future) this is a chance to experiment with putting things together for more than one person. Group ritual can have some different considerations than solo ritual.

For every Sabbat in this year, we will take the time to talk about some of the Mysteries, themes, taboos, and traditions you might draw from. You are also encouraged to revisit the Sabbats in Years 1 and 2 for inspiration.

Seasonal Themes, Traditions, and Taboos

My experience of Yuletide traditions has been very focused on keeping the solar vigil and celebrating with Family (both Witch Family and also bio/chosen family). Unlike secular Christmas, it isn't focused so much on gifting — though it could. Instead, I've tried to convey to my own Coven and children a sense of coziness, watchfulness, crafting, and camaraderie. Feasting, storytelling, and crafting (especially of talismanic ornaments) features heavily in the traditions we have shared over the years. And wassailing! Oh, the wassailing!

Rituals might include: a Fire Vigil until sunrise, Wassailing the Trees, Yule Log, Oak King/Holly King Battle, Morris Dancing, Mari Lawd, Julbock (Yule Goat), as well as ritualized or magical baking, feasting, and gifting.

You can look to the Year 1 and Year 2 rituals, BoS pages, and study notes for inspiration and guidance; but also feel encouraged to do your own digging into the folklore and folk magick surrounding this holiday to see if there are other aspects you would like to explore or incorporate. Maybe something stands out to you from a cultural tradition that we haven't studied as a group, but which nevertheless informs your personal practice.

Mysteries Associated with this Sabbat

Within the framework of the lesson, our goal cannot be to transmit the Mysteries, themselves. We can only hint at them here. These are opportunities to consider the underlying Truths and to allow them to reveal themselves to you.

These are not necessarily the ONLY Mysteries that we could approach or contemplate at this season. I recommend jotting down other big Truths that are very present for you at this time of year.

"Robin and Wren"/"Oak King and Holly King" — Here in the darkest time of year is a good time to consider the power of solitude, contemplation, and thriftiness (as well as how these things balance with community, activity, and abundance).

"What is seen by Odin's eye" — The Glass Orb is the vessel associated with the Winter Solstice. It can be thought of as Odin's eye, in addition to its associations with the Adder's Egg or glain. Spend some time with this vessel and consider what it reveals.

Assignment

Write and perform a Yule ritual. This can be a group or personal ritual. Debrief the ritual with the other participants (if applicable) and also by writing a reflection of your experience.

Your debrief should include:

- any impressions you had or challenges you experienced during the set-up
- how you might alter this ritual for solo/group use
- a notation of the date and general time you did the ritual
- who (if anyone) was with you
- impressions, insights, and sensations you had throughout the ritual (during the opening portions, the working, or the meal)
- any challenges you experienced while executing the ritual
- ideas that this ritual sparked for you (either for other rituals or for other creative/philosophical endeavors in your world)
- anything else that you feel should be noted

Additional Resources

None

BoS Pages Included

Laying the Compass
Opening the Gates
Raising the Castles
Calling the Realms
The Housle
Yule Mysteries

Imbolc

Prerequisite Lesson

None

Objective

To align with the seasonal energies of the Sabbat

To explore the Mysteries related to the Sabbat

To create an Imbolc ritual (or hedge-crossing) for personal and/or group use

To practice and perform ritual

Materials Needed

Stang, candle, lighter

Cauldron, water, lancet

Anvil, hammer

Three knives (red, black, white)

Triple Cord

Service Cord

Bread, lipped dish or bowl

Red wine, cup

Incense, holder, charcoal

Other materials, as dictated by the rite

Note: This list represents general ritual materials. Add or subtract whatever is needed for the ritual you choose to experience.

Study Notes

For this and all Sabbats in Year 3, you will be writing your own ritual. This is an opportunity to explore, experiment, and create. The ritual does NOT have to be complicated or include lots of steps. In fact, if your sense of the Magical Artes is more simple, this is a great opportunity to tailor workings to match your proclivities.

If you are working with a group (or plan to do so in the future) this is a chance to experiment with putting things together for more than one person. Group ritual can have some different considerations than solo ritual.

For every Sabbat in this year, we will take the time to talk about some of the Mysteries, themes, taboos, and traditions you might draw from. You are also encouraged to revisit the Sabbats in Years 1 and 2 for inspiration.

Seasonal Themes, Traditions, and Taboos

Imbolc is usually the coldest and most bitter part of winter — or rainiest and dreariest, depending on where you live. At least, as someone who has lived all over North America (and in Northern Germany), this is my experience. If you are somewhere else in the world, your experience may be different. Bleak and bitter though it may be, Spring is so close. As such, it is the "most Kolyo time" of the year — covered and hidden.

Rituals might include — Fire and Ice themes, the Lady's Mantle, Kolyo Oracle, candle creation & blessing.

You can look to the Year 1 and Year 2 rituals, BoS pages, and study notes for inspiration and guidance; but also feel encouraged to do your own digging into the folklore and folk magick surrounding this holiday to see if there are other aspects you would like to explore or incorporate. Maybe something stands out to you from a cultural tradition that we haven't studied as a group, but which nevertheless informs your personal practice.

Mysteries Associated with this Sabbat

Within the framework of the lesson, our goal cannot be to transmit the Mysteries, themselves. We can only hint at them here. These are opportunities to consider the underlying Truths and to allow them to reveal themselves to you.

These are not necessarily the ONLY Mysteries that we could approach or contemplate at this season. I recommend jotting down other big Truths that are very present for you at this time of year.

"Uneasy Seat Above Caer Ochren" — This is a wonderful time to explore the Mysteries of oracular work. Our Tradition associates Imbolc with invoking Kolyo and asking for Her guidance and wisdom on Her most holy day. She often reveals Her own Mysteries, but the process itself has much to impart, as well.

"The Light in the Darkness, the Darkness in the Light" — Kolyo and Goda share this Mystery, which they teach us using different methods. Starlight in an inky sky. Stark shadows in the brightest sun. Nakedness. Cloaking. Youth. Age. Nothing is as straightforward as it seems. First impressions are often deceiving.

"The Staff" — All of the weapons and vessels of the Spiral Castle carry their own Mysteries. When contemplating the lessons of the Staff, think of its many forms and functions — walking stick, battle-staff/quarter-staff, lantern pole, sounding rod, spear, arrow, wand, hobby horse, tein, distaff.

"Fire and Ice" — Climate change notwithstanding, Imbolc tends to be the coldest and bleakest of the Sabbats in North America. But "far beneath the winter snows, a heart of fire beats and glows." This is a great time to ponder what unseen things are happening during periods of rest.

Assignment

Write and perform an Imbolc ritual. This can be a group or personal ritual. Debrief the ritual with the other participants (if applicable) and also by writing a reflection of your experience.

Your debrief should include:

- any impressions you had or challenges you experienced during the set-up
- how you might alter this ritual for solo/group use
- a notation of the date and general time you did the ritual
- who (if anyone) was with you
- impressions, insights, and sensations you had throughout the ritual (during the opening portions, the working, or the meal)
- any challenges you experienced while executing the ritual
- ideas that this ritual sparked for you (either for other rituals or for other creative/philosophical endeavors in your world)
- anything else that you feel should be noted

Additional Resources

None

BoS Pages Included

Laying the Compass

Opening the Gates

Raising the Castles

Calling the Realms

The Housle

Imbolc Mysteries

Spring Equinox

Prerequisite Lesson

None

Objective

To align with the seasonal energies of the Sabbat

To explore the Mysteries related to the Sabbat

To create a Spring Equinox ritual (or hedge-crossing) for personal and/or group use

To practice and perform ritual

Materials Needed

Stang, candle, lighter

Cauldron, water, lancet

Anvil, hammer

Three knives (red, black, white)

Triple Cord

Service Cord

Bread, lipped dish or bowl

Red wine, cup

Incense, holder, charcoal

Other materials, as dictated by the rite

Note: This list represents general ritual materials. Add or subtract whatever is needed for the ritual you choose to experience.

Study Notes

For this and all Sabbats in Year 3, you will be writing your own ritual. This is an opportunity to explore, experiment, and create. The ritual does NOT have to be complicated or include lots of steps. In fact, if your sense of the Magical Artes is more simple, this is a great opportunity to tailor workings to match your proclivities.

If you are working with a group (or plan to do so in the future) this is a chance to experiment with putting things together for more than one person. Group ritual can have some different considerations than solo ritual.

For every Sabbat in this year, we will take the time to talk about some of the Mysteries, themes, taboos, and traditions you might draw from. You are also encouraged to revisit the Sabbats in Years 1 and 2 for inspiration.

Seasonal Themes, Traditions, and Taboos

Both equinoxes are times of balance, and are linked to the Queens of our Tradition. The vernal equinox is a time of dawn, birth, and freshness. Furthermore, the month of March is associated with Birch — with February and April being linked to Willow and Ash, respectively. These are the 3 woods of the traditional broom, a tool our Tradition closely associates with the Golden Queen.

Rituals might include egg balancing, egg decorating, egg cleansing, broom riding, broom cleansing, lantern lighting, and more.

You can look to the Year 1 and Year 2 rituals, BoS pages, and study notes for inspiration and guidance; but also feel encouraged to do your own digging into the folklore and folk magick surrounding this holiday to see if there are other aspects you would like to explore or incorporate. Maybe something stands out to you from a cultural tradition that we haven't studied as a group, but which nevertheless informs your personal practice.

Mysteries Associated with this Sabbat

Within the framework of the lesson, our goal cannot be to transmit the Mysteries, themselves. We can only hint at them here. These are opportunities to consider the underlying Truths and to allow them to reveal themselves to you.

These are not necessarily the ONLY Mysteries that we could approach or contemplate at this season. I recommend jotting down other big Truths that are very present for you at this time of year.

"The Broom" — In his letters to Joe Wilson, Robert Cochrane discusses what we call "The Mystery of the Broom." He sums it up using the enigmatic phrase "spinning without motion between three elements." The Broom as a transvective tool allows us to MOVE between the Realms — without necessarily moving our bodies at all.

"The Golden Lantern" — All of the vessels and weapons of the Spiral Castle impart their own Mysteries. To better understand the inspiration, poetry, art, and illusion of the Golden Lantern, consider the Sun in alchemy and classical astrology, will o' th' wisps and foxfire in Irish and Appalachian lore, the rays of Awen, and tales of magic lamps.

| Assignment | Write and perform a Spring Equinox ritual. This can be a group or personal ritual. Debrief the ritual with the other participants (if applicable) and also by writing a reflection of your experience. |

Your debrief should include:

- any impressions you had or challenges you experienced during the set-up
- how you might alter this ritual for solo/group use
- a notation of the date and general time you did the ritual
- who (if anyone) was with you
- impressions, insights, and sensations you had throughout the ritual (during the opening portions, the working, or the meal)
- any challenges you experienced while executing the ritual
- ideas that this ritual sparked for you (either for other rituals or for other creative/philosophical endeavors in your world)
- anything else that you feel should be noted

Additional Resources

None

BoS Pages Included

Laying the Compass

Opening the Gates

Raising the Castles

Calling the Realms

The Housle

Spring Equinox Mysteries

Beltaine

Prerequisite Lesson

None

Objective

To align with the seasonal energies of the Sabbat

To explore the Mysteries related to the Sabbat

To create a Beltaine ritual (or hedge-crossing) for personal and/or group use

To practice and perform ritual

Materials Needed

Stang, candle, lighter

Cauldron, water, lancet

Anvil, hammer

Three knives (red, black, white)

Triple Cord

Service Cord

Bread, lipped dish or bowl

Red wine, cup

Incense, holder, charcoal

Other materials, as dictated by the rite

Note: This list represents general ritual materials. Add or subtract whatever is needed for the ritual you choose to experience.

Study Notes

For this and all Sabbats in Year 3, you will be writing your own ritual. This is an opportunity to explore, experiment, and create. The ritual does NOT have to be complicated or include lots of steps. In fact, if your sense of the Magical Artes is more simple, this is a great opportunity to tailor workings to match your proclivities.

If you are working with a group (or plan to do so in the future) this is a chance to experiment with putting things together for more than one person. Group ritual can have some different considerations than solo ritual.

For every Sabbat in this year, we will take the time to talk about some of the Mysteries, themes, taboos, and traditions you might draw from. You are also encouraged to revisit the Sabbats in Years 1 and 2 for inspiration.

Seasonal Themes, Traditions, and Taboos

Beltaine is a festive and generally jovial time, but there is a sort of "memento mori" feeling in our celebrations, as well. Enjoy this life in all of its fullness and fervor, but remember that you will die. At Beltaine (or Walpurgisnacht), we encounter "Death in Life" — the little death, perhaps.

Rituals might include a balefire, passing between two fires, flying to the Brocken for the Great Sabbat, a maypole dance, the Great Rite, etc.

You can look to the Year 1 and Year 2 rituals, BoS pages, and study notes for inspiration and guidance; but also feel encouraged to do your own digging into the folklore and folk magick surrounding this holiday to see if there are other aspects you would like to explore or incorporate. Maybe something stands out to you from a cultural tradition that we haven't studied as a group, but which nevertheless informs your personal practice.

Mysteries Associated with this Sabbat

Within the framework of the lesson, our goal cannot be to transmit the Mysteries, themselves. We can only hint at them here. These are opportunities to consider the underlying Truths and to allow them to reveal themselves to you.

These are not necessarily the ONLY Mysteries that we could approach or contemplate at this season. I recommend jotting down other big Truths that are very present for you at this time of year.

"Life in Death; Death in Life" — This is a phrase we use to reference something very fundamental to this Tradition. While the WitchMother isn't particular prominent at this Sabbat, this phrase IS. (And this phrase is very much associated with Her.) This Mystery is also very present with us at Samhain.

"The Sword That Cuts Both Ways" — All of the weapons and vessels of the Spiral Castle impart their own lessons and Mysteries. The Sword (weapon of the East Gate) has much to teach. One of the ways it shows up is as the Sword Bridge that we cross into the place of Initiation. As such, we name the Coven Sword as "The Sword That Cuts Both Ways."

Assignment

Write and perform a Beltaine ritual. This can be a group or personal ritual. Debrief the ritual with the other participants (if applicable) and also by writing a reflection of your experience.

Your debrief should include:

- any impressions you had or challenges you experienced during the set-up
- how you might alter this ritual for solo/group use
- a notation of the date and general time you did the ritual
- who (if anyone) was with you
- impressions, insights, and sensations you had throughout the ritual (during the opening portions, the working, or the meal)
- any challenges you experienced while executing the ritual
- ideas that this ritual sparked for you (either for other rituals or for other creative/philosophical endeavors in your world)
- anything else that you feel should be noted

Additional Resources

None

BoS Pages Included

Laying the Compass

Opening the Gates

Raising the Castles

Calling the Realms

The Housle

Beltaine Mysteries

Midsummer

Prerequisite Lesson

None

Objective

To align with the seasonal energies of the Sabbat

To explore the Mysteries related to the Sabbat

To create a Midsummer ritual (or hedge-crossing) for personal and/or group use

To practice and perform ritual

Materials Needed

Stang, candle, lighter

Cauldron, water, lancet

Anvil, hammer

Three knives (red, black, white)

Triple Cord

Service Cord

Bread, lipped dish or bowl

Red wine, cup

Incense, holder, charcoal

Other materials, as dictated by the rite

Note: This list represents general ritual materials. Add or subtract whatever is needed for the ritual you choose to experience.

Study Notes

For this and all Sabbats in Year 3, you will be writing your own ritual. This is an opportunity to explore, experiment, and create. The ritual does NOT have to be complicated or include lots of steps. In fact, if your sense of the Magical Artes is more simple, this is a great opportunity to tailor workings to match your proclivities.

If you are working with a group (or plan to do so in the future) this is a chance to experiment with putting things together for more than one person. Group ritual can have some different considerations than solo ritual.

For every Sabbat in this year, we will take the time to talk about some of the Mysteries, themes, taboos, and traditions you might draw from. You are also encouraged to revisit the Sabbats in Years 1 and 2 for inspiration.

Seasonal Themes, Traditions, and Taboos

Midsummer is a time of activity — hands-on, boots-on-the-ground, nitty-gritty. It is a time of both work and play, which we see in our vision of the Stone Castle as a warriors' fort — train hard all day, play hard all night. We are awash in the verdant landscape, embodied by the Oak King. It is also a time that it linked to the Good Neighbors (the fey).

Rituals might include: bonfires, fireworks, revelry, Oak/Holly King battles, fairy houses, and more.

You can look to the Year 1 and Year 2 rituals, BoS pages, and study notes for inspiration and guidance; but also feel encouraged to do your own digging into the folklore and folk magick surrounding this holiday to see if there are other aspects you would like to explore or incorporate. Maybe something stands out to you from a cultural tradition that we haven't studied as a group, but which nevertheless informs your personal practice.

Mysteries Associated with this Sabbat

Within the framework of the lesson, our goal cannot be to transmit the Mysteries, themselves. We can only hint at them here. These are opportunities to consider the underlying Truths and to allow them to reveal themselves to you.

These are not necessarily the ONLY Mysteries that we could approach or contemplate at this season. I recommend jotting down other big Truths that are very present for you at this time of year.

"Robin and Wren"/"Oak King and Holly King" — Here in the lightest time of year is a good time to consider the power of community, activity, and abundance (as well as how these things balance with solitude, contemplation, and thriftiness).

"The Stone Bowl" — All of the vessels and weapons of the Spiral Castle carry their own Mysteries. The Stone Bowl reminds us that "There is no magic without sacrifice" — a phrase which we often paint or carve on the bottom of this dish.

Assignment

Write and perform a Midsummer ritual. This can be a group or personal ritual. Debrief the ritual with the other participants (if applicable) and also by writing a reflection of your experience.

Your debrief should include:
- any impressions you had or challenges you experienced during the set-up
- how you might alter this ritual for solo/group use
- a notation of the date and general time you did the ritual
- who (if anyone) was with you
- impressions, insights, and sensations you had throughout the ritual (during the opening portions, the working, or the meal)
- any challenges you experienced while executing the ritual
- ideas that this ritual sparked for you (either for other rituals or for other creative/philosophical endeavors in your world)
- anything else that you feel should be noted

Additional Resources

None

BoS Pages Included

Laying the Compass

Opening the Gates

Raising the Castles

Calling the Realms

The Housle

Midsummer Mysteries

Lammas/Lughnasadh

<u>Prerequisite Lesson</u>

None

<u>Objective</u>

To align with the seasonal energies of the Sabbat

To explore the Mysteries related to the Sabbat

To create a Lammas/Lughnasadh ritual (or hedge-crossing) for personal and/or group use

To practice and perform ritual

<u>Materials Needed</u>

Stang, candle, lighter

Cauldron, water, lancet

Anvil, hammer

Three knives (red, black, white)

Triple Cord

Service Cord

Bread, lipped dish or bowl

Red wine, cup

Incense, holder, charcoal

Other materials, as dictated by the rite

Note: This list represents general ritual materials. Add or subtract whatever is needed for the ritual you choose to experience.

<u>Study Notes</u>

For this and all Sabbats in Year 3, you will be writing your own ritual. This is an opportunity to explore, experiment, and create. The ritual does NOT have to be complicated or include lots of steps. In fact, if your sense of the Magical Artes is more simple, this is a great opportunity to tailor workings to match your proclivities.

If you are working with a group (or plan to do so in the future) this is a chance to experiment with putting things together for more than one person. Group ritual can have some different considerations than solo ritual.

For every Sabbat in this year, we will take the time to talk about some of the Mysteries, themes, taboos, and traditions you might draw from. You are also encouraged to revisit the Sabbats in Years 1 and 2 for inspiration.

Seasonal Themes, Traditions, and Taboos

This Sabbat can be viewed within our Tradition as either Lughnasadh or Lammas. The traditions associated with the two holidays are different, but they offer wonderful opportunities to explore the seasonal energies of this time. Furthermore, we tend to honor Goda at this time, as it is Her sacred day — including possessory and oracular work with Her.

Rituals might include: Uneasy Seat, Goda Oracle, corn dollies/bread men, oath-taking, games and competitions, 7 veils/gates, shield-making, and more.

You can look to the Year 1 and Year 2 rituals, BoS pages, and study notes for inspiration and guidance; but also feel encouraged to do your own digging into the folklore and folk magick surrounding this holiday to see if there are other aspects you would like to explore or incorporate. Maybe something stands out to you from a cultural tradition that we haven't studied as a group, but which nevertheless informs your personal practice.

Mysteries Associated with this Sabbat

Within the framework of the lesson, our goal cannot be to transmit the Mysteries, themselves. We can only hint at them here. These are opportunities to consider the underlying Truths and to allow them to reveal themselves to you.

These are not necessarily the ONLY Mysteries that we could approach or contemplate at this season. I recommend jotting down other big Truths that are very present for you at this time of year.

"What songs the siren sings?" — Goda is Our Lady of Lammas — a time of sacrifice and also joy, abundance, and oaths. This is a great time to contemplate Goda and her associations with love, loss, reunion of the Soul, and song.

"Uneasy Seat Above Caer Ochren" — This is a wonderful time to explore the Mysteries of oracular work. Our Tradition associates Lammas with invoking Goda and asking for Her guidance and wisdom on Her most holy day. She often reveals Her own Mysteries, but the process itself has much to impart, as well.

"The Dance of the Seven Veils" — Goda stands naked, having shed the veils already. What do we find when we strip away our careers, relationships, memories, bodies, desires, etc. Consider Inanna's descent, and the jewelry/garments she relinquishes at each gate. Consider the 7 classical planets, and the 7 most commonly discussed chakras. Consider the process of aging and death, and how we all eventually "stand naked."

"The Shield" — Each of our vessels and weapons unfolds its own Mysteries. Some are better documented than others in the traditions of the Craft and other Mystery Schools. The Shield is one that gets short shrift in most places, but it is still present and powerful. It is related to the Witch's Glove, the Pentacle, and even the Cloak (which is a shielding device in myth and literature).

"The Light in the Darkness, the Darkness in the Light" — Kolyo and Goda share this Mystery, which they teach us using different methods. Starlight in an inky sky. Stark shadows in the brightest sun. Nakedness. Cloaking. Youth. Age. Nothing is as straightforward as it seems. First impressions are often deceiving.

| Assignment | Write and perform a Lammas/Lughnasadh ritual. This can be a group or personal ritual. Debrief the ritual with the other participants (if applicable) and also by writing a reflection of your experience. |

Your debrief should include:

- any impressions you had or challenges you experienced during the set-up
- how you might alter this ritual for solo/group use
- a notation of the date and general time you did the ritual
- who (if anyone) was with you
- impressions, insights, and sensations you had throughout the ritual (during the opening portions, the working, or the meal)
- any challenges you experienced while executing the ritual
- ideas that this ritual sparked for you (either for other rituals or for other creative/philosophical endeavors in your world)
- anything else that you feel should be noted

Additional Resources

"Siren Song" by Ian Chambers — http://www.clanoftubalcain.org.uk/sirensong.html

BoS Pages Included

Laying the Compass

Opening the Gates

Raising the Castles

Calling the Realms

The Housle

Lammas Mysteries

Fall Equinox

Prerequisite Lesson

None

Objective

To align with the seasonal energies of the Sabbat

To explore the Mysteries related to the Sabbat

To create a Fall Equinox ritual (or hedge-crossing) for personal and/or group use

To practice and perform ritual

Materials Needed

Stang, candle, lighter

Cauldron, water, lancet

Anvil, hammer

Three knives (red, black, white)

Triple Cord

Service Cord

Bread, lipped dish or bowl

Red wine, cup

Incense, holder, charcoal

Other materials, as dictated by the rite

Note: This list represents general ritual materials. Add or subtract whatever is needed for the ritual you choose to experience.

Study Notes

For this and all Sabbats in Year 3, you will be writing your own ritual. This is an opportunity to explore, experiment, and create. The ritual does NOT have to be complicated or include lots of steps. In fact, if your sense of the Magical Artes is more simple, this is a great opportunity to tailor workings to match your proclivities.

If you are working with a group (or plan to do so in the future) this is a chance to experiment with putting things together for more than one person. Group ritual can have some different considerations than solo ritual.

For every Sabbat in this year, we will take the time to talk about some of the Mysteries, themes, taboos, and traditions you might draw from. You are also encouraged to revisit the Sabbats in Years 1 and 2 for inspiration.

Seasonal Themes, Traditions, and Taboos

Both equinoxes are a time for contemplating balance. The autumnal equinox is also associated with sacrifice and feasting, hunting, and the cauldron/cup/grail.

Rituals might include: Broom-Standing, Cauldron scrying, harvest feast, Hunt for Mabon, masking, story-telling, etc.

You can look to the Year 1 and Year 2 rituals, BoS pages, and study notes for inspiration and guidance; but also feel encouraged to do your own digging into the folklore and folk magick surrounding this holiday to see if there are other aspects you would like to explore or incorporate. Maybe something stands out to you from a cultural tradition that we haven't studied as a group, but which nevertheless informs your personal practice.

Mysteries Associated with this Sabbat

Within the framework of the lesson, our goal cannot be to transmit the Mysteries, themselves. We can only hint at them here. These are opportunities to consider the underlying Truths and to allow them to reveal themselves to you.

These are not necessarily the ONLY Mysteries that we could approach or contemplate at this season. I recommend jotting down other big Truths that are very present for you at this time of year.

"What the Mask Reveals" — The Spiral Castle Tradition often performs a "Hunt for Mabon" at the Fall Equinox. During this ritual, we usually mask — either as a Hunter or as one of the Five Animals that the hunting party queries. We work with the Mask in order to better understand both ourselves and That which is represented by a specific mask.

"The Mystery of the Cauldron" — Robert Cochrane wrote about the Mystery of the Cauldron in this letters to Joe Wilson. He poses a riddle to Wilson, asking him what can't exist within the Cauldron. "Two words: Be Still." The Cauldron holds all — all life, all hope, all desire, all abundance, all possibility. It is always moving. Always shifting. Always becoming. There is no stillness in the Cauldron. (But there can be stillness within us, which we find within this tumult.)

"The Bloody Cup/The Holy Grail" — All of the vessels and weapons of the Spiral Castle impart their own Mysteries. This is probably the most well-known of all the Mysteries we seek. The San Greal — or Sang Real.

"The Five Transformations" — Ceridwen is one of the ladies whom we see most clearly as our Silver Queen. She is the keeper of the Cauldron, and her story of flight, pursuit, and transformation with the young Gwion Bach (who becomes Taliesin) is most revealing.

Assignment	Write and perform a Fall Equinox ritual. This can be a group or personal ritual. Debrief the ritual with the other participants (if applicable) and also by writing a reflection of your experience.

Your debrief should include:

- any impressions you had or challenges you experienced during the set-up
- how you might alter this ritual for solo/group use
- a notation of the date and general time you did the ritual
- who (if anyone) was with you
- impressions, insights, and sensations you had throughout the ritual (during the opening portions, the working, or the meal)
- any challenges you experienced while executing the ritual
- ideas that this ritual sparked for you (either for other rituals or for other creative/philosophical endeavors in your world)
- anything else that you feel should be noted

Additional Resources

Avalon Within — Jhenah Telyndru — https://amzn.to/3OZ0EMs

BoS Pages Included

Laying the Compass

Opening the Gates

Raising the Castles

Calling the Realms

The Housle

Fall Equinox Mysteries

Ethics, Revisited

Prerequisite Lesson

None specified

Objective

To revisit the "Ethics Statement" written in Year 1

Materials Needed

Your "Ethics Statement" from Year 1

Study Notes

The consideration and discussion of ethics is not a "one and done" practice for a Witch of the Spiral Castle. We understand that our experiences shape us. Bearing witness to the experiences of others shapes us. These lives we live are circuitous, and they are designed to bring us to the most clear understanding of our own Selves (or own Souls) that we can achieve.

To hold doggedly to a set of ethics might actually be unethical. To never revisit and reconsider. To never allow for a place of grace or a place of continued growth …

Well, if not "unethical," then certainly something less than rigorous.

Every few years, I encourage you to look at (and revise, if warranted) your statement of ethics. Journal about it, if you work solitary. Discuss these as a group, if you work with a study group (or later, a coven). Poke at each piece, and ask:

- Does this piece reflect what I have done?
- Does it reflect how I see myself?
- Where did I acquire this piece? Am I comfortable with its origins?
- Do I judge others and their actions by the same standard? (If not, why not? If so, how so?)
- Are there shades of grey? Is there room for grace?
- What does accountability look like?

Other questions may arise that are particular to your ethics. Flow with those questions. Dig into them.

If you lead or participate in a study group (or if you plan to lead a coven) within this Tradition, ask yourself some questions about how you will handle working with students/group-mates who may have different ethical standards than your own. For instance, if you are personally opposed to hexing/blasting magick, are you able to be tolerant of those practices in others?

Assignment

Write a brief reflection regarding your personal ethics. Be sure to include the following:

- How they have changed/adapted.
- How they have remained the same.
- Answer as many of the questions from the lesson as you can.

Additional Resources

None

BoS Pages Included

None

Cautions

Prerequisite Lesson   04-01 Ethics, Revisited

Objective   To reflect on the possible repercussions of baneful magick

Materials Needed   Journal, pen/cil

Study Notes   When we are talking about ethics, it is worthwhile at some point in the process to take a deep look at the baneful or blasting magicks that are part of the spectrum of magick available to us.

To do this, I feel that we need to establish a certain foundational principle within this Tradition. As Hassan-i Sabbah (founder of the Order of Assassins) said on his death-bed in 1124: "Nothing is real — everything is permitted." This is to say that there are no natural, empirical laws that govern ethics. Only the codes we agree to live by circumscribe our reality. Nobody can stop us from doing what we please. Ultimately it is we ourselves who must choose.

Robert Cochrane wrote shared the following "old Witch Laws" in one of his letters to Joe Wilson:

> *Do not do what you desire - do what is necessary.*
> *Take all you are given - give all of yourself.*
> *What I have - - - I hold!*
> *When all else is lost, and not until then, prepare to die with dignity.*

In a letter to William G. Gray, Cochrane said:

> *Nothing is purely good or evil, these are relative terms that man has hung upon unacceptable mysteries. To my particular belief the Goddess, white with works of good, is also black with works of darkness, yet both of them are compassionate, albeit the compassion is a cover for the ruthlesness of total Truth.*

61

There is a lot to unpack in both of those pieces of wisdom. One of the things Glaux and I gleaned from them is that baneful acts of magick (ie, magick that is intended to cause harm) are not inherently bad or negative — even though the results would be negative for the person on the receiving end of that magick. However, if these acts of blasting magick (such as banishing and cursing/hexing) are being undertaken in order to protect someone who needs protection (including ourselves) OR keep what is ours (or help a another person keep what is theirs), then they are part of "doing what is necessary."

What about baneful magick that is undertaken in retribution — an act of vengeance for a wrong already committed? Again, I can't say for another person what is necessary, nor can I necessarily understand what part of themselves they are protecting or keeping by lashing out. I have no power to permit or deny their actions, but I can absolutely choose the extent to which I participate (and whether or not I need anything from a raincoat to a nuclear bunker to avoid the backlash, if it comes).

That brings me to the first caution that I would offer any student of this path who is considering baneful workings:

> *Remember that all magick requires sacrifice.*

No matter how justified you feel, how dire the need, how beneficent or benign the act of magick — it all comes with a cost. That DOES actually seem to be something of a natural (or supernatural) law. Physics and metaphysics seem to share the concept that every action causes a reaction. Whether that reaction in magick is always "equal and opposite" is fuzzier in my mind. But it is there.

This isn't a caution away from performing spellcraft. Rather it is a reminder to be honest about the need, to investigate the cost before taking action, and to take accountability for the price when you choose to proceed.

Other cautions that I would give, include:

- Trauma creates energetic links between people. Be aware of the bond you already have with the person who would be the target of your blasting. Be as fastidious as you can in severing links (using our Link Cutting Ritual). Understand that you may be intensifying those links by taking magickal action.
- Blasting magicks are very often viewed with revulsion and suspicion — even from the Witches who love us (sometimes even when they agree that some type of drastic action was needed). This is an area where the Sphinx's power "to keep silent" is useful — to protect both your own "reputation" and the magick itself.
- If you are going to do any sort of banishing or hexing magick with a partner or group, everyone present must be "of a mind." Everyone who is contributing energy needs to be clear on the What, the Who, the Why, the How, the How Much, etc. Not just clear on it, but in total agreement about it. (And everyone needs to understand and accept their price for participating.)
- Play out a "worst case scenario" of the after-effects of the magick you are considering, and be honest with yourself regarding whether or not you can accept those consequences. Very often, the worst case is actual literal death. (I know that sounds far-fetched, but I assure you, it isn't. I've witnessed a person pushing themselves through the "fiery wall of protection" as they single-mindedly came after someone who was surrounded in witchy protections. At any time, they could have stopped attacking, and they would have been fine. The person wouldn't stop, though, and the spell played out when that person ultimately died — I would argue, at their own hands — due to complications from substance abuse.) You need to ask the hard questions, and be sure you are okay with a result like that before proceeding.

- It is easy to become desensitized to the plight of others if/when baneful work becomes your favorite tool. Remember the old adage, "If all you have a is a hammer, every problem starts to look like a nail."

There is probably more that could be said, but most of it boils down to staying open and honest with yourself and accepting the full responsibility for your actions (both mundane and magickal).

Assignment

Write a brief reflection regarding baneful magick. Be sure to consider the following:

- Any spellwork you have done that has had an unintended negative impact on someone else (or even, had the intended impact, but it was more negative than you had anticipated) — such as in the case of a protection spell.
- Situations that you think could warrant baneful magick — regardless of whether or not you might take that step.

Additional Resources

None

BoS Pages Included

None

Banishing

Prerequisite Lesson

04-02 Cautions

Objective

To look at the mechanics of banishing

To practice creating a spell with the intention of banishing a threat/enemy

Materials Needed

Journal, pen/cil

Study Notes

For this lesson and the next, I am going to ask you to do something that many Witches would consider unthinkable. I am going to ask you to write two baneful spells.

I am NOT asking that you perform them. (Nor will I ask IF you performed them.)

In this case, the performance isn't the point.

What IS the point? Well, there are a few points.

1) I want you to know that you CAN do this darkside magick, if the need is great enough. Not just "know" in a theoretical way, but really know that you have the ability to protect you and yours with a very full arsenal.

2) I believe that we have to have some familiarity with how blasting magick works in order to counteract it.

3) Blasting and blessing both exist along the same continuum. To deny ourselves access to one is to limit the other.

4) If you plan to teach/lead within this (or any) Tradition, someone will eventually ask questions about this realm of magick. It is hard to give answers that come from a place of experience if you don't have some basic experience.

This is an intellectual exercise intended to sharpen and improve your skills as a Witch. I am in no way trying to push you into performing any type of magick with which you are uncomfortable. Indeed, I would challenge you to find those "grey places" within this task where you ARE comfortable.

Banishing Magick

We've discussed banishing before — in the Year 1 lessons on Energy Work. Of course, at that time, we were talking about banishing energies or entities, which is a different sort of thing than banishing a person. (Not really, in fact. But it feels different since most people don't think of energies or entities as beings with freewill and conscious desires.)

To banish a person means to make them leave whatever space it is that they occupy as it relates to you. It may involve their physical relocation, a redirection of their attention, or a sort of "report and block user" to the Universe.

Banishing, in my mind, doesn't inherently harm the target of the spell.

A major school of thought when I was coming up in the Craft was that any act of magick that interfered with the freewill of another person was a negative or baneful magick. I whole-heartedly disagree. For one thing, I am not entirely convinced that a person's freewill can be overridden like that. I think that even in cases of love spells, domination spells, etc, the spell is a magickal nudge (or permission slip) that allows the target to go along with a desire they already had but were denying to themselves. It is NOT some sort of magickal roofie that obliterates their ability to choose.

I make a super effective GTFO Oil (which is basically a banishing oil). It uses cayenne, sage, sea salt, sulphur, asafetida, and crossroads dirt. All of that is mixed into castor oil using a coffin nail. (Yep. Yowzers!) Clients and friends have used this oil with truly remarkable results. Targets get amazing job offers and move across the country, take advantage of fantastic opportunities that get them out of the professional/social sphere of the petitioner, get new housing opportunities (in neighborhoods far removed from the petitioner who used to be their neighbor), or decide that they are bored with bothering the petitioner and just sort of bugger off.

I will admit that I know of some targets who have gotten divorced, gotten fired, and gotten evicted as well — none of which are "super happy fun time" results for them. But also, I would absolutely argue that the factors that culminated in those results were brewing for a lot longer than my oil was at play — and they were always results that the targets could have avoided by making better choices (in both the mundane and the magickal senses).

<u>Assignment</u>

Research various methods of banishing, and write a spell that you could use to "send away" a target, if needed. Consider for yourself what sort of circumstances would need to exist for you to perform this spell. Be sure to include as much detail as possible regarding the spell's materials, planetary/lunar factors, Spirits/Godds, etc.

<u>Additional Resources</u>

None

<u>BoS Pages Included</u>

Be Gone/GTFO

Banishing Spells

Hexing & Cursing

Prerequisite Lesson

04-03 Banishing

Objective

To look at the mechanics of cursing/hexing

To practice creating a spell with the intention of cursing/hexing an enemy

Materials Needed

Journal, pen/cil

Study Notes

Again, I feel that I need to reiterate (as I did in Lesson 04-03 Banishing) that this lesson and assignment are theoretical in nature and that I am not asking or even suggesting that you perform a curse or hex on someone. Nor am I judging or criticizing you, if you do perform one.

All of the same reasons apply to this work, as they did in Lesson 04-03.

1) I want you to know that you CAN do this darkside magick, if the need is great enough. Not just "know" in a theoretical way, but really know that you have the ability to protect you and yours with a very full arsenal.

2) I believe that we have to have some familiarity with how blasting magick works in order to counteract it.

3) Blasting and blessing both exist along the same continuum. To deny ourselves access to one is to limit the other.

4) If you plan to teach/lead within this (or any) Tradition, someone will eventually ask questions about this realm of magick. It is hard to give answers that come from a place of experience if you don't have some basic experience.

This is an intellectual exercise intended to sharpen and improve your skills as a Witch. I am in no way trying to push you into performing any type of magick with which you are uncomfortable. Indeed, I would challenge you to find those "grey places" within this task where you ARE comfortable.

Hexing & Cursing Magick

Whether you call it a curse, a hex, or something else, magick of this type is intended to cause harm to a target. You can't curse them "for their highest good, and harm to none."

Okay. Because I so often play Devil's Advocate, I'll say that sometimes the swift kick in the butt that this sort of magick delivers could cause them to rethink their life choices and set them on a better path — hence, being ultimate "for their highest good." But I don't necessarily want us to fool ourselves that we are really doing this for them, to help them learn, etc.

No. A curse or hex is designed to hurt/harm the target, and we do it for ourselves (or our petitioner, if we choose to do work for other people). Maybe it is part of a protection working. Maybe it is part of a working for retribution/justice. Yes, indeed, the action and result of both of those spells can be a hex/curse on the target, whether we consciously phrased it as such or not. (I mean, what do you think you are casting on a trespasser when you piss into a bottle of rusty nails and glass shards? Is it any less of a curse because they wronged you first? Or because you didn't attach a specific target's name to the spell?)

Or maybe it is a straight-up John Wick-worthy vengeance working you are doing. (Wouldn't that still be a justice spell? Someone wronged you in a way so egregious that you are calling for their total or partial destruction — in repayment of what they took/did?)

Some of the curses and hexes that we see from historical and folkloric sources seem petty and unprovoked, but I have to worder if the Witch who wrote/cast them would agree. Was that Witch possibly defending (or avenging) the last ragged piece of identity, ownership, or joy that was left to them? Or maybe they were trying to claw and scrape something for themselves — something of value, of beauty, of pride — in a world where they were born with nothing, given nothing, and seen as deserving of nothing. It is impossible to know, but it is worth remembering that magick doesn't exist without context, and that it is often the tool of the oppressed who have few physical, legal, social, or other practical choices left to them.

I only make a mild distinction between the terms hexing and cursing, and there doesn't seem to be a standard differentiation between the two. For me, this is what I mean when I use these terms:

Hexing — Unintentional magick that causes harm to a target (such as the Evil Eye or other big emotions from one person causing a change in another person's circumstances). This might almost fall into the category of "Accidental Magick."

Cursing — Intentional magick to cause harm to a target

| Assignment | Research various methods of cursing/hexing, and write a spell that you could use on a target, if needed. Consider for yourself what sort of circumstances would need to exist for you to perform this spell. Be sure to include as much detail as possible regarding the spell's materials, planetary/lunar factors, Spirits/Godds, etc. |

| Additional Resources | None |

BoS Pages Included	Be Still/STFU
	Fiery Wall/Watch Over Me
	All is Fair
	Domina
	Protection Spells
	Ruination Spells
	Domination Spells
	Justice Spells
	War Water
	Witch Cake

Historical Research

Prerequisite Lesson

None specified

Objective

To research the historical/cultural symbols, relationships, and stories connected to your Godd-Friend or Familiar

To research how that Godd/Spirit was worshipped/worked with by others

Materials Needed

Internet

Library access

Note-taking materials

Study Notes

Traditional and folkloric Witches have a bit of a reputation for being bookworms and academics. Not all of us are those things — but a lot of us are! If our practice is rooted in historical and folkloric ways of working, chances are good that you've needed to unearth some of that history and folklore on your own.

Our Spirit relationships — whether with a Godd-Friend/-Spouse or a Familiar Spirit — deserve the same level of research and devotion. We owe it to both ourselves and to Them to know some things about who They are (or have been), separate from what we have intuited.

Intuition and Personal Gnosis are both great! More than that, they are important components of building your personal relationship with Deity/Spirit. In fact, other lessons in this unit are going to ask you to dig deeply into those kennings.

It is my deeply held belief (based on years of experience) that a historical grounding and an intuitive understanding are the two halves of a great whole when it comes to knowing a Spirit/Godd.

For this lesson, I want you to do some research. Look to books in print, books online, credible websites, sacred texts, etc. You are trying to find what has been written about how others worked with and/or worshipped your Godd-Friend or Familiar Spirit.

Some Deities and Spirits are relatively easy to find information about. Others are not, I'm afraid. For the ones who aren't, unturn every rock you can. If they were a living person, see what you can discover about their life. If they are, for example, a leanan-sidhe (or a whatever type of Spirit), research what you can about that type of Spirit.

Questions you want to be able to answer at this stage include:
- What are their major stories/myths/accounts?
- What do we know about others who have worked with them? Do/did they have clergy or sacred servants? Did those people share any common features?
- What offerings, sacrifices, or rituals are associated with them?
- Do they have cognates (counterparts) in other cultures or eras?

As you gather information, you will most likely come across answers to questions in 05-02 (Associations & Areas of Influence). I recommend taking a look ahead at that lesson so you don't discard or lose track of details as you work.

Include a Works Cited/Consulted (Bibliography) page. I don't expect you to write your "paper" using MLA, APA, or the Chicago Style Manual format. I'm not looking for a particular word or page count. But for your own sake (and mine, if you are engaged in mentoring with me), you should absolutely make note of where your information originates.

I'm hoping that you'll be able to dig deeply into the source material. Look for the sorts of books and articles that also cite their sources, and then go check out those for yourself. Dig into the originals, as much as your topic allows — translations of the first written records of the myths or history around your Godd or Spirit.

Record-Keeping Suggestion: Make an effort to save a printed or digital copy of any online sources you use, for your own future reference. Even the very best stuff on the Internet tends to go away after a decade or so — or become impossible to find again due to the overwhelming amount of people writing about a given search term. I have been grateful over the years that I saved things like the 1734 Papers from Joe Wilson's website or favorite essays from Sarah Anne Lawless. And I have kicked myself for NOT saving other bits that would have been so helpful for projects that I didn't know at the time I would undertake (like this series of courses).

<u>Assignment</u>	Write a research paper (with bibliography) that answers the questions:
	• What are their major stories/myths/accounts?
	• What do we know about others who have worked with them? Do/did they have clergy or sacred servants? Did those people share any common features?
	• What offerings, sacrifices, or rituals are associated with them?
	• Do they have cognates (counterparts) in other cultures or eras?

<u>Additional Resources</u>

Internet Sacred Text Archive — https://www.sacred-texts.com/

Theoi Greek Mythology — https://www.theoi.com/

Norse Mythology — https://norse-mythology.org/

Journals for Folklore Studies (Ohio State University) — https://cfs.osu.edu/about/resources/journals

Mythology, Fairy Tales, and Folklore Journals (NYU) — https://guides.nyu.edu/fairytales/journals

<u>BoS Pages Included</u>   Gods, Goddesses, and Mighty Ones set (in Year 1 book)

Associations & Areas of Influence

Prerequisite Lesson

05-01 "Historical Research"

Objective

To explore a chosen Godd's/Spirit's historical associations, symbols, and areas of influence

To recount your own Personal Gnosis regarding associations, symbols, and influ-

Materials Needed

Internet

Library access

Note-taking materials

Study Notes

This piece of research will blend your recent historical research with your personal experience. The key is to make sure that you are clear about which is which — both in your own mind, and also in work that you present to others.

This level of academic honesty was once the norm within Traditional Witchcraft. I'm sad to say it isn't, any longer. The Internet has offered such ease of access to sources and content, making it a real boon to those of us thirsty for information. Sadly, it has also made the promulgation of half-facts and unsubstantiated drivel all too easy (and abundant). There are a lot of tropes that exist on the premise of "common knowledge" that began they're existence as someone's UPG (Unverified Personal Gnosis). The issue isn't that those exist — rather that they are no longer credited as such.

Part of the culture of the Spiral Castle Tradition is that we still hold ourselves accountable for honesty (academic and otherwise)— and give credit where it is due. We value UPG (and also Group Gnosis), and we attempt to verify it through documented sources, other practitioners, etc. whenever possible. But we always own up to it (and don't try to pass it off as something historical).

Again, I don't necessarily expect MLA or APA formatting for your citations. (Don't get me wrong. I love them, and I will be giddy with academic shivers if you share work like that in the mentoring relationship or in the community app. I just don't require it.)

Crediting sources can be as simple as including tags like "According to so-and-so ..." or "In my personal experience ...".

Questions you want to be able to answer at this stage include:

- What are the symbols associated with this Godd/Spirit? And why?
- What colors are associated with Them? And why?
- Which animals, trees, herbs, stones, landmarks, actions, etc are associated with Them? And why?
- What types of magick do They excel at?
- Are there healing modalities within Their purview?
- Are there types of divination that They interact best with?
- What sort of communication methods do They enjoy?

You will be creating something like a Table of Correspondences (or at least a list), in a sense. It doesn't have to be a table at all — although feel free to use a format like that, if you find it helpful. Just be sure to include a column for your source. And also, don't shy away from digging into the rationale and stories for the correspondences in a more narrative way. Both approaches may be needed.

This is a great opportunity to take stock of what you know, what you think you'd like to know, and what you learned as a part of this process. It also will help you identify the gaps that still exist for you, which in turn gives you the opportunity to communicate directly with the Godd/Spirit and/or expand your research.

Be creative and don't feel constrained to the categories/questions I've listed above. Your Godd/Spirit may have unique features that you know and understand, but which I can't account for in this lesson. Explore and include those!

Assignment

Write a paper/essay regarding the associations and areas of influence (on record and also based on personal experience) for your Godd-Friend/Spirit. Questions might include:

- What are the symbols associated with this Godd/Spirit?
- What colors are associated with Them?
- Which animals, trees, herbs, stones, landmarks, actions, etc are associated with Them?
- What types of magick do They excel at?
- Are there healing modalities within Their purview?
- Are there types of divination that They interact best with?
- What sort of communication methods do They enjoy?

Additional Resources

None

BoS Pages Included

None

Personal Relationship

Prerequisite Lesson 05-03 "Associations & Areas of Influence"

Objective To document your personal experience of your Godd-Friend/Familiar Spirit

To notate your observations and kennings related to Them

Materials Needed Note-taking materials

Study Notes This section of your work is going to give you space to explore the personal relationship you have developed with your Godd-Friend/-Spouse or Familiar Spirit in a more narrative format.

YOU are the source here. Well, you and Them. There is no need for documentation, per se — aside from a heading or intro that clearly identifies this piece as based on personal experience.

I feel that this section might be easiest to approach from a sort of "interview" perspective. We're going to pretend that I am asking you all about your experiences and your kennings (intuitive knowings). You can add questions, if your experience covers something that I haven't asked.

1. How did you first encounter this Godd/Spirit?
2. What were your first impressions?
3. Describe what you remember of your earliest encounters? ("Encounters" might include dreams, visions, hedge-crossings, possessory work, intimacy.) Note: do not feel obligated to share intimate details with me/RTA peers. Do record and reflect on these experiences for yourself, though.
4. How often do you typically encounter Them now?
5. Describe the nature of those encounters. Are they always the same? Or is there a lot of variety?
6. What sort of rituals, offerings, or energy exchanges do They ask of you? (Or what do They particularly enjoy that you do for Them?)
7. In what ways have They assisted/guided you?

8. Have They asked for services, tasks, or work from you?

9. How would you characterize your relationship, as this time? (Friends, professional, lover/spouse, parental/familial?)

10. Do you feel bonded to Them? Or is there a sense that this is a temporary arrangement?

11. What have you sensed of Their personality? How does that experience compare with what you have researched?

12. Do you have any funny, poignant, or unexpected stories of your encounters?

13. What would you like to explore in the future related to Them?

Be as detailed and thorough as you are able with your answers. If you typically share your work as part of a mentoring relationship with me (or with the RTA community via the app), you can always edit the parts that feel too sacred or private to share. But this is a great time to record for yourself what your journey with Them has been like.

Assignment

Write a reflection that answers the questions posed in the Study Notes. Be as thorough and detailed as possible.

Additional Resources

None

BoS Pages Included

None

Representing Deity/Spirit

Prerequisite Lesson

05-03 "Personal Experiences"

Objective

To assess your role as an agent of your Godd/Spirit
To define what that work looks like for you now
To consider what that work might be in the future

Materials Needed

Note-taking materials

Study Notes

I want to state (clearly and unequivocally) here that having a relationship or bond with a Godd/Spirit does not, ipso facto, anoint anyone as a Priest/ex of that Godd/Spirit. Nor does it compel anyone into that type of service.

Also, you aren't obligated to offer a Spirit or Deity any service, even if they ask (or TELL) you directly that they want it. I know I have said this before, but it is worth repeating again and again. I've seen too many Witches use some variation of "The Devil made me do it" when rationalizing their own poor choices. No. No, He didn't. The Devil (or Aphrodite, or Cernunnos, or whomever) presented you an opportunity and you *pounced* like a lion on an antelope. You always have the right to say no. Granted, there could be consequences (a change in your relationship with Them, less frequent offers of cool opportunities, harder work that you have to do elsewhere, etc), but consequences are the reality of declining any offer or opportunity.

You are only obligated to perform services based on the commitments you have made based on your oaths and compacts.

We are exploring what this type of service *might* look like — and that includes both service to the community and also service to Deity.

The Focus Area you explored last year culminated in what we call "Service Cords," so this is the time to start planning and implementing that service. (Remember that you can always add other Focus Areas — other ways to serve.)

This is also the year in which we talk about Coven/Trad-wide leadership and explore the roles of Queen/Devil/Consort. Whether or not you ever choose to take on those roles, finishing this year's work (along with the previous two years' work) will qualify you to receive a Coven Charter. That means that you CAN become a Coven leader, if you choose. People in these roles within the Spiral Castle Trad work in service to both community and Deity. (We will explore the major aspects of service to Coven-community in Units 6, 7, and 8.)

So, let's think about what your service to Deity/Spirit might look like.

Again, the Focus Area you chose in Year 2: Practicum might be a good indicator of the shape that your service to Deity/Spirit may take. You could be their Warrior, their Healer, their Oracle, etc.

As you add skills and pursue other Focus Areas (using the progression laid out in Year 2, or a study program of your own devising), you may find that your service is multi-faceted and complex.

Let's explore some potential expressions of that service:

Artisan of [Deity/Spirit] — Some of the most moving and powerful art/statuary/talismans etc are fashioned by people who are devotees of the Godd or Spirit depicted. Selling your work is not discouraged in this Tradition, nor are other forms of public display. Sharing these acts of service with the Coven, local, regional, or global community may offer inspiration to the public and increase their positive awareness of your Godd/Spirit.

Bard of [Deity/Spirit] — Perhaps you create and share ritual, poetry, or music related to Them. Or perhaps your Bardism takes the form of teaching and sharing resources. If this is a Godd/Spirit for whom resources have not been gathered together, you could find yourself using the work you've done in this unit as the foundation for a book, website, etc — as an act of service to Them and a resource to others who are drawn to Them. My first book, *Aphrodite's Priestess*, came together in exactly this manner. I was tasked in my own studies with writing a research paper about Her — back in 2001/2002. There were no books or websites about being a Priestess of Aphrodite at that time, so I created an email group (early social media) where devotees could share resources. Eventually, I expanded on the paper I had written and published the book.

Conjurer of [Deity/Spirit] — As a Conjurer in service/relationship with a particular Godd/Spirit, you serve Them by helping them be palpable and present in the world. This could be invoking/evoking them at rituals. Or it could mean sharing your experiences of them with others. Or it may be more private, and involve rituals and workings that you undertake for their edification — away from the public gaze.

Healer of [Deity/Spirit] — You offer healing services (potentially for pay/barter, if you choose) to family members, Covenmates, or the local community in Their name and/or drawing on Their power. If this is a public service, you might not necessarily advertise that you are doing so, but you are mindful and grateful for the role They play nonetheless.

Seer of [Deity/Spirit] — You perform divinatory or oracular services in Their name and/or drawing on Their power. Again, you may not always share your source with the public, but you are nevertheless doing Their work in the world.

Votary of [Deity/Spirit] — You facilitate ritual experiences related to your Godd/Spirit for members of your Coven or community. Or maybe you only undertake private rituals. The choice is yours.

Warden of [Deity/Spirit] — As a Warden, you act as a Warrior and/or Guardian. Your Godd-Friend/Spirit has probably already pointed you in the direction of that which they want you to protect, whether that be a person, group of people, idea, or place.

These are just ideas. Starting places. You know your Godd-Friend/Familiar Spirit, and you know your own talents and interests. Examine for yourself where those overlap. Listen to your intuition and inclinations about the kind of work you feel drawn to. If you find yourself thinking (repeatedly), "What I really wish existed was X" or "Wouldn't it be great if someone did X" then chances are good that you are being tapped on the shoulder to make/do that thing.

I feel like this is the right place to note (or repeat) that you don't have to comply with that "tap." There may be repercussions/consequences if you don't take up the work, but you always have a choice.

Assignment

Write a reflection regarding your representation of (or service to) your Godd-Friend/Familiar Spirit. Consider:

- Are there public elements that you are being drawn to do?
- Are there private elements that you are being drawn to do/continue?
- What terms do you feel comfortable using for yourself within this role, and why? (Artisan/Bard/Conjurer of …, Priest/ex of …, Devotee of …, etc)
- Do you currently foresee your service changing or evolving in the future?

Additional Resources

None

BoS Pages Included

None

Rites of Passage

Prerequisite Lesson

None specified

Objective

To discuss the Rites of Passage that are honored within the Spiral Castle Tradition

To consider your role in facilitating these Rites of Passage for members of your own Family and community

Materials Needed

Note-taking materials

Study Notes

I want to start the discussion within this unit of lessons by beginning with a candid talk about the nature of the Spiral Castle Tradition and the roles of its 3rd Degree members.

First, I want to acknowledge that Witchcraft isn't a religion or a religious practice for everyone. I believe that Witches of the Spiral Castle can decide for themselves where they land on this question. We might be animists, theists, atheists, polytheists, pantheists, panentheists — or something else. The Spiral Castle Tradition doesn't dictate that for people. We know and understand that Witchcraft can be practiced with or without the things that make it a religion. And while those religious markers do distinctly exist within this Tradition, I believe that it is possible to be a Witch of the Spiral Castle and NOT subscribe to it as a religion.

Witches who DON'T relate to this Tradition as a religion (or through a religious lens) may view the cycle rituals and entities (Godds, Spirits, etc) as allegorical, metaphorical, or otherwise symbolic. And that is not only valid, but it is accepted here.

Witches who DO relate to this Tradition as a religion recognize that we have all the hallmarks of that category, and that the expression of those religious elements is meaningful to them on a spiritual level (rather than a purely psychological or metaphysical one).

The Oxford English Dictionary offers these definitions for "religion":
- the belief in and worship of a superhuman controlling power, especially a personal God or gods.

- a particular system of faith and worship
- a pursuit or interest to which someone ascribes supreme importance.

I would argue that the Spiral Castle Tradition has all of these characteristics — or CAN have, depending on the individual.

We are unusual compared to many other religions in the sense that we don't have an orthodoxy (or system of "right belief"), and we have very loose guidelines regarding orthopraxy (or "right practice") — except when it comes to initiations. There, our guidelines are more strict. We don't tell our members what they need to believe or not believe. We don't dictate their ethics. We don't name their Godds for them, or even insist that they have any at all. We offer a framework for ritual and ceremony, without proscribing the contents of those celebrations and workings.

We hold certain tenets and concepts as sacred, though. The autonomy, self-accountability, and authority of the individual Witch, for instance, is a core belief for us. The search for Truth as the highest goal of the human Soul is another core belief. Indeed, the pursuit of enlightenment is our most sacred value.

This unit (which focuses on the ministerial aspects of being a Queen, Devil, or Consort of the Spiral Castle) and the next two units (which focus on the leadership and teaching aspects) ask you to think deeply about how you see your role, how others will see your role, and how you plan to be present in what you ultimately choose as your role.

When you take your 3rd Degree vows and oaths, you will be declaring yourself a Queen, Devil, or Consort of this Tradition. You will be invested with the authority to lead, teach, and care for the members of your own Coven, if you choose. But the choice to do any or all of those things is ultimately yours. You are under no obligation to take on a role as a teacher, a group/ritual leader, or (dare I say it?) a minister. Alternatively, you may feel comfortable with all of these — or with only one or two. (Sibling mine, this Tradition is even okay with you picking and choosing among the pieces associated with each of these. You could say, "I feel good about teaching a study group, but not a Coven. I want to lead Dedication rituals, but not Initiations. And I am good with facilitating Rites of Passage, but I don't want to engage in any pastoral care.")

We also honor that your position on these questions may change over time.

By engaging in the study and discussion around these topics (3rd Degree Witch as Minister, Teacher, Leader, and Initiator), you will go into the next phase of your practice with your eyes open and a personal map to help you navigate the experiences that are ahead of you.

Rites of Passage in SCT

You can view the life cycle rituals either through the lens of spirituality or through the lens of culture. All societies honor what they consider the sacred or important stations on the wheel of one's life. They don't all agree about what they are, of course.

The Spiral Castle Tradition has its own culture, its own norms. Some of these are reflected or echoed in the larger culture that surrounds us, while some others are not.

We recognize and honor these sacred times as portals or gateways. We are noting and celebrating the life of the individual at each station. In some cases, these portals are subtle (like the transition into one's Wisdom years). In other cases, they are distinct (like the crossing — in either direction — between Life and Death). We see all of them as an opportunity to bless, celebrate, and reflect on both what has been and what is to come.

Third Degree Witches may very likely find themselves asked to facilitate these rituals by members of their Coven, folks in their community, or by their own family.

There are no "set" or prescribed rituals for these times. (Our Initiations are the only ones that must be performed "just so.") Instead, we try to create meaningful experiences that are reflective of the individual whom we are celebrating. We might use the Compass Rite and Housle, if we are honoring someone with whom we share Cords — or their children. We might not use them if we are facilitating the ritual for a member of our greater community.

This text has sample Rites of Passage in the BoS section (at the back of the book). Use them as they are, or use them as inspiration for creating Rites that ring true for your Coven/People.

Within this Tradition, we have honored (and encourage you to honor) the following Life Cycle Rites:

WITCHING — This is a celebration and blessing for an infant. We perform this ritual when they are one year and one day old. During this ritual, we offer blessings to the child, the parents, and the Godd-parents. The parents and Godd-parents are also tasked with protecting the child's autonomy, personal authority, and accountability — and about teaching them about those things.

MENARCHE / THORARCHY / PUBERTY — Adolescence is often a confusing and difficult time for young people. The body is going through radical changes, the hormones are in flux bordering on chaos, and whole new vistas of thought and independence are starting to blossom. How we frame the celebration that honors this change can vary depending on the young person's gender identity. Or, if we choose, we can develop a standard ritual within our Covens that is not gender-specific. Such a puberty rite might be called a "Feast for Water and Fire" — honoring that the changes the young person is experiencing (regardless of gender or sex) are alchemical, awakened by both Water and Fire. This ritual is performed shortly after the onset of menses or semenses — or some other hallmark, as you will.

COMING OF AGE — This ritual marks the transition from childhood into adulthood. It should be performed no earlier than the Age of Majority (18 in the US, UK, and Canada). But it could happen later, depending on the individual. This ritual honors and celebrates the independence and full adulthood of the individual. It recognizes that they are legally and ethically responsible for themselves and invites them fully into the community of adults.

HANDFASTING — This ritual celebrates the committed bond of a romantic partnership. It CAN be performed as a legal wedding, but that legal/civil bond is not required. The union can be made for a specific period of time (year and a day, three years, nine years, etc), or it might be a lifetime commitment. Some folks like to specify that the union is "for as long as the love shall last." I would personally advise against this wording, for several reasons. One is that the lastingness of the love is frequently not the reason that people part. Ultimately, those wording choices lie with the partners who are entering into union.

HANDPARTING — This ritual honors the ending of a committed relationship. It is a beautiful and useful ritual that not enough people engage in. It offers the opportunity to consciously and compassionately separate the lives that had previously been bound, offering thanks for what has been and looking ahead to what is to come. It offers those former-partners a greater sense of closure than is often found in the over-cultures in which we live and love. This ritual can be held with only one of the individuals present, if needed.

WISDOM / ELDER RITE — We don't mark this passage based on physiological changes, and we don't call it a Croning or Saging within the Spiral Castle Tradition (as those terms linguistically demean one group and elevate the other). It is not part of our cultural values, as a Tradition, to commemorate life cycles in terms of reproductive fertility. Instead, we honor the awakenings that happen both in our youth and in our age, irrespective of how those awakenings may correspond to our personal fertility. Elders have proven themselves Wise in one or many ways. They are invited to offer that wisdom with the Family and community, as they choose.

CROSSING — This is the funerary custom of our Tradition. We honor the life and impact of the friend who has gone ahead of us to That Which Lies Beyond. This ritual can be conducted with or without the participation of the decedent's family, as we recognize the need of the Craft Family to say farewell and to honor the Crossing of a fellow Witch according to the customs and values that we shared with them.

Any of these rituals might be performed privately within a Coven, privately or semi-privately with family or guests, or publicly with a larger community. Where, how, and with whom they are celebrated is a matter for discussion and consideration of the parties involved.

Additionally, you are welcome to lead other rites that honor or bless a person undergoing a transition or marking a significant milestone. These portal times are often fraught with challenges, obstacles, personal victories, and big emotions. A person passing through those gates would benefit from the support, protection, and blessing of their community. (Some examples that come to mind are pregnancy, gender transition, moving out of a parent's house, having an empty nest, etc.) Those rites can be held under the auspices of the Spiral Castle Tradition — or not! Use your judgment.

Assignment

Answer the following questions for yourself:

- How do you see facilitation of Rites of Passage? Does this fall under the umbrella of Witchcraft, religion, both, neither?
- Which of these Rites do you have personal experience with? Describe those experiences.
- Please express any other thoughts, concerns, or insights you have about Rites of Passage.

Additional Resources

Check out the Ministerial Reading List for books related to Rites of Passage.

BoS Pages Included

Witching Ritual

Puberty Ritual

Coming of Age Ritual

Handfasting Ritual

Handparting Ritual

Wisdom Ritual

Crossing Ritual

Pastoral Care

Prerequisite Lesson

06-01 "Rites of Passage"

Objective

To consider the various areas of Pastoral Care as they relate to leading a Coven

To make a plan for expanding your skills in the area of Pastoral Care

Materials Needed

Note-taking materials

Study Notes

I'm going to be frank. Whether you see this branch of the Craft as a religion or not, whether you see yourself as a minister/pastor or not, if you lead a group or facilitate a community of any kind, you will likely be called upon to perform some Pastoral Care.

What is Pastoral Care?

According to Wikipedia (citing four separate sources for this definition):

> Pastoral care is an ancient model of emotional, social and spiritual support that can be found in all cultures and traditions. The term is considered inclusive of distinctly non-religious forms of support, as well as support for people from religious communities.

Yep. Emotional, social, and spiritual support for the people in your group. You probably do some level of this already with people in your family or friends' group. Humans are social animals, and look to each other for comfort, aid, and guidance. We particularly look to those we see as leaders (whether officially or unofficially).

Pastoral Care is a range of supports that can include, but isn't limited to:

- "Counseling" (to be distinguished from therapy)
- Visitation of sick, house-bound, elderly, military, and/or imprisoned members of your group
- End-of-life care and Death Doula care

If there is an element of religion in the mix, this care becomes a "ministry." Facilitating Sabbat celebrations for incarcerated folks is a Prison Ministry, for example. The distinction may be semantic, but it might be an important distinction for you.

Witchy Pastoral Care guides are thin on the ground. Non-Wiccan ones, even more so. I've included a couple of resources to get you started (both here and also in the Ministerial Reading List), but you might consider reading some of the work that has been created for Christian ministers, as well. If you can find texts that aren't so heavy-handed, they could be a useful reference. (Yes, you'd have to wade through the Bible verses and doctrine, but I trust that you're able to do that.)

Pastoral Counseling

When I was first coming into my 3rd Degree (2005), the general consensus in the Witchy (and NeoPagan) community was that our Priest/exes had no place or purpose in the counseling of our Coveners. This was, once again, largely due to fear regarding our reception and also over the very litigious landscape that we have here in the States. ("What if someone comes to us for counsel, they don't like what we say, and they sue us for practicing without a license?" That was the general line of thought.) Those are still concerns, and they are valid.

From what I have read and experienced, though, Coven leaders (whom we reference as Queens, Devils, or Consorts, at their preference) are still engaging in a level of counseling. They just don't call it by that name, and they try to avoid formalizing the relationship. The coaching model, which has gained popularity and public presence, has also helped provide us with some extra tools that distinguish what we offer from clinical forms of therapy.

Andrew Copton (in his foreword to David Savage's book *Non Religious Pastoral Care*) says it well. "Someone less than a counsellor, more than a friend, who can listen and be present with us."

It takes some skill-development to do that well, but this is often the role of a Coven's leader in helping their fellow Coveners find their footing in hard times.

Visitation

This is an aspect of Pastoral Care that is spotty at best within our communities. Some NeoPagan, Wiccan, and Heathen groups have gotten very involved with prison ministries — and I have linked a few of those in this lesson's resources. But it seems that very few are involved with hospital, nursing home, or other types of visitation. (One of my besties is the Quality of Life Director at a care facility, and I know she has been called on multiple times to plan activities specifically for the Pagan/Heathen/Witchy residents — and also to act as a Death Doula.) These services are going to be more in-demand as our community ages. It is important that we don't neglect the social, emotional, and spiritual needs of our Siblings when they become unable to attend our gatherings. They are still Family, after all, and it is a comfort and balm for them to know we are still with them.

End-of-Life Care

Our Tradition does not have "Last Rites." Maybe we should? We don't need them in the Catholic/Christian sense of a final confession and absolution, final communion, etc. But I could see the benefit of a final ritual and act of magick in a life that has been filled with ritual and magick. We do a Crossing Rite, after all, following the death. Maybe a Preparatory Rite is in order.

Either way, everybody should have a supportive person or group with them when they are preparing to cross. Nobody should die alone in a hospital, hospice, or home. As Family, we would do well to be there for each other, offering succor and love, when a member of our Coven is crossing the veil.

Assignment	Respond to the following questions as you reflect on Pastoral Care :
	• What experience have you had in receiving Pastoral Care ?
	• What experience have you had in providing Pastoral Care ?
	• Where do you anticipate that you already have strengths in this area?
	• What would you like to learn more about?
	• Are there areas of Pastoral Care that you would prefer to avoid (or decline to offer)?

Additional Resources

Non Religious Pastoral Care — David Savage — https://amzn.to/3hb9tGo

The Pagan Clergy's Guide for Counseling, Crisis Intervention, and Otherworld Transitions. — https://amzn.to/3H3Hhj9

Starhawk and M. Macha Nightmare. *The Pagan Book of Living and Dying.* — https://amzn.to/3iA65Fe

West, Carrie and Phillip Wright. *Death & the Pagan: Modern Pagan Funerary Practices.* — https://amzn.to/3EXKUVh

Fenley, Judith Karen and Oberon Zell. *Death Rights and Rites.* — https://amzn.to/3XQ4lYP

Mortellus. *Do I Have to Wear Black?: Rituals, Customs, and Funerary Etiquette for Modern Pagans.* — https://amzn.to/3Fndb9b

Butler, Charles. *Pagan Prison Ministry.* — https://amzn.to/3UB2cgU

Kaldera, Raven. *Candles in the Cave: Northern Tradition Paganism for Prisoners.* — https://amzn.to/3ixWYFg

Appalachian Pagan Ministry — https://appalachianpaganministry.com/

The Pagan Federation — https://www.paganfed.org/

"The Limits of Ministry" — https://wildhunt.org/2018/01/the-limits-of-ministry-pagan-clergy-and-serious-situations.html

"Pagan Ministry" — https://www.patheos.com/blogs/paganrestoration/2013/07/pagan-ministry-serving-the-pagan-peoples/

BoS Pages Included

None

Weddings & Ordination

<u>Prerequisite Lesson</u>

06-01 Rites of Passage

<u>Objective</u>

To consider some of the factors, issues, and elements of legal weddings

To begin thinking about ordination from both a legal and spiritual perspective

<u>Materials Needed</u>

Note-taking materials

<u>Study Notes</u>

Candidly, I will say that the government doesn't care about any of the ceremonies or rituals we (or members of other faiths) perform, with the exception of the Handfasting/Wedding. Even then, they only care in the event that the partners wish to recognize their union as a marriage in the legal sense.

The legal arrangement known as marriage is a contractual agreement that comes with tax benefits, inheritance considerations, decision-making rights (as the "next of kin," for instance, when the other partner is unable to make decisions for themselves), and inclusion in benefits programs. For this reason, many states and territories stipulate who they consider ordained or authorized to solemnize this ritual (in a legal sense). They do NOT (and cannot) stipulate who has the authority to facilitate the union in a spiritual sense (at least not in the US).

For all other "ministerial" or "pastoral" duties, the government is largely uninvolved. They figure that if you see the person as qualified to provide guidance, comfort, and facilitation related to spiritual matters, then they are qualified.

The Spiral Castle Tradition agrees. We believe that Witches can act in all aspects of ministerial/pastoral capacity for themselves and for others, if those involved are comfortable with that arrangement.

As such, every 3rd Degree in our Tradition is considered "ordained." By the time you have taken the 3rd Degree initiation, you have been fully trained in the cosmology and culture of our Tradition, have undergone training related to pastoral care, and are free to exercise that training as you deem appropriate. That includes the solemnizing of matrimonial rites, from our perspective.

As discussed earlier in this lesson, we recognize ourselves as a religious body, and we recognize all of our members as the ultimate religious authority in their own lives.

However, you will need to check with your state or territory regarding their requirements. The Spiral Castle Tradition and its Clannad (family group) are not incorporated as a church and currently have no plans to do so. I make that note because it is an important distinction in some areas.

I have performed handfastings/weddings in both Indiana and Kentucky. About half of them have involved signing a marriage license, and only one of those was ever challenged by the county who issued the license. When requested, I supplied them with copies of my own 3rd Degree cert, my Coven Charter, and — for what it was worth — my Minister's credential from the Universal Life Church. Those documents held up, and the County Clerk filed the license. (I think that one got extra scrutiny because it was the first same-sex marriage in the county where it was filed, to be honest. It was in 2015 shortly following the Obergefell decision, and many smaller counties were taking no chances about making sure the i's were dotted and the t's were crossed.)

The ULC credential hasn't held up under recent state Supreme Court scrutiny, so I don't recommend relying on it (or any other online church who is offering ministerial credentials) alone. Indeed, if you decide to get an online credential as a back-up, choose one of the organizations that includes some sort of review process of an application. (There is a link in the resources for this lesson titled "10 Simple Steps to Ensure Legal Ordination." It is worth the read, just to get a broad overview of the issues and concerns around "legal" ordination.)

After you have taken your 3rd Degree initiation, you will receive a certificate that specifically states that you are ordained by the Spiral Castle Tradition Clannad. If you take your initiation in-person, you will receive it then (along with the designation of Magister of the Lineage, if your initiator is either myself or someone whom I have personally initiated). If you self-initiate into the 3rd Degree, you must contact me for that cert. I will ask a couple of questions, and then email it to you.

In either case, you will have an ordination certificate from this religious body.

Some states include language like "minister of a congregation" as a stipulation for who can officiate weddings. In this Tradition, a "congregation" is a Coven. For us, this doesn't mean that you have to be the one and only Queen/Devil/Consort within that Coven. You may share duties with another 3rd Degree. You may run a subgroup within the Coven. Those are all valid. Maybe you run a study group or offer classes regularly within your community. We see these all as valid "congregations" that are on-par with ministries we observe within other religious organizations.

If you run into issues, please reach out to Laurelei or one of the other members of the Grand Coven.

For more information about ordination, the Grand Coven, or chartering a Coven, check out the information in the back of this book.

Other Considerations

Because the handfasting is a union of lives, and the wedding is a union of legal entities, you may want to consider whether or not you will require some pre-ceremony meetings or sessions. You might also want to think about what (if anything) you will require to be in place before you facilitate this particular magic. Also, you will want to consider your fee. (It is customary to give an honorarium to the officiant. Know how you want to answer this question when a couple asks.)

The ritual itself is a Whole. Other. Thing. Entire books have been written on this subject, one or two of which are in the resources below. Entire careers are centered around facilitating this ceremony. I can't hope to break down the entire process in this single lesson.

More than any other Rite of Passage that I've conducted, I find Handfastings/Weddings to be very personalized to the couple. That is due in part to the public nature of the rite. Some couples choose to soften the edges of the ritual for their extended families. Others come in with full frontal magick. Many couples have specific language or acts that they want included.

Read up on both wedding planning (in general terms) and also handfastings (in more specific terms) if you plan to officiate this rite for people.

Finally, it is my hope for the SCT to offer a library of rituals (on the Thread app or other electronic means) to help our members. That doesn't exist at the time of this writing, but it will soon.

Assignment

If you think that you would like to be able to solemnize marriages (now or in the future), fill out the Planning Worksheet on the next page.

If you don't think this is something you will want to do, write a reflection in which you explore for yourself why that is.

Additional Resources

"10 Simple Steps to Ensure Legal Ordination" — https://www.startchurch.com/blog/view/name/10-simple-steps-to-ensure-legal-ordination

Kaldera, Raven and Tannin Schwartzstein. *Handfasting and Wedding Rituals*. — https://amzn.to/3Vuuivj

Williams, Liz. *Modern Handfasting: A Complete Guide to the Magic of Pagan Weddings*. — https://amzn.to/3H6EpSB

Ferguson, Joy. *Magickal Weddings*. — https://amzn.to/3VtN4TG

BoS Pages Included

None

Planning Worksheet for Officiating Weddings

Step 1: Find your state's/territory's criteria for wedding officiants.	
Criteria 1:	**Criteria 2:**
Additional Criteria:	
Step 2: Plan for acquiring/providing documentation.	
Step 3: List any criteria you will have for the couple before agreeing.	
Step 4: Consider the process you want to use for building the ritual (meetings, samples, rehearsal, etc) .	

Children

Prerequisite Lesson

06-02 "Pastoral Care"

Objective

To consider the role of children in the Spiral Castle Tradition and Clannad

To take stock of personal concerns, hopes, ideas related to children in the SCT

Materials Needed

Note-taking materials

Study Notes

In my observation, the inclusion of children in Witchcraft groups has been controversial ever since the anti-witchcraft laws were repealed in England (and later in the US) in the middle of the 20th Century. Whether you consider this Tradition of Craft to be religious or not, NeoPagan or not, other Traditions of NeoPaganism (including Wicca) are the closest corollaries we have to what we do. It has really only been in the last decade or two that we've seen conscious inclusion of minors within those groups.

There has been "good" (or at least *valid*) reason for that. The general public hasn't been ready to hear any conversation that included "children" and "Witchcraft" in the same breath. The strange reality there is that most people still harbor the fear that Witches cannibalize infants and children. Don't believe me? Take a poll of your witchy friends and see who has been asked about that very fact. My Coven in California was once accosted on a public beach because on-lookers feared for "the baby's safety" and wanted to make sure we had no intention of harming her. (The baby was my eldest. Her father and I were absolutely enraged at the insinuation.)

And we should be. We should be outraged that people still think we harm children. We should be outraged that parents still have their parental rights challenged, based solely on the fact that they practice Witchcraft. Members of the home coven of SCT (Coven Caer Sidhe) know the family in the Jones v. Jones case in Indiana from 2004. That was a divorce case between two Wiccan parents in which the presiding judge ruled that both parents would take steps to "shelter the child from their nonmainstream religious beliefs" as part of the custody agreement. The now-divorced parents joined together to file an appeal, which they ultimately won when the appellate court ruled that the first judge had overstepped their bounds. (No kidding!)

The Joneses were pretty well-known in Indianapolis at the time, as their family organized a large eclectic working group and were also heavily involved in the local Pagan Meetups and Pagan Pride Day. We all watched the case with great anticipation due to the implications that it could have on our own families. Neither parent had asked the court to intervene regarding religion. They were both in agreement about the rearing of their child. But the Court still involved itself "to protect the child" — from our Craft, ostensibly.

And these examples don't even touch on the many trials in which divorcing parents seek a divorce court's ruling on the extent to which a Witchy parent is deemed fit for custody, largely on the basis of their religion or practices. One of my best friends has incurred a huge amount of debt fighting her ex for the right to include her children in her religion (she is heathen) and the subculture that is the greater NeoPagan community.

Nor do they touch on the job loss, housing insecurity, or other hate-informed consequences that we face. (Did I ever tell you about that time an angry student obliterated my teaching career by doxing me and "exposing me as a Witch" to the school and community where I lived and taught?)

When I say that we had "good" reason not include the kids until the last couple of decades, it's because we've had to fight. We were not poised to win that fight during the height of the Satanic Panic. And maybe, as the Vox article in this lesson's resources claims, that moral panic is still with us. Certainly, Witches and NeoPagans still face challenges and sometimes dire consequences related to their practices (religious or otherwise).

So, why even consider including our children? Well, because we DO have the right to teach our children our religion, even if it is "nonmainstream." We have the right to educate them about our spiritual and metaphysical practices, even if we don't consider them religious in nature. As was reiterated in the Jones appeal decision, "[P]arents have a fundamental right to control the education, upbringing, and religious training of their children." We have that right legally in the US (and elsewhere, but I am just citing US law because it is where I live and what I know). And we have that right morally everywhere.

Witches historically have passed on their Craft to the younger generations of their family — either their children or grandchildren. We did that even before the anti-witchcraft laws were repealed.

Minors in the Spiral Castle Tradition

When my ex-wife and I first started practicing together, we discussed the place of my own children within this Tradition. We agreed that the people of the Craft are a Family. That family structure (dynamic? philosophy?) was an inheritance from the traditional, family-based strains of British Craft where we took much of our inspiration. To exclude our children would be to deny them access to something vitally important.

However, we had stipulations and rules about when, how, and to what extent they children could be involved. These weren't just for my children, but for any child of a Coven Caer Sidhe member. There are 9 such "children" currently. (Five of them are now adults, but those five have been raised in the Craft — together — since the Laughing Dragon days. The youngest two of those five are about to turn 20 years old and are halfway through their Bachelor's degrees.)

Here are the guidelines we set:
- No minor would be trained or corded in the SCT unless at least one parent was a Red Cord member.
- No SCT parent should feel compelled to train their child in our ways. Their children were welcomed, but there was no judgment regarding their participation — or lack thereof.
- Minor children of the Coven could receive a Green Cord at the Age of Reason, which is around 7 years old (give or take).

- Minor children of the Coven could take a Red Cord at the Age of Puberty.
- Only persons of the Age of Majority would be eligible to take the Triple Cord (1st Degree).
- Children would not be permitted to attend rites or discussions that the Coven agreed were inappropriate for their age. In these cases, none of the children were in attendance. At any time, according to their own discretion, a parent could choose to exclude their child from a ritual, lesson, or meeting.
- Minors at the Red Cord level were given the same rights within our Coven as adults at the same level in terms of having their opinions heard, voting on certain issues, etc.
- We would never pressure one of our children to participate longer or to a greater extent than they chose for themselves.
- We would allow the children to come and go from meetings, lessons, and rituals as they saw fit. If they were uncomfortable or bored, that was a good enough indication for us that they weren't ready for that particular concept/material.

In our Coven, we never created or implemented lessons that were specifically intended for use with children of any age. We weren't specifically opposed to it, and in fact I have started a project of a more eclectic nature along those lines. (I started that project in 1998, before I ever had kids of my own; and we used some of the lessons for littles within Laughing Dragon. The parents rotated the supervision and/or activity facilitation amongst ourselves. There were times when we had 6-8 young children present, all under the age of 8, and the lessons were a blessing when we had them.)

We found that separate lessons/activities for the children were somewhat impractical for Coven Caer Sidhe, which is the main reason why we didn't have them. No more than three children were ever present simultaneously (due to the gap in their ages and other factors, like custodial visitation). And since there were frequently only 4 or 5 adults present, sending one of us off to facilitate a children's circle would mean that we had a significant gap in our own attendance.

Assignment

If you run a coven or study group, at some point one or more of your members will have young children that they can't leave with a sitter — or simply have children that they wish to include. Take some time now to think about how you might handle that. SCT allows for children of Coveners and has a culture of Family. We also have a culture of autonomy and would never tell a Coven's Queen, Devil, or Consort that they were required to include children. Consider these questions in your reflection:

- Will you permit minors to attend? If so, are there parameters for their inclusion? If not, be clear with yourself as to why not.
- How do you feel about minors taking Green and then Red Cords?
- If minors are included, do you foresee creating special lessons or activities for them?

Additional Resources

Jones v. Jones case — https://law.justia.com/cases/indiana/court-of-appeals/2005/49a02-0501-cv-64-0.html

"Why Satanic Panic Never Ended" — https://www.vox.com/culture/22358153/satanic-panic-ritual-abuse-history-conspiracy-theories-explained

BoS Pages Included

None

Roles & Rules

Prerequisite Lesson

None

Objective

To consider the roles Witches might fill within a Coven

To consider the rules or norms that might serve a Coven well

Materials Needed

Note-taking materials

Study Notes

Let's start talking about the structure of a Coven within the Spiral Castle Tradition.

As frustrating as you may find this in the beginning when you're trying to set things up, the Spiral Castle Tradition holds personal autonomy and authority at such a high value that we refuse to dictate the Coven structure or management for any of our Covens. We believe it is the Coven Founders' right and responsibility to put policies, procedures, and systems in place that make sense for that group.

To that end, I can offer some suggestions, but I will never say "It MUST be this way."

Roles versus Offices

This isn't really an either/or proposition. You can have both Roles and Offices in your group. You can have Officers who hold one or more Roles as part of their stated duties. You can have Officers who choose additional tasks from a pool of unrelated Roles. You can have no Officers at all, and only Roles. Or you can have none of the above and "wing it."

I don't recommend "winging it," to be honest. That system usually breaks down fast, with the lion's share of the work reverting to Coven's Queen/Devil/Consort.

Delegation is good. It is good for you, it is good for the other individuals, and it is good for the group as a whole.

Clarity is also good. Be clear in what each Office or Role involves. Be specific about the What, Where, When, How Often, and How Much of each. Also be clear about the term of office/role. Is it one year, three years, lifetime? And how are those officers/roles chosen? Are they selected by the Queen, etc? Are they elected by the Coven? (And who gets to vote? Red Cords and up? Triple Cords and up?)

Some Titles, Roles, and Offices to Consider

There are some titles that are inherent in the Tradition, by virtue of the Initiations we take.

- Adoptee (aka Red Cord, Dedicant) — A person who has dedicated to the Craft and the Trad and is working through the "Foundations" lessons. This person is considered Family.

- Witch of the Spiral Castle (aka Triple Cord, Initiate, Full Witch) — Someone who has completed all of the "Foundations" lessons and has taken the first trials (initiation) and been Raised to a Witch of First Admission. This person is considered a Full Witch within our Trad (or, more accurately, a fully-trained Witch).

- Artisan, Bard, Conjurer, Healer, Seer, Votary, or Warden of the Spiral Castle — This person has completed a path of study (as outlined in "Practicum") and has taken their 2nd Degree initiation. A person can hold more than one area of service, if they choose to undertake the study and projects.

- Queen, Devil, or Consort of the Spiral Castle — A Witch who has completed the "Mastery" coursework and been initiated to the 3rd Degree. They are ordained to charter a Coven, teach, and perform all rituals within the Spiral Castle. A Witch can choose which of these titles they prefer. These can absolutely be applied without consideration of gender, as the Witch bearing that title chooses. They reflect how the "Master" Witch sees themselves in relationship to our Great Powers — the WitchFather (Folkloric Devil) and WitchMother (Queen of Elfhame). It is the experience of Witches in this Tradition at this level to personally identify as the embodiment of one while being the Consort of the other. Our titles reflect where we would like to place that emphasis.

- Magister of the Lineage — A Queen, Devil or Consort who was initiated to 3rd Degree either by Laurelei or by a Queen, Devil, or Consort that Laurelei initiated.

- Regent — The Magister serving in the primary leadership role for the Tradition.

We also have three group names that are worth noting here.

- Spiral Castle Clannad — This is the entire family group for the Tradition. It is our Family. Anyone who has taken the Adoption Oath is a member of the Clannad, whether they performed a Self-Dedication or the rite of Adoption within a Coven.

- Grand Coven — This body is the entirety of the Magisters of the Lineage. We convene only occasionally, with the purposes of discussing issues and concerns related to the Clannad, performing workings, and sharing fellowship.

- Home Coven — The founding Coven of the Tradition (Coven Caer Sidhe). If at anytime that Coven disbands, the Coven of the current Regent becomes the Home Coven. (Currently, the founding Coven is also the one led by the Regent.)

The primary Coven offices that have been recorded and shared publicly tend to be based on gender, which SCT roundly rejects. Nor do we use the terms "Priest" or "Priestess" (or High Priest, High Priestess) in this Tradition. They aren't taboo, per se. They just don't resonate with the source material or traditions from which we draw inspiration.

We also don't particularly idealize the concept of a dual-partnered, gender-influenced leadership model, the way is seen in most Covens. This idea isn't isolated to Gardnerian forms of Craft. We also see it in Clan of Tubal Cain, 1734, and most other TradCraft groups. Why we don't hold to this notion is perhaps complicated enough to warrant its own "Mystery" discussion. The super-short version is that we see each individual as autonomous and whole, just as they are. Therefore, they do not need another human as a partner to "complete the circuit." (We're not even touching on the gendered philosophies about "holding power" or "issuing power" — or about who is the ultimate authority within the Coven, relative to their gender.)

Finally, we don't insist that our Covens adopt any sort of hierarchical structure, but we do agree that they are welcome to do so if they feel it makes sense. (For the first decade of its existence, the Home Coven was egalitarian and non-hierarchical. That is no longer the case since we are at a place where members don't equally share in the teaching of lessons, leading of rituals, or administration of business.)

Offices that we see across the "Witch-o-sphere" and/or that speak to our folkloric roots:

- Queen, Dame, King, Devil, Consort, Robin — for the leader(s) of the Coven. They usually have the primary teaching responsibility, preside over meetings to make sure things run smoothly, and are often looked to for Pastoral Care (as discussed in 06-02). They are a 3rd Degree. In some groups, this position is held until the bearer passes it on to their successor. In others, it is rotated between qualified and interested Witches for a specified term.

- Maid, Squire, Jack, Verdelet, Summoner, Black Rod, Page — sometimes seen as the understudy(ies) to the leader(s). They facilitate in the absence of the leader(s), and are usually tasked with making sure the people of the Coven know when and where the meeting will take place. Some groups specify that a Witch of a certain degree holds this office.

- Elders — This term is often used for Witches of the 3rd Degree who are not the main leader of the Coven. Sometimes a Coven is run by a Council of Elders, rather than one or two individuals.

For ideas about Roles (which could be the same as Offices, but also could be different), I've taken a lot of inspiration from *Coven Craft* by Amber K. I highly recommend adding this book to your library if you intend to facilitate any sort of group of magickal humans. Some roles might include:

Roles for Facilitating Meetings

- Gatekeeper — makes sure everyone has a chance to be heard without dominating the floor
- Focuser — gets the group back on target
- Parliamentarian — reminds the group of procedural rules
- Peacekeeper — helps with conflict resolution
- Vibeswatcher — monitors mood of group and suggests remedies when needed
- Timekeeper — notes beginning and end times; enforces time limits for individual speakers
- Scribe — takes notes for the group

Roles for Running the Group

- Scribe — secretary
- Pursewarden — treasurer
- Watcher — security officer
- Minstrel — music director
- Lorekeeper — scrapbooker/storyteller
- Ranger — environmental officer
- Archivist — librarian
- Guide — youth advisor
- Herald — public outreach (website, etc)
- Dean — educational coordinator

An SCT Coven might also consider Roles or Offices that are connected with the Focus Areas from Year 2: Practicum. Perhaps, you might use "Chief," "Head," "Lead," or "Director" to the title to designate that individuals are serving as the primary representative of that service-related role for the Coven. (Chief Bard, Head Artisan, Director of Healing, etc)

Rules (Policies and Norms)

Some new leaders balk at identifying the rules for their group. They often feel uncomfortable with the perceived boldness of saying, "We do things this way," or "This behavior is not tolerated here." They feel like a dictator — or a school board, or a corporation.

My advice to Witches who are stepping into leadership and facilitation roles within the SCT is to: A) remember that nobody among us is the Witch Police or a tyrant who has control over anyone else's magick, lifestyle, behavior, choices, or contribution; B) adopt the old adage "Good fences make good neighbors." (Go read "The Mending Wall" by Robert Frost, if you haven't ever done so — or haven't since school. There is wisdom there that I didn't appreciate at age 16.); and C) don't assume that any policy or norm is "common sense" and therefore shouldn't be stated.

Partnerships, friendships, and all other manner of affiliations benefit from boundaries that are clear and consistently maintained. If the boundary matters to you, it matters. And it is worth stating so that folks can honor it.

Witchcraft tends to draw people who think differently than the rest of society. We are liminal people — on the edges, different. It stands to reason that there is a wide variety of neuro-types among us — and that has been my experience, for sure. One of the things that people on the Autism Spectrum, for example, really value is clear boundaries. Too many have experienced embarrassment and isolation because of the unspoken rules of engagement in society.

My recommendation is to write down your policies and make them available to all members of your group — including prospective members, who should review them before officially joining. After all, if the boundaries you and your Coven have put in place are untenable to someone seeking entry into your Coven (your family unit within the Clannad), then they aren't going to be a good fit as a Sibling. (And you know what? Witchcraft — and even SCT Craft — is still available to them. You aren't denying them anything at all, except access to your time, energy, and personal space.)

Your rules (policies and norms) might include, but aren't limited to:
- Expectations regarding behavior during classes, business meetings, and rituals
- Expectations regarding communication during classes, business meetings, rituals, and electronic means (social media, chat threads, etc)
- Expectations regarding privacy
- Expectations regarding shared monies and supplies
- Expectations regarding set-up/clean-up
- Corrective measures for unmet expectations
- Terms of office/roles
- Duties and obligations of office/roles
- Selection/election of officers/facilitators
- Screening and acceptance of new members;
- Hiatus/sabbatical of members
- Active/inactive members
- Decision-making (voting/consensus or under direction of Leaders/Elders?)

Assignment

Start jotting down your ideas about how you would ideally like to run a Coven. If you plan to Charter a Coven within SCT, you will need at least two other Chartering Members, so your ideas may get refined or amended as a result of your discussions with them. But you will be a step ahead of the game if you have already starting drafting the documents you will need.

Additional Resources

11-02 Coven Leadership Reading List (lots of worthwhile titles)

BoS Pages Included

SCT Titles and Offices

Coven Caer Sidhe Guidance (set)

Meeting Structures & Schedules

Prerequisite Lesson

07-01 "Rules & Roles"

Objective

To consider the pros and cons of various meeting schedules and methods

To review some of the considerations for setting a Coven schedule

Materials Needed

Calendar

Note-taking materials

Study Notes

I've seen (and done) a wide variety of scheduling options for Covens. None are perfect. Likewise, none are inherently wrong. The trick is finding the balance for you and your group — and then re-finding it when need demands a change.

My biggest piece of advice here is to have a plan, but stay flexible.

When I am organizing events (like large, week-long camping festivals), I plan everything meticulously beforehand. And then, when I arrive on the grounds and unforeseen events and circumstance poke holes in my plans, I go with the flow. My plan then becomes the touchstone that we all refer back to. I carry a notebook where I scribble down ideas and suggestions about how the process can be improved. My two mantras (which I find applicable for Coven facilitation, as well) end up being:

"Relax. Nothing is under control."

and

"Always building the better mousetrap."

Considerations

In the beginning, you are likely to be the only member of your group that is familiar with Spiral Castle Tradition. You are the link between the new students and the Clannad (entire Family). Well, you and their RTA course manual(s). That can feel like a lot of pressure. And also, understand that we all experience Imposter Syndrome at some point. Often at many points. Remind yourself as often as you need to that in addition to being a well-trained Witch, you are also a human with imperfections, personal opinions, biases, and gaps in your knowledge. It is okay to say, "I don't know." It is okay to say, "I personally prefer this." It is okay to say, "I need help."

In deciding how often, where, and for what purpose your Coven is meeting, you need to consider your own needs and preferences first. If you, as the facilitator, can't adhere to the schedule, aren't comfortable with the meeting location, or are feeling frustrated by teaching more than doing, then the group will fall apart. Be honest with yourself — now and as you progress.

The things you need to consider include:

Purpose — Why is the Coven coming together? Maybe you want a place to work through the lessons together and get feedback, ideas, and clarity from people in your local area. Maybe you want to do ritual with others, to share those experiences, and feel the power raised by a group of Witches. Maybe you want fellowship and social connection with people who are immersed in the same work and study as you. Because the RTA materials exist and everyone has equal access to them, it is possible to meet for just one of these reasons, with the expectation that folks are handling the other two independently. Of course, if you and your group want all three, that is valid, too. (Valid and typical, actually.)

Timing — Some Covens meet weekly. Some bi-weekly. Some monthly. I've known of Covens who only met for the Sabbats (or Full Moons). Your purpose for meeting will likely influence how often you meet. The day of the week and time of day that you choose, though, is more likely to be impacted by your group's social and professional circumstances. Maybe Friday and Saturday nights are a no-go because you have a fairly young and/or single members, and those are "date nights." Maybe Saturday and Sunday aren't good because your group has parents with young children, and that is "family time." Maybe certain weeknights are unavailable due to various commitments. Again, you need to consider your own availability first.

Duration — How long do your meetings last? Is it "until the work is done," or do you have a hard limit on when it needs to end? Both of these have their own benefits and challenges. Both of them require that the group stay committed to its purpose and not get drawn into distractions that could result in either an inordinately late dismissal or work left undone.

This is a great time to NOTE: Most groups experience a certain "New Relationship Energy" when they are first formed. Folks want to do all the things, all the time. They are enthusiastic about weekly meetings that last as long as they need to — and there is a lot of social content involved. Be warned: NRE fades. I've never seen it not fade. When it fades, if the group doesn't take a beat to refocus on their aims and possibly reconsider their schedule, there are difficulties. People — maybe even you — feel put-upon because they aren't getting what they actually need from the group. Coven longevity is sustained from a strong core, good leadership, compassionate communication, enough flexibility, and clarity of both purpose and boundaries.

Differentiation — I'm borrowing this term from world of education because, just like in a classroom, not all of your members will be at the same learning level. In a healthy Coven that has been operating for years, you'll have a mix of Elders, students at all three Degree-levels, and the occasional Green Cord or visitor. You might also have children present. You'll need to think about how to address all those different learning needs. Even if your Coven isn't a place where classes happen (because you expect members to work through the RTA curriculum independently, for example, and you only gather as a group for ritual), there are often allowances that need to be made. For example, you might have a Red Cord meeting that happens weekly and forms the basis of your schedule. Let's say that in this case, you use the Suggested Weekly Progression from Year 1: Foundations. You might use the full Compass Rite that is taught in the Year 3: Mastery curriculum, but only expect students to call the Gates, Castles, or Realms according to what they have been actively studying. (So, everyone can Raise the Stang and call Gates, Practicum students and higher call Castles, and Mastery students and Elders call the Realms.) You might rotate Sabbat rituals between the three books: Samhain rite from Foundations, Yule rite from Practicum, Imbolc rite written by a 3rd degree, etc. Doing this, you change the progression every year so that over a 3-year period, a person can experience all of the SCT standard rituals and also plenty of experimentation. Children of Coveners are welcome at both rituals and classes, at their parents' discretion, and they participate with the adults once they have reached the Age of Reason (and taken a Green Cord). Before that, they play or do activities nearby under light-to-moderate supervision. Maybe in your group, all the adult members rotate that supervision. You might have a Practicum group that meets monthly to share their progress and talk about concerns related to their Specialties. You might have a Mastery/Elders group that meets quarterly to seek the Mysteries and discuss Coven leadership. (This is one possible model. Others might occur to you that are a better fit for your group.)

Attendance — Consideration of attendance is a policy issue, but it is also a very real factor when trying to figure out which type of schedule is going to be a best fit. Coveners are people with lives, and lives are often messy and don't stick to our schedule. We need to have some grace regarding that. But we also need to provide a reliable structure that folks can count on. You have an advantage that I didn't have a few years ago. You have the RTA books. If someone is absent — even if multiple people are absent, or you choose to cancel the meeting due to weather, illness, etc — your Coven or study group can hold the expectation that folks will review that lesson and do the accompanying assignment individually. You don't have to be delayed or derailed. Remember, the SCT puts a high value on autonomy and accountability. Everyone should be able to go it alone for a week or two, if needed. (As a policy issue, you'll want to decide if you require a certain level of attendance to stay active in the Coven — particularly if you rely on people to fill certain roles or duties.)

Punctuality — This might be another one for policies and expectations, but it also very much impacts the flow and function in a group, so it is worth mentioning here. Think about what you value when establishing the culture of your group on this issue. Some of us feel that we show respect for each other's time and energy by being on time and sticking to a schedule. Others of us feel that a little laxity is in order within our spaces, since we are often held to strict schedules in other parts of our lives. (I'll let you know now, for Clannad-wide gatherings like our monthly Zoom social, retreats, webinars, and festival(s), we run on time. No "Pagan Standard Time" for us in those spaces.)

Assignments — If your Coven meets for lessons, what you are covering at those lessons? (No, not in terms of curriculum. The RTA books include a curriculum.) Basically, are you taking a high school (secondary school) approach to the curriculum, in which you read and discuss the lessons together, and assignments are done afterwards and submitted to the Queen/Devil/Consort later for review — or are considered duly "reflected upon" as part of the group discussion and verbal debrief? Or are you taking more of a university approach in which students read the material and complete the assignment independently, and you expand on that work together by sharing your reflections, projects, insights, and process? There is no "right way" to approach this. It's all about what works for you and the group.

Location — You should give some consideration to the options you have for meeting place. The most traditional version is to meet in-person at a residence that is deemed "Covenstead" — usually the home of the Queen, Devil, or Consort who is the primary facilitator of Coven activities. But there are other options. You could rotate between the homes of different members. You could meet at location A for classes, location B for rituals, and location C for social activities. You should almost certainly have a separate location from any/all of the above for initiations and retreats, so you can get away from the familiar/mundane. (Alternatively, you could have a plan in place for transforming a familiar space into the private, isolated, liminal, and unfamiliar space that is needed for initiations and retreats.) You can hold some meetings virtually. Maybe that is something you reserve for exceptional circumstances (weather that impacts travel, isolation due to illness in a Covener's home, etc). Or maybe you meet virtually for all classes, and in-person for rituals. You'll also want to consider some points of boundary– and expectation-setting for your chosen location — such as privacy, allergies, accessibility, cleanliness, and distractions.

Turn-Taking — Some groups might find it needful to implement a speaking order, time-limits, or other procedures around turn-taking. The "talking stick" is a very common tool in groups like ours. I like to use a rattle with "fiddly bits" like strings, beads, and charms because it gives the speaker something to do with their hands while sharing (which is often needed when talking about raw, personal reflections — or when they just have a little stage fright), and it also gives the speaker a noise-maker to remind others that they have the floor. I also like establishing the norm of using silent ways to convey certain types of info. Wiggling the fingers of a hand or hands held upright (aka "sparkle fingers" — as it has been dubbed by my retreat community) to note personal agreement or shared experience. ASL applause (rotating the upright rands) for "BIG YES/YAY." Crossed fingers held up to "bookmark" a comment/thought/point while waiting for the speaker to finish. Consider what you might implement to ensure efficient and equitable discussion in your group.

Built-In Social Time — Covens should be groups of people who get along and generally enjoy each other. (It is part of SCT culture to require consensus for admission of all new members at a local level, after all.) That means that we often want to share bits of our lives with each other. I've used a few different methods for giving space for that social time in groups whose major purpose was study and ritual. One is a monthly social moot (or meet-up) in which members gather for a party, stitch-and-witch, or mixer that wasn't topic-driven.   Another option is allowing for a "Weather Report" from each member at the beginning of every meeting/gathering, providing the space of 5 minutes to each person to share what they've been up to since the last meeting. Another option that I've enjoyed is allowing members to gather anywhere from 30-60 minutes before the official meeting start to eat a meal and talk. The meal could be a family-style pitch-in, or it could be bring-your-own. (It was often pitch-in when we met on the weekends, and fast food BYO on weeknights). All of these options allow folks to share the joys, challenges, worries, and interests of their personal lives without eating up significant amounts of time that were intended for class or ritual.

<u>Assignment</u>

Continue jotting down your ideas about how you would ideally like to run a Coven. If you plan to Charter a Coven within SCT, you will need at least two other Chartering Members, so your ideas may get refined or amended as a result of your discussions with them. But you will be a step ahead of the game if you have already starting drafting the documents you will need.

Add your thoughts about meeting structure and schedule to your thoughts about rules and roles — and now you have a real plan in place!

<u>Additional Resources</u>

Check out the Ministerial and Leadership reading lists for titles that can help.

<u>BoS Pages Included</u>

Coven Caer Sidhe Guidance

Interpersonal Dynamics

Prerequisite Lesson

07-02 "Meeting Structure & Schedule"

Objective

To consider the interpersonal issues of Coven management

Materials Needed

Note-taking materials

Study Notes

A truth: Everyone says they hate drama.

A truth: Every group experiences some drama.

Why is that, do you think? Well, I think there are a few reasons for this, based on my years of experience in group process.

One of the reasons I think both of these truths exist is that people tend to feel strongly about whatever it is that they value. This means that they are willing to engage in conflict and/or "rigorous collaboration" (which is conflict that isn't viewed as inherently negative or riddled with abusive language) in order to preserve those values within the relationship/community. When "it is important" to someone, they don't necessarily view the conflict as "drama."

Another reason that both of the above are true is that conflict which arises in a relationship or group that isn't about a deeply held value to the observer seems frivolous. ("You two are arguing over nothing. Let it go.")

Another factor in this paradoxical dilemma is that conflicts and disagreements are going to happen eventually — despite the idealization of the partnership or group that often happens due to "New Relationship Energy." Individuals value different things — or value the same things in different ways. We also disagree about "facts" — and there are often less actual "facts" than we think there are. So much of our experience of the world (of "reality") is subjective. We can't process it through anything except our own "filters." Those filters can get expanded and changed, but we always have one, and it is always pretty unique to us — based on our experiences, observations, and training.

Finally, drama happens even when everyone involved hates drama because we have communication styles that don't always mesh well — and that aren't always consistent. Some people come across blunt, argumentative, demanding, or undermining. Others might come across as wishy-washy, two-faced, vague, or weak. All of those traits are subjective and come down to preferences. We might rephrase all of them if we are describing a person we admire or who communicates similarly to us. (We might use descriptions like direct, forthright, honest, decisive, and thorough — or for the other group: flexible, diplomatic, visionary, and compassionate.) To add complication to the mix, being hungry, tired, ill, or under-pressure can change our baseline communication.

Truthfully, there are a lot more than three or four reasons why communication goes wonky. Whole fields of study are devoted to communication and group dynamics. These are a few factors that I've seen play out over and over within Covens and larger pockets of the community.

Spiral Castle Covens tend to be small and very close-knit. We take blood oath beginning with Adoption, and that isn't a widespread practice within many Craft Trads. We value consensus in our decision-making whenever possible, and most especially on Adoptions and Raising Rites. That does tend to keep us on the same page a little more. But even then, disagreements happen, outside factors contribute to stress, and everyone is capable of having a bad day/season.

Aside from learning a little about interpersonal and group dynamics through leadership seminars, books, etc — which I highly recommend you do — there are some basics you can remind yourself of to help navigate choppy waters.

- Consensus-building is a powerful decision-making tool. It takes longer, but it is worth it. Everyone is heard, solutions can be explored, and there is a lot more buy-in once the decision is made because everyone had time to get to a conclusion with which they feel comfortable.

- "Problems" can often point the way to unmet needs. I've always loved the quote by Henry J Kaiser that says, "Problems are only opportunities in work clothes." When I was a teacher, it was one of the quotes that decorated my classroom walls. When issues come up, don't reactively consider it a setback. It's actually an opportunity to move forward. It may even give you the chance to innovate and create something really meaningful.

- Relationships become exponentially more complicated when there are more people in them. "Complicated" doesn't equal "worse," just … more challenging. Let's say your Coven is chartered with three people — whom we'll call Anna, Bea, and Carlos. Each of the two has their own relationship — patterns, history, etc. Anna and Bea. Bea and Carlos. Carlos and Anna, PLUS there's the whole group relationship. That's four systems of relating for three people. They bring Donovan into the group, and now we add not just Donovan and Anna, Donovan and Bea, Donovan and Carlos; but also the subgroup relationships between any three of them. (Anna, Bea, and Carlos... Anna, Bea and Donovan... Bea, Carlos, and Donovan … Anna, Carlos, and Donovan, etc.) With four people, your group has now jumped to over 20 (24, in fact) — and it requires an algebraic formula just to calculate the combinations. (Remember permutations and combinations from school?) If this makes your brain hurt, don't worry. Nobody expects algebra from you in the Spiral Castle. Just awareness. Be cognizant of the fact that there's going to be more going on than you can see from your own place in the group. And larger groups can be a Gordian Knot of interconnected relationships.

- The empowerment / enlightenment of the Self is our highest aim within SCT. Use that as a touchstone when making decisions and mediating conflicts.

- We have adopted each other as Family. Shared blood bonds. A bell can't be un-rung. A Coven can decide to exclude a Sibling-Witch from their group process due to malfeasance, or a Witch can decide to separate from the Coven; but the Oaths and Vows are still in place. The Family ties are still there. Be cautious about who you share those with, and keep them sacred. We are a Family by choice, by intention, by magick.

<u>Assignment</u>	Write a brief reflection regarding group dynamics and interpersonal relationships. Be sure to include the following:

- Good, healthy group experiences you've been involved in
- Toxic or uncomfortable group experiences you've had
- Family dynamics that you've encountered that might shape your experience of a Craft Family
- Hopes, fears, and ideas you have for facilitating this aspect of Coven life

<u>Additional Resources</u>	There are several titles on the Coven Leadership reading list that can be helpful for this topic.

You might also want to check out these:

Communication Coach Alex Lyon — https://www.youtube.com/@alexanderlyon

Organizational Communication Channel — https://www.youtube.com/@orgcomm
(This is also Alex Lyons)

Antagonists in the Church: How to Identify and Deal with Destructive Conflict — by Kenneth Hauck — https://amzn.to/3FE9cnN

<u>BoS Pages Included</u>	None

Puppy Papers, Lineage & "Authority"

Prerequisite Lesson

07-01 "Rules & Roles"

Objective

To consider the relative value of "lineage"
To understand the place of lineage documents (or "puppy papers")
To reflect on "authority"

Materials Needed

Note taking-materials

Study Notes

Like most of this year's study, the topics we're covering in this lesson are nuanced and very personal. It may take you some time to fully appreciate their complexity — and your circumstances may lead you to have very different thoughts and feelings than mine have. As I've said many times before (on other topics), I'm comfortable with that.

Some History Regarding Lineage

As I understand it, most British Traditional Witches (Cochranian or other family based and/or folkloric groups) and British Traditional Wiccans (Gardnerian, Alexendrian, etc) living in the UK don't fuss with lineage documents. "The proof is in the pudding," as it were. If you know the ways, you know them, and you are considered "legitimate" by whatever group or person with whom you are trying to establish that point of commonality.

Lineage documents (dubbed "puppy papers") are a fairly American addition to the Craft, starting with the Long Island line of Gardnerian Witches. I've linked a fascinating book that explores the whole issue (in the chapter on USA) in the resources, for those who are interested in learning more of our history. (Don't be dissuaded by the word "Wicca" in the title. The author talked with the many of the keepers of the Trads from which we are descended — 1734, Roebuck, Clan of Tubal Cain.)

These puppy papers are a big deal in some lines of American Craft. But why?

In my mind, it all boils down to legitimacy and authority. Who has the right to claim a title? Who has the right to lead the rituals? Who has the right to teach and to initiate?

Americans so often struggle with identity and with imposter syndrome. The nations of North, Central, and South America are all relatively young political entities. Most of us share a history and ancestry of some combination of First Peoples, enslaved (and/or indentured) peoples, colonizers, and refugees. We have complicated relationships with ourselves, our histories, our culture(s), and our identities.

Lineage documents in Witchcraft were born out of a desire or need, I think, to establish some point of legitimacy. "I AM a Witch! It's not all in my head. Here's my proof."

"Puppy Papers" in the Spiral Castle Tradition

I have mixed feelings on lineage documents. I use them, but only cautiously.

Until I was in relationship with my ex-wife (and co-founder of this Tradition), I didn't even know they existed. My initiating HPS (Mary) had started her own Tradition after working in and learning from Gardnerian Wicca, Roebuck/ Ancient Keltic Church, and a pair of Welsh Druids. She was a 3rd Degree Gardnerian, but she rejected a whole lot of the customs, practices, and philosophies of that path — including the puppy papers, it seems.

And I understand why. In "proving" one person's "legitimacy," they can also serve to disprove another's. There are whole lines that are considered "not really part" of various Craft Trads because somebody was discredited, and everything they did after that was considered null and void — including the initiations. So, generations of Witches went through the training and initiation, carried the customs, and are nonetheless "illegitimate" in the eyes of their greater Craft family.

That doesn't seem right to me.

These documents were also developed in a Craft community that worked hard to maintain its Mysteries and many of its customs as "oath-bound secrets" — making the open exchange of information impossible. Glaux and I rejected the concept of "oath-bound secrets" when we founded this Tradition. The only information that we have ever considered "subrosa" (sacredly confidential) are the identities and personal experiences of our Witches. In other words, we can all talk about our own experiences and understandings, but we can't "out" our Covenmates or name them when talking about their function in our experiences.

When we went public with our Trad through the American Folkloric Witchcraft blog, we let all the horses out of the barn. No idea or concept was so sacred that we couldn't write about it. (Well … we didn't write about the initiation rituals, but that was more an issue of practicality than anything else. We have both received initiations in other magickal systems, and we know the value of surprise in those rites. When I decided to write these course guides, which include self-initiation rituals, I took steps to differentiate self– versus coven-initiation, while preserving the power and impact of both.)

So why do we have lineage documents, at all, in SCT? If both self– and coven-initiations are considered equally valid, all of the information is publicly accessible, and we reject the idea of one Witch being any more or less valid or legitimate than another, why bother with certificates and lineage at all?

There are a few reasons. If they matter to you, they matter — and these items are here for you. If they don't matter, then they don't — and you don't have to use them.

The first reason is that they are an acknowledgement of your hard work and achievement, and also of the environment in which you did that work. There is a structure in place here. A certain level of rigor. People who have engaged in the same or similar levels of study will relate to that. In this sense, our certificates and lineage letters act something like a diploma. (We are, after all, talking about "degrees.")

Another reason is that you may need all or part of this documentation in order to achieve other goals in your personal path. If it is important to you to be able to officiate wedding ceremonies (as we discussed in 06-03 "Weddings & Ordination), you might need some documentation in order to satisfy your state's or province's requirements.

The final reason, in my mind, is to identify your branch on the family tree. It is my hope that this will only ever be an informational and relational sort of identification. I see it as something akin to other genealogical research — or figuring out "who's you are" at family reunions. ("Oh! You're Ronnie's oldest? You have his eyes. How's he doing? I haven't seen him twenty years.") Our Covens will have their own personalities and customs, just like we do as Witches. Our lineages — our genealogies — help us celebrate our connections and honor our differences.

What is in a "Puppy Paper?" (And how do I get one?)

There are a couple of kinds of documents involved, in our case. One type is a certification. We issue these at each degree, and they are signed by your initiator — and given to you following the initiation. If you complete your work independently through these books, you probably already know that you can contact me to have them emailed to you.

The other type is a sort of letter or short biography prepared by each initiator in your line. So you might only have the one I provide (if I directly initiate you — or if you are self-initiated and wish to have one). Each person in the initiate-line adds their own "letter" explaining who they are, and they provide copies of the letters for their whole line to the new initiate (at 1st Degree). These letters usually contain a public name, a Craft or Family name (the one you were given at 1st Degree), a picture (often in regalia), the dates of your initiations, titles you hold, the name of your Coven if applicable, and sometimes a short paragraph.

It is shockingly difficult to find copies or examples of these documents online, despite so much information being published by and about various Trads. I have only ever seen one set in person from a Tradition other than ours. I have included a version of mine in this book, as an example. It is the version I use with remote students — initiates with whom I do not have a blood-bond of my own. (I differentiate in this way because I harbor some beliefs about the power of the Name and of the Stars. I don't want to give my initiation dates and Craft name to folks I don't actually know and who have made no promise to me directly regarding privacy.)

Some Thoughts on Authority

Ideas of lineage and legitimacy are tied to ideas of authority. "Who has the right?" and "Who has the power?"

These ideas will come into places of prominence or concern — or just discussion — for you at different times in your life as a Witch.

Mainstream society and the larger Craft community have been moved along a continuum from secrecy and guardianship of information into a much more open-source, freeware, wiki kind of world. I could share stories from my early experiences in the Craft that would absolutely sound like gatekeeping, abuse, toxicity, hostility, and domination. Frankly, I believe that some of them were — from my perspective twenty years later. I had no frame of reference to, though, to recognize these dangers at the time. (More worrisome, perhaps, is the fact that I might still have subjected myself to them in order to get to the lessons and Mysteries, even if I did recognize them.)

I have done my best to root these out of the Spiral Castle Tradition. But I am human, and I am sure I have blindspots even now.

In our ongoing quest for enlightenment and empowerment (which I think are two ways of naming the same Truth — which is our inherent Divinity), let us always remember that there is no authority — no power — except where we bestow it.

Assignment

Create your own lineage letter.

Write a brief reflection regarding your thoughts on lineage, documentation, and authority.

Additional Resources

Wicca: History, Belief, and Community in Modern Pagan Witchcraft — by Ethan Doyle White — https://amzn.to/3HnvInf

---

BoS Pages Included

Laurelei's Lineage Letter

Study Group & Chartered Coven

Prerequisite Lesson

None specified

Objective

To consider your role as a teacher within the SCT/RTA, if applicable

To think about ways to adapt the rituals in Years 1 & 2 for group use

---

Materials Needed

RTA Year 1: Foundations book

RTA Year 2: Practicum book

Note-taking materials

Study Notes

Whether you ever considered or wanted the role of teacher or not, if you form a study group or charter a Coven, the people who join you will see you as one. That's true whether that group operates within the Spiral Castle Clannad ("Clan" — extended family) or not. If you've already started a study group or some other gathering of Witches, you've probably already experienced the Truth of that.

In some ways, the heavy-lifting of curriculum transmission has already been done within the Spiral Castle Tradition, in the form of the three books that comprise the Red Thread Academy. You don't have to create your own curriculum to encapsulate the major ideas, experiences, and considerations at the right stages for others. Nor do you have to figure out the best progression to share those ideas and experiences.

The expectation is that every Witch in this Trad (from at least the time of Adoption/Red Cord/Dedication) will have their own copies of the books for the level(s) they have studied or are currently studying. This is a way to ensure that everyone has the same access to the teachings and rituals of this Tradition, and it helps to eliminate some of the "telephone game" effect of a purely oral tradition.

I hope that I have conveyed strongly enough, too, that our having this material written does not mean that we are lock-stepped into uniformity and synchronization with each other. There is a lot of room for Covens and individuals to explore and express their cultures, interests, and "sense of the Arte."

Also, the fact that these books are used across the Spiral Castle Clannad doesn't deny you the opportunity to take an active role as a teacher within your group, if that is where your talents and interests are. If you go with the teaching model (discussed

109

in Lesson 07-02 "Meeting Structures & Schedules") in which you require the reading and activities for a lesson to be completed prior to the meeting, and that participants come ready to share and explore that work more deeply, there is a lot of room for you to bring your knowledge, wisdom, and nuance to the group in the form of group discussion questions, activities, additional resources, and more.

You might also revise or adapt the lesson progression, alter the rituals so they work better for groups, or assign certain lessons as purely independent work to make room for exploring some aspect of Craft that you or your group has an interest in. You could, for instance, decide that you want to talk about poppets or dream pillows or magickal bath recipes for a class session as a hands-on workshop. Alternatively, you might explore those things together as a lunar working.

There are some pointers that I would like you to consider as you make plans to teach and lead a group.

- The one who does the work is the one who gets the experience and wisdom. (Think about the lessons in the stories of Finn MacCool frying the salmon and Gwion Bach stirring the cauldron. They themselves received the reward for their efforts — not the person who set them to the tasks, thinking the reward could be handed off at the end.) Don't intercede for your students and rob them of the opportunity to grow and learn. Think of yourself as the "Guide on the Side" (and not the "Sage on the Stage") and work toward facilitation, rather than lecture, whenever possible. Along these lines, when you ask a question of the group and are met with silence, give it time to grow until someone answers. Don't jump in with the response you are looking for. Let it be uncomfortable, if it needs to be. Repeat the question, maybe, but give the students a chance to do that mental work. It's a very rewarding sort of awkwardness because when the answer comes, it will be from a place of original thinking, and not from a place of mirroring back to you the thing you just said.

- In ritual settings, get everyone involved. New members can help with set-up and learn where things go. Anyone can be invited to call a Gate, once they've seen it done once or twice and have had some exposure to the symbols. (They'll be nervous because they don't "know the words," but we thrive on extemporaneous calls and language. Only our oaths and vows are scripted, really.) If there is something to be made in the ritual, everyone should have one — unless it is specifically a group-held item.

- There is no Witch Police. We have customs and cosmology in common, but there is a great deal of flexibility in how we approach those things. This Tradition (any Tradition) is a duplicatable framework, but there are infinite idiosyncrasies that can complement that frame. Using the Great Powers as an example, some members of the Trad see them as merely archetypes while working within an Energy Model, others see them as titles that are applied to specific Deities with whom they have affiliation, and yet others honor and work with the specific trio that is Goda, Kolyo, and Tubal Cain. None of these are "wrong." Whenever you have the desire to tell another Witch they're "doing it wrong," explore where this impulse is coming from, who it serves, and if there might not be something YOU are not understanding. Approach it as a dialogue in which either party (or both) might walk away with new insights. Offer your own experience as something to consider, but not as the metric by which all other experiences must be judged.

- It's okay to not know something. It's also okay to say, "I don't know" out loud to someone who thinks you ought to know the answer. As teachers and leaders, we are modeling practices. Take opportunities like this to show that none of us can know all there is to know about the Craft, that we all continue to be students, and that "problems are opportunities in work clothes." Not knowing something is a gift! It is an invitation to explore, learn, and grow.

- We don't invite specific individuals to join the Coven. We can let the "community" know that we are starting a group, and then let folks self-select themselves. But we don't add a layer of hand-picking or anointing (because that is how it seems to play out in the minds of the prospective members) to our group formation. (Where I've seen invitations happens, it always does very hinky things to the group dynamic — and the specially-invited person is often set up for failure, disappointment, and a special brand of ego-tripping.)

Teaching is a craft of its own. It can be learned, and also, really gifted teachers often have a combination of talent and skill-development. By the time you are at this stage of your own studies, you definitely have the knowledge and experience to start teaching others — if that is something you choose to do.

Assignment

Write a brief reflection regarding teaching this Craft to others in a group setting. Be sure to include the following:

- Your experiences with teaching other types of material, if any.
- Your initial thoughts regarding teaching methods and approaches.
- Your reactions to any points that stood out to you from this lesson.

Additional Resources

None

BoS Pages Included

None

Mentorship

<u>Prerequisite Lesson</u>

08-01 "Study Groups and Chartered Covens"

<u>Objective</u>

To explore some of the differences when teaching a single person

To explore the distinction between teaching and mentoring

<u>Materials Needed</u>

Note-taking materials

<u>Study Notes</u>

Not only is there a precedent or model in the RTA of engaging in one-on-one mentorship, but that model also exists in the larger world of the Craft. In fact, the mentorship model might actually be the more common framework for learning the Craft, from a historical and folkloric viewpoint. We certainly see lots of examples in the folk tales, trial records, and legends about a Witch or Sorcerer learning from a much older and more experienced practitioner in a one-on-one setting.

Often what we see in the folklore is based around the apprenticeship model, and that can certainly still work in the Craft today. There is a lot of "learning on-the-job" that happens in this method, and that is certainly appealing. We've built as much of that into the RTA as possible, actually — while working with the challenge of being separated by time and space.

Another aspect of apprenticeship that we experience here is the idea that, once the student/apprentice is fully trained, they are capable of breaking off on their own, starting an independent practice away from the teacher, and taking on students of their own.

Mentorship differs slightly from apprenticeship in the sense that it might be a more theoretical sort of guidance and instruction. I'm thinking all the way back to ancient Greece and the origin of the term "mentor" — back to Athena showing up as an old man of Ithaca who was named Mentor and who had been a faithful friend to Odysseus and a trusted advisor and counselor to Odysseus' son, Telemachus. Athena Mentor modeled this way of teaching and advising for us. (The personal name Mentor came to be associated with someone in this type of role much, much later.)

In my experience, the mentorship relationship is very similar to the coaching relationship, if you are familiar with the work of life coaches, business coaches, relationship coaches, etc. A person with expertise or experience acts as advisor to someone who needs some assistance getting through a challenging time or situation. That assistance or support often comes in the form of goal-setting, fresh perspective, accountability, encouragement, feedback, etc — much like a sports coach gives to an athlete.

That is what mentorship within the Red Thread Academy looks like. It usually starts with a conversation about the person's goals — what they need and want from the coaching relationship, what they are working toward in their Craft studies and practice. Then the mentor and mentee create a plan together, schedule check-ins, set some tasks for achieving the goal, and dig into the work.

In our case, the schedule might follow the Suggested Weekly Lesson Progression in the curriculum. A lot of Witches just want someone specifically to be accountable to — or to get feedback from.

If it seems to you that folks who want that "external accountability" are short-circuiting their own personal accountability, I'd like to suggest a different perspective. Many folks — and especially neuro-divergent folks — really benefit from a "body double" in order to achieve certain tasks. A coach/mentor can basically act as that body double simply by being present in the mentee's life and holding the expectation that the mentee has for themselves.

One of the other great benefits to this relationship is the perspective that the mentor can bring. Years of experience and study can be a great asset when trying to troubleshoot or work through a thorny issue. I've worked with folks in a mentoring relationship who struggled with scrying, seething, and who had aphantasia — to name a few tricky areas. Because we were meeting one-on-one, we had the opportunity to figure out where and what the challenges were and to try some different ways of approaching the task (or the end goal). Sometimes we need to focus on the forest, but sometimes we need to see the specific trees.

You'll find that mentorship can be very flexible and look different from one student to the next. Some mentorships can last for months or years. Others are a single session. Most are somewhere in between.

The power of this type of relationship really comes from the flexibility to address the specific needs of the mentee in a way that makes sense to them. They have a goal, and you can change things up to help them find ways to achieve it without disrupting the Coven's schedule or someone else's learning style.

Coaching Fees

Coaching often comes with an investment. Teaching the Craft often does not. And here we have a disconnect and need to reflect for a moment.

In this Tradition, we do not adhere to the Ardanes (which are the "Old Laws" of the Craft as notated by Gerald Gardner — and which might have actually been written by him in the creative sense, rather than having been handed down from the lineage of his tradition). Even so, it is shocking how far-reaching the admonition is to refrain from "accept[ing] money for the use of the Arte." I've known many an eclectic Witch — and a few folkloric ones — who are very repulsed by the idea of money changing hands for anything related to the Craft. For a great many, that includes teaching the Craft, as well as performing spells. (Interestingly … and ironically …, most of those same Witches have no problem at all with taking money for divination.)

Within this Tradition, we have our own customs and expectations around the exchange of money for services that emerge from the Craft. I think they are sensible, and I hope you will see their sense and logic, too.

Our governing customs in this realm are based on the following philosophies:

- All persons deserve to be appropriately compensated for their time and energy.
- Family relationships are not a commodity or a billable service.

We do not charge a fee for membership in our Covens, nor for the classes and rituals that we perform within our Covens for corded members of our Family. This includes initiations. (We might need to collect dues to pay for supplies or space for day-to-day operations and for special rituals and events, but that is not the same as a membership fee. No single Covener — not even the Queen, Devil, or Consort — should ever have to bear the financial burden alone.)

We absolutely can and do charge fees to the public for workshops, mentoring, and rituals — including both rites of passage and initiations. (And we set our own consistently-applied policies about charging Coveners for individual services like mentorship, pastoral counseling, etc.)

"But, Laurelei," (I hear you saying), "are we ever really offering mentorship or initiations to the 'general public'? If the person is a Red/Triple Cord member of the Tradition — even at a distance — aren't they Family?"

That's an excellent question, Sibling, and I am glad you asked!

Yes, the corded members of the SCT who work at a distance from us are definitely part of the Clannad — the extended Family. The difference between close Family and extended Family really lies in the energetic exchange and bond that is possible. The members of a Coven (close Family) know each other's partners and kids, bring each other soup when one is sick, swap babysitting nights, call to check-in, let each other vent. That happens as much with the Queen/Devil/Consort as it does with others. There is a deep connection as well as reciprocity there.

We are absolutely able to have similarly close relationships with Piblings, Niblings, and Cousins as we are with Siblings, but the farther out the extension goes, the less likely it is that there is the same sort of natural bond and reciprocity. In these cases, it is best to plan for a sort of reciprocity that ensures that nobody is being taken advantage of.

Teaching, mentoring, and ritual facilitation are work. They are time-consuming and energy-consuming. They take some mental, emotional, and physical resources on the part of the person providing them. Offering these without compensation to folks with whom we do not share a Coven-bond is a recipe for burnout.

In setting your fees for these services and learning events, you should look to your local marketplace for the price-point. What are others charging for a skills-based workshop or a "night with a guest lecturer"? What are coaches in your area charging for their services? What would a local psychic reader get paid for an hour of their time? (Or a dance instructor, massage therapist, or other professional, etc?) What is the nearest retreat center charging for a weekend-long event?

Also, you need to factor in your costs and materials. You may have to rent space, make photocopies, buy refreshments, buy or replenish supplies, spend time hand-crafting items, etc.

Of course, if you want to offer these services as "acts of service," that is your choice, too. You can also offer your service to the Clannad and to your local community by offering free workshops at Pagan Pride Day, hosting public rituals in the park, and creating publicly-accessible video or blog content, if you are so moved.

<u>Assignment</u>	Write a brief reflection regarding the mentoring relationship. You might choose to include the following:
	• Experiences you've had in the past as a mentor or mentee, and how these might impact your role as a mentor in the SCT/RTA
	• Your thoughts and feelings regarding your comfort-level with charging for teaching and ritual services
	• The boundaries/protocols you might implement to comply with your own ethics around ideas of service and compensation
<u>Additional Resources</u>	None
<u>BoS Pages Included</u>	None

Initiations

Prerequisite Lesson

08-02 "Mentorship"

Objective

To discuss some of the considerations particular to facilitating initiation rituals

---

Materials Needed

Note-taking materials

Study Notes

Initiations are truly magickal and memorable rituals. I'm hoping you can look at the Dedication and both Admissions you have taken within the Spiral Castle Tradition and see the truth of that.

If you run a Coven, you will undoubtedly have the privilege and pleasure of facilitating initiations for Coveners, when their times come. Since these rituals don't happen very often, and we therefore get significantly less practice in facilitating or observing them, I thought it prudent to share some advice that might help you get started.

Privacy

There are a few considerations for privacy to consider. The most basic of these is that you should perform the initiation ritual in a place where there is no chance that an uninitiated person will come into close enough range of the ritual site to see or hear what is happening. These are intense and personal rituals, and all care must be taken to allow them to happen without interruption or intrusion.

Pictures and recordings are not appropriate during the ritual itself. Feel free to take pictures of the space, the set-up, and each other before or after. Just not during.

Coveners and other Family who are not of the same degree or higher than the initiation being performed should not be present during the ritual. Everyone might come to the site, but there needs to be separate and secluded space for the initiation. My preference is to rent a cabin — or cabins (plural) if there are Coveners present who have not reached that degree. This allows for a departure and return in the initiatory cycle that can help everyone process it as the "hero's journey" — with its corresponding call to adventure, departure, crossing the threshold into the underworld, trials, apotheosis, crossing the threshold back to the Greenworld, return, and reintegration. I feel strongly, though, that what happens during ritual should retain an air of unfamiliarity and mystery. If we include the members who aren't yet at that stage, we risk normalizing the initiation in such a way that it loses much of its power.

Facilities

For the best experience, you're going to need a ritual site with some level of climate control, plumbing, electricity, lighting, food prep area, and a separate room for sections of the ritual that require the candidate be alone. If any member of the initiation group has a mobility impairment, you're also going to need to make sure that the space is accessible for them.

If your preference is to handle the initiation outdoors, I would recommend arranging for a portion of it to happen outside, but only if a few circumstances are in place.

1. The weather isn't too hot or too cold. Remember that you need to make sure not to shock or stress the candidate's system in such a way that they are hurt or thrown into a state of medical distress.
2. The outdoor site still needs to be totally secluded. If there is a chance of a neighbor, fellow camper, or random passer-by to see or hear the ritual, the candidate is likely to be so "on guard" that they struggle to immerse fully in that portion of the ritual.
3. All participants need to be able to fit in the space and navigate it safely by candlelight.

I really don't recommend attempting to perform the entire initiation outdoors. All of our initiations last somewhere between four and eight hours, depending on a few factors (like how much of the cord is braided beforehand). Unless you are able to rent or use a large area for your private group, it will be difficult to stage it appropriately entirely outside.

A "different" space than your regular Coven meetings is preferred for initiations, in most cases. It is best to take this as an opportunity for retreat, if at all possible. Very familiar surroundings can make the ritual feel mundane. If you must use the regular Coven space, take care to move unneeded furniture and cover or remove unneeded items from view in the primary ritual room.

The candidate and all ritual participants should take a preparatory ritual bath (with their own sachets and candles). You'll want a place with bathing facilities.

Time

Again, I suggest you treat initiation weekends as opportunities for Coven retreat. Don't try to knock it out in a single evening, with everyone returning to their separate homes at the conclusion of the ritual.

Rather, plan on arriving as early on the day of the initiation as possible to get "landed," ritually bathed, and set-up before commencing the ritual sometime after sunset. Once the ritual is started, don't rush. Allow each section to take as long as it needs. That includes allowing for some periods of debrief.

After the three trials is a great time to talk about the experiences and insights attached to those trials. During the cord-braiding is a good time to talk, as well — though, I caution you to be mindful with this. Whatever you're discussing gets tied into the cords. Be sure to allow some time for debrief after the ritual officially ends, as there is often stuff that comes up for people during the Oaths, Vows, and Presentation. This last debrief goes nicely with food! You'll all need it, at this point.

The next day can be given over to journaling, bonding, recovery, some planning with the new initiate, etc. It's a great time for mentoring or coaching, and also a wonderful opportunity to enjoy each other's company.

Fasting

The fasting that we do prior to initiation is important to help alter consciousness for the ritual and trials ahead. Everyone who is participating in the ritual should participate in the fast.

We don't dictate the type of fast that anyone must do. This is about consciousness-shifting, not deprivation or control over others.

A good guideline for the length of the fast is:

No fast for Adoption/Dedication

3 days for 1st

5 days for 2nd

7 days for 3rd

The last day of the fast should be the same day that the initiation begins. Anyone who can safely move into a liquid fast that last day are often rewarded for doing so.

Equipment

There is nothing on the materials lists for our initiations that I personally consider optional. If you are performing the rituals as a self-dedication, I tend to be lenient about some substitutions or small changes. If you are facilitating these initiations for others, try to have everything you need and stick to the ritual outline.

Bring more candles than you think you need. You can use electric lighting in some part of the ritual without killing the vibe (such as during the cord braiding), but having to work through harsh lights during much of the ritual just so you can see the outline is problematic.

Cost

The initiation has a lot of costs associated with it. Space rental, travel, food for the weekend, gift, sachets, candles. And more candles.

I've performed and received initiations in three magickal traditions, and they have all had similar cost considerations. When I look at what I can see of the initiations in traditional cultures, I can see that there is a cost involved.

It is a hardship for many of us to pay this cost. At this point, I am convinced that this is one of the thresholds we must cross — one of the guardians we must face — in order to fully engage in the death and rebirth of initiation.

In some Covens, the costs are split equally between all participants, including the candidate(s). In others, the cost is split between everyone, except the candidate(s). In other systems of magick, I have seen the cost borne entirely by the candidate(s). All of these are viable options within SCT.

Setting Up

For an in-person ritual, the candidate should not be involved in setting up the ritual space, and they should be prevented from seeing the ritual space until the ritual has begun.

Trials

The trials have some nuanced elements when administered from one person to another. For one thing, the "final exam" is handled differently. The form that accompanies the self-initiations in all three books is fine and can be used in or prior to Coven-based initiation, of course. Often, though, this piece is drawn fully into the ritual as a "Trial of Inquisition" — and also includes questions the candidate isn't anticipating. In fact, all Initiates of that Degree are encouraged to bring some of their own questions to ask.

In the 1st Degree, the candidate is left alone during the scrying/journey portions of the ritual. The others take turns checking on them to see when they have emerged from this journey. (We try to be as quiet and unobtrusive during these checks as possible — observing from the shadows at their back, if at all possible.)

In the 2nd Degree, the Mazey Stone path is travelled by everyone except the primary initiator, who taps a simple beat with the Stang during the journey. When the candidate has emerged, they change the beat to bring the others up to the surface so the work can proceed.

Also, in the 2nd, it is worth noting that the candidate still performs a SELF-sacrifice (OF themselves, TO themselves, FOR themselves). Nobody else has the right to make that sacrifice. The biggest difference in the group-based ritual, though, is that the candidate is called back to Life by the Stang-playing and singing of the others who are present.

The 3rd Degree initiation includes elements of sex magick. At no point ever do we, as initiators, require a candidate to participate with us or perform for us in an overtly sexual capacity. We'll talk more about this in Unit 10, but it is important to reinforce that norm here, as we discuss ritual variations. None of our variations include sex with or in the presence of an initiator.

Discomfort/Fear/Triggers

In the Year 2: Practicum book, there is a trigger warning. I believe that it is worth having a conversation with all candidates for initiation regarding triggers in initiation, in a general way.

I've done a good study of initiations, and I am going to share a "hot take." Initiations are supposed to be triggering. Not traumatizing, but triggering. There should be a point in the initiation when you are so far out of your comfort zone that you fear genuine failure — or maybe that you experience panic, despair, embarrassment, or a desire to tell off the initiator and storm out of the room.

You're supposed to face that experience (that Guardian of the Mysteries) so you can figure out how to get past it. It is ONLY by confronting that Guardian that you can gain access to what lies beyond.

Not every trial is designed to be triggering, but all of them are capable of it. A knife at your throat. Your hands bound. Nudity. Your eyes covered and having to trust a guide to lead you. Long silences after you answer a question. These are a few examples of things that have happened in initiations that I've participated in. I've known of all of these things being triggering for me or my fellow-initiates. The catch is that what is triggering for one of us might be within the norm for another.

One of the questions that I pose to candidates — who usually don't know what triggers await them — is: Do you trust the initiator/team to see you safely through this ordeal? Another valid and useful question is: If not to be tested and reborn into the Mysteries, why have you come to these ordeals?

Physical discomfort (including non-damaging aches and pains) is sometimes a by-product of the process. It is never the goal. Not in the Spiral Castle Tradition. You will not undergo a "Trial by Pain" here (such as flogging).

Hoodwinking and Warricking

"Hoodwinking" means blindfolding. "Warricking" means binding. For in-person initiatory rites, these are elements that are involved, to one degree or another.

These are done symbolically, for us, and they are not part of any supposed BDSM urge or undercurrent in the Craft.

At Adoption, we are brought to the space hoodwinked and vouched for by a Sibling. The blindfold here symbolizes that we don't (and can't) really know what is ahead of us.

At Raising (1st), we are brought to the space both bound and blindfolded, symbolizing our willingness to trust our Siblings and seek the Mysteries.

The binding is not intended to cause pain, but sometimes it does cause some intense discomfort because of the way it alters blood flow in the shoulders and arms. We have to be very aware and sensitive to a person's level of flexibility when administering the binding, and we have to be aware of what is happening with them energetically and physically to know when it needs to be removed.

The traditional warricking cord loops fully around the candidate's neck and ties the hands in place at the small of the back. This is NOT the method we use. We either tie the hands in a manageable position in front of the body, or we tie them in a reachable position just behind the hips. The cord drapes across either the front or back of the neck. Nothing is tied or stretched so tightly as to dig into the skin, although as the candidate tires and shifts their position within these limits, the cord may feel very noticeable where it lays across the throat/neck.

When we are leading a person who is blindfolded, we need to clear tripping hazards and give clear verbal and physical directions. Our hands should always be on their shoulders or arms to help guide and steady.

Additions/Subtractions

If you are administering an initiation in the Spiral Castle Trad, stick to the outline. Our initiations are very purposeful in terms of their progression and the pieces that are included. Don't add things because you think they would be cool — or remove things because you don't see their value. If something like this comes up for you, talk with me or with the other 3rd Degrees.

Medical and Emotional Concerns

Because we are putting candidates in uncomfortable, triggering, or off-balance circumstances for the initiations, it is very important that we have some training in crisis management techniques and also first aid. Our rituals are genuinely quite safe, but it is still possible for someone to experience a crisis. That might happen because they are so off-balance and tense, or it might be purely bad timing.

Regardless of the cause, we need to be able to either help them navigate and emerge from the crisis — or we need to call in professional help in an emergency.

We also need to be as aware as is reasonably possible regarding medical or emotional states that could contribute to crisis during the ritual. We have a myriad of ways to make adjustments for disability and past trauma without compromising the initiation.

Multiple Candidates

The preference within Spiral Castle Trad is that each candidate will have their own initiatory experience, not shared with another candidate or two. That being the preference, we are also sensitive to the fact that initiations require a commitment of both time and money that many Coveners can't invest many multiple times per year. If you do choose to initiate multiple candidates on the same weekend, here are my recommendations:

- Only group candidates together if they are taking the same initiation. The energies, trials, and workings associated with each initiation are different. Keep them separate.
- Try to initiate them on separate nights, if possible. The cost of another night's lodging is usually cheaper than making the whole trip multiple times.
- If initiating two people together on the same night, separate them for each of the trials, coming back together for the cord-braiding, oath-taking and presentation. You might move the candidates in and out of the same room, using a separate waiting room as a holding space. Or you might set-up two separate rooms as the trial rooms.
- Be cognizant of how sound travels. Provide a candidate who is waiting with white noise and a blindfold so they aren't drawn into what is happening in the main room and also aren't distracted out of the initiation current by their surroundings in the waiting area.
- Be aware that a special bond or link is often created by two people who initiate together like this. That can be both a blessing and a curse for them. Candidates should always be given that warning — and a chance to make a different arrangement.
- Everyone involved is likely to be exhausted by the end. Whether you do one extra long night or two regular long nights, it is hard on everyone who participates.

Assignment

Write a brief reflection regarding initiation considerations. Be sure to include the following:
- Any suggestions or cautions that particularly resonated with you
- Any suggestions or cautions that do NOT resonate with you
- Memories regarding your own self-initiations, and places within them that you instinctively applied the considerations discussed here (and/or places where you didn't, but wish you had)
- Hopes, fears, concerns regarding leading initiations for others

---

Additional Resources

None

BoS Pages Included

None

Secrecy, Ethics, Mysteries

<u>Prerequisite Lesson</u>

08-03 "Initiations"

<u>Objective</u>

To reflect on considerations around the imparting of privacy, ethics, and the Mysteries

<u>Materials Needed</u>

Note-taking materials

<u>Study Notes</u>

Teaching the Craft is not like teaching a dance workshop, a leather-working class, or a new language. All of these include the teaching of skills and the modeling of subtleties that are needed to be truly masterful. The Craft has those, too. But the Craft also has an edge to it that demands some other considerations.

Perhaps that is because we are working with forces that aren't understood by most — forces that they don't want to understand. These forces include Spirits, magick, and the Mysteries that reveal the true power of ourselves.

As a Queen, Devil, or Consort of the Spiral Castle, you may find yourself in a deeper relationship with those forces than you had before.

Secrecy/Subrosa

Our teachings aren't a secret. Glaux and I opened that box for the world to peek inside more than a decade ago, when we started the AFWCraft blog.

Our rituals aren't a secret, in their own right. They have been published and shared across three course manuals. Anyone who seeks to know them, can read them and perform them.

What happens at those rituals during the spaces between the text — the messages we get, the wounds that get lanced and cauterized, the intimacy that is shared — *those* are private. We can share what happened for us, but it is a violation of trust to share what happened to someone else without their express consent.

The same is true for revelations and recollections that are shared from assignments, class discussions, and other meetings. We can share our own stories, but not those of others.

It can be hard to master the impulse to share a great story, but I can speak from personal experience how much of a shock and a violation it is to hear your story (even a funny one that the group bonded over) told back to you from someone who wasn't present. For example: Say your Coven uses the talking board a lot to communicate with Familiar Spirits. Everyone in the Coven has gotten to know the personalities of everyone else's Familiars, and there are often inside-jokes within the group that pull from those personalities or from the specific things the Spirits have said via the board. It feels like someone ran your comfiest pair of underwear up a flagpole for the world to see if you hear those jokes parroted back to you by someone who wasn't there — someone who doesn't share that bond and trust and intimacy. Maybe the thing itself wasn't so private, but it was shared in private space, and it was yours.

It should be obvious, but I'll say it anyway: The identities of our Covenmates is entirely confidential. We don't name them to people who otherwise wouldn't have access to that knowledge. For example, if we choose to perform ritual publicly as a Coven, then the folks who attend will have some sense of who is in the Coven. That does not give us permission to write an article about that ritual in which we use the names of the Coveners — or to tag them in photos of that public ritual on social media. These things can have dire consequences for their jobs, their custody of children, their housing safety, and more.

We work subrosa, despite the public availability of our teachings and rituals. Subrosa means "under the sign of the rose" and is an ancient way of indicating that the contents of a meeting (as well as the identities of the participants) are held in sacred trust. Teach and model the significance of subrosa for those in your group. You might even place a rose on the table, have a rose banner that hangs within your space, or incorporate a rose into your "talking stick."

Ethics

We've spent some time talking and thinking about our own personal ethics. If you lead a group, you will also be talking and thinking about your group members' ethics and how those impact the group as a whole. The Tradition doesn't dictate what another person's ethics are, but we also have no compulsion to welcome people into our homes, into our Family, if their ethics are wildly out of line with our own.

And I do mean "wildly" out of line. I think the choice to use or not use blasting magick, for instance, isn't a deal-breaker — and I hope our Covens always allow folks the space to explore differences like this. The choice to violate another person's consent, on the other hand, IS a deal-breaker.

This area can be tricky to navigate, and it requires that you hold yourself accountable to your own ethics and to your oaths. We have support in place to talk through these issues with other Queens, Devils, Consorts, and Magisters, should you find yourself in need of that — via either the RTA Advanced section of the Thread App or through the Grand Coven.

The Mysteries

In *The White Goddess*, Robert Graves describes the three sacred guardians of the Mysteries — the lapwing, the dog, and the roebuck. The lapwing "disguises the secret," the dog "guards the secret," and the roebuck "hides the secret." My experience has been that we ourselves take part in this guardianship, whether we mean to or not.

In fact, we often make a point in this Trad that "the secret" (aka, the Mysteries) is much like Goda riding through town naked on her white horse. They are right there! And yet, most people don't see them for what they are. People say, "Oh, that's obvious. Everyone knows that." And by saying so, they deny themselves the time and care to explore and really KNOW the thing they have dismissed as "obvious."

Maybe another way to think of it is that the Mysteries disguise, hide, and guard themselves — with no help from us.

As a Queen, Devil, or Consort of the Spiral Castle, you might spend a lifetime in contemplation of these Mysteries. To Witches who come to you for training and fellowship, you might be viewed as the dog, the lapwing, or the roebuck based on the role you play in their study and experience. You might come to know our own Goda, Kolyo, and Qayin as expressions of these Guardians, too.

Assignment

Write a brief reflection regarding the topics discussed today, and most especially about secrecy and working subrosa.

Additional Resources

None

BoS Pages Included

Subrosa

Skull & Bones

Prerequisite Lesson

None specified

Objective

To obtain a skull and two leg bones for necromantic rituals

Materials Needed

Animal skull

Two leg bones from the same animal

Study Notes

NOTE: I want to make a statement regarding the acquisition and use of tools within the Spiral Castle Tradition.

Absolutely no tool is mandatory for the practice of our Craft. Not even the Stang. You — your body — is the Stang at the crossroads, the tree on the hill. Tools are all metaphors and symbols made solid, giving us physical means to interact with energetic and esoteric constructs. They are allies and partners in the work. We recognize them as enspirited (or capable of being enspirited). They aren't stage props or knick-knacks.

The tools we have covered in Foundations and Practicum — and also here in Mastery — are the most commonly used tools of this Tradition. They are the ones that I felt you, as a student, would get the most benefit from working with.

They give a flavor — a distinct character — to our rituals. They are part of our tradition, part of our culture. But they are not required.

You might have some of them, but not all. You might use all of what you have in some rituals — and none at all in others. You might deepen your relationship with this one, but not that one. All of these are valid.

In a Coven setting, it can be very helpful to have all of them. They are helpful in the learning process, and your Coveners may be drawn to tools that you aren't. Some of the tools, then, may be Coven tools, and not personal ones. Others may feel far too personal to share. I feel this way about my knives, my gandried, and my cup; and in my Coven, those things are not shared. We each have our own. However, until folks have their own gandrieds and cups, our Coven also has some that aren't bonded to a particular person and are available as loaners. (This is also useful for guests.)

I give this note now because many of the tools described in this book are more likely to be Coven tools, as opposed to personal ones. You are more likely to have them all, if you are operating a Coven, running public rituals, or otherwise involved in group Witching.

The Skull & Crossed Bones

Most SCT/RTA Witches have their own working skull by this stage in their journey, though it might be glass, ceramic, or stone. You might even have an animal skull, which will be helpful.

In a full ritual set-up where all of the gear is out and being used, the skulls of the Coveners are placed at the base of the Stang, along with the cauldron and anvil. A pair of crossed leg bones is also placed there, as is the Dolly (which we'll cover in lesson 09-03).

Actually, the bones are crossed when we are not doing necromantic rituals. But if we want to talk to the Dead, we open the leg bones so they make a vertical channel facing out from the skull. This opens the path of communication.

I recommend that the skull and bones used for this are from a once-living being. I find them much more effective than stone, paper mache, ceramic, or glass. But, if you must, use an alternative that feels good to you.

I recommend avoiding plastic for all ritual gear, if you can avoid it. The synthetic structure doesn't carry energy well, and I feel like we can do better for our Ancestors than this — even on a tight budget. I would rather a Witch carve an apple into a crude skull shape and "skin" a couple of sticks to act as the bones, than use plastic ones. It would only cost you the price of the apple, and the preparation would be its own sort of offering.

Of the animal bones you might choose, medium to large mammals are best, for practical reasons. The bones are sturdier and less like to break from being held and moved. Horned/antlered animals are the most preferred, due to their association with the Witch Father. Deer and bull skulls are probably the easiest to locate at flea markets, depending on where you live. For the leg bones, check with a butcher or someone in your area who processes game for local hunters. (Tell them it's for a "craft project." You're not lying, and they are probably happy to let you walk away with something they would just throw out.)

Personal animal Allies are also great candidates for skulls and bones, as long as they're sturdy enough for this use and legal to own. Check the laws in your area regarding protected and endangered species.

You probably also want to vet your bone dealer to make sure the animals are being handled in a way you consider humane and ethical. All of the animal bones I use, for instance, are from animals who died naturally, accidentally, or during controlled hunts by hunters I know and trust. It is important to me not to support hunting for sport or methods of husbandry that I consider cruel.

Assignment	Obtain a skull and bones. If this is something that is beyond your means at this time, write a reflection about that. Be sure to include what you would consider an ideal set — or an adequate substitute. Share a picture, if possible.

Additional Resources	Left-Hand Rabbit — https://www.etsy.com/shop/Lefthandrabbit — I'm friends with Ashley and have bought some great furs from her. If she doesn't have what you want, she probably knows who does. She's also on Instagram and Facebook, if you want to reach out there.

BoS Pages Included	Skull & Bones

Weapons & Treasures

Prerequisite Lesson

08-01 "Skull & Bones" (specifically, the note about Tools)

Objective

To identify the Weapons and Treasures that are still needed

To create a plan for obtaining them

Materials Needed

Note-taking materials

Study Notes

There are four Weapons associated with the Gates, and four Treasures kept by the Castles. We strive to have all of them within our Covens, even if we don't have them all personally.

You have made a start on this list, already, if you completed all of the lessons in Years 1 and 2.

I have no expectation that Witches approaching their 3rd Degree will have all of these at this time. Some of them can be very pricey — like the Sword. Others are very art-and-crafts intensive. Some are even rare (Helm).

Instead, I ask you to take stock of what you have, and make a plan for what is missing. Some items will have a more pressing need than others. You'll want some sort of Sword, for instance, before you conduct in-person initiations of your own, as that is a Weapon we use in those rituals. For others, you'll need time to make them or find something in your price range. You might even find that one of your Coveners brings one to the group for use in ritual.

The Weapons

Staff — Someone's personal Staff might serve as the Coven Staff during rituals where you want it present at the North Gate. Or, you might take on the project of creating and blessing a Staff together — perhaps as a lunar working. Staves can be decorated or simple, as you prefer. If you choose to decorate yours, be aware that you may decide to strip it and re-adorn it at some point in the future. (Both myself, my, ex, and my daughter have all done this with our own. It may be that Staves just like to change their clothes every so often.)

Shield — While any style of Shield will do, we tend to favor the Targe in this Trad. A targe is a round shield made of iron or wood that's been plated in iron. It has come to be associated with the Scottish Highlands, though its use was more widespread than that. It is worn on the forearm and has a hand-grip and a strap (usually with a buckle) to secure it to the arm. Shields made for battle were concave, but ours are usually flat. I've made several targes over the years, with most of the supplies being readily available at hardware, leather crafting, and sewing shops. (Instructions are included in the BoS pages in the back of this book.)

Sword — Each Coven will want a Sword to represent the Sword That Cuts Both Ways — the Sword-Bridge that we cross into initiatory rites. The Sword can be a replica or costume sword (like those found at Museum Replicas and Windlass), or it can be a functional sword that holds an edge (like those at Cold Steel). Just be aware that the functional swords are very, very sharp. (My husband has a Grosse Messer, and the half-joke/half-warning in my family is that it cries out for blood. If it is unsheathed, especially by someone other than my husband, chances are high that someone gets cut before it is back in its sheath.) Whatever kind you get, I recommend a double-edged blade to reinforce the symbolism of "cutting both ways." Some blades that might be considered long knives (by blade aficionados) could also work nicely. These might include the Seax, the Arkansas Toothpick, the Gladius, the Tanto, a "hand and a half" dagger, or others along these lines.

Helm — The Helmet is the weapon of the West, guarding the head and the seat of the White Soul. As with the Sword, a replica or costume piece (not made of plastic) would work. There are leather helmets of both historical and fantasy origins, as well. It is possible to even construct a leather helm for yourself, if you desire. Alternatively, you could display a Coven Mask (or multiple masks) in the West. (Look to the Dorset Ooser and the Head of ATHO for both inspiration and connection of these symbols. In fact, a Coven Ooser is an excellent choice here!)

The Treasures

Stone Bowl — You've already made one for yourself, as part of Year 2: Practicum. If you decide to work with a Coven, you might choose to make a Stone Bowl for the Coven, or just use yours to answer Coven questions, as needed.

Glass Orb — This is one of the trickier tools to make or find. My training HPS found a glorious Glass Orb at an overstock store called Tuesday Morning. It was a clear glass sculptural piece that featured a hollow orb about the size of a grapefruit atop a solid glass pedestal. I have never seen its like again. It was all one piece. A similar (but smaller) construct can be made using a clear glass fishing float, a glass candlestick, and a clear-drying super glue. (You could also use a clear Christmas bauble, but the glass is very thin and brittle on those. You might find yourself replacing it more frequently than you'd like. My own Glass Orb is a clear and translucent white glass paperweight — hollow, but with thick glass and a slightly flat base so it doesn't demand a holder. The Glass Orb should be glass or crystal, be hollow, and be clear (or a very translucent white or blue). If you have a solid (not hollow) glass or crystal ball that you love, that can work, too.

Golden Lantern — I don't think any of us could afford a lantern made of actual gold, so "golden toned" is often what we achieve. There are lots to choose from. You could also use gold paint or gold leaf to transform a lantern. Any style of lantern is acceptable. Mine is an amber glass lantern for candles in a style that was popular in the 1970's.

Silver Cup — I don't recommend Covens drink from a shared cup. Silver cups are (at this time) both abundant and relatively cheap at flea markets. The quaich (a Scottish, two-handled, shallow cup) is the preferred style for the Housle Bowl (which is the Cup of the Bloody Castle), but other styles are equally acceptable. I have a coupe-style silver cup for myself, but I plan on buying a proper quaich for the Coven's Housle.

Assignment

Make a list of the tools for yourself and note what you have and what you still need. For items you still need, describe what you would like to find, make, or be given. If you make or acquire any of these items this year, share pictures.

Additional Resources

None

BoS Pages Included

Sword

Helm & Mask

Staff

Shield

Glass Orb

Sone Bowl

Golden Lantern

Silver Cup

Dolly

<u>Prerequisite Lesson</u>	None specified

<u>Objective</u>   To provide a vessel for the Coven Familiar

<u>Materials Needed</u>   A doll (or doll-making supplies)

<u>Study Notes</u>

The Dolly is one of the less common bits of folkloric Craft that occasionally shows up in the writings of published Witches. As with many other folkloric pieces, the traditions that have been handed down around the Dolly can vary widely, as do the origin stories or rationales given for her existence.

In Spiral Castle Trad, the Dolly is representative of the Coven Guardian or Familiar. Witches who practice independently might still have one as a House Guardian/ Familiar for the home where they live.

This question of "what solitaries among us do differently than Covens" is uncharted territory for SCT, in some ways. It has only been with the publication of the RTA Course Guides that there have been "solitary Witches of the Spiral Castle." So, in some ways, RTA students who share their work are showing me what it means to be a solitary on this path. For that reason, you are invited to explore the Dolly and see how she fits, if you plan to continue a solo practice.

The "Hearth Doll" of Old Craft became the "Kitchen Witch Doll" for many Appalachian and Ozark families. All of my grandmas, aunties, and both moms have these dolls hanging in their kitchens. I was given one when I first got married and established my own home. Later, when my first husband's grandma passed, she made sure I received hers, since I'd openly admired it several times. (She's still with me.) These days, they are seen simply as "good luck" — with little awareness of their traditions.

In different parts of the UK, we still see the Hearth Doll (or Chimney Doll) in her place upon the hearth. The Ros and Bucca Coven of Cornwall used to maintain a website that showcased several images related to their practice of the Craft. The House Doll pictured there is very much akin to the Coven Dolly that I am presenting here. (The website has gone defunct or been removed, though I believe the Coven still operates under the leadership of Gemma Gary. Thanks to the Wayback Machine at InternetArchive.org, this resource can still be referenced and viewed. Link in the additional resources.)

The Dolly can be simple or elaborate. You can make it according to any number of traditional doll-making methods — or you can purchase a doll (again, not plastic please) to act as the vessel for the Spirit of your home or Coven. Wooden, corn husk, porcelain, and cloth dolls are all good choices.

I personally love the detail that is given to the House Doll on the website referenced above. She is fully decked out with talismans, a beaded and knotted rowan berry necklace, and a hare, and she is provisioned with a chair, cauldron, and wee blackthorn staff. In essence, she has all the tools she needs to do the work she's been engaged to do.

The Coven's Dolly (within the SCT) is kept at the home where the Coven meets (the Covenstead) and is present for most, if not all rituals. Fashioned as an adult figure (not a child), the Dolly is the vessel of the Coven Familiar and should convey something of that Spirit's nature, if possible.

Assignment

Make or otherwise acquire a Dolly. Write a reflection regarding the elements of its design and construction. What tools does s/he need or have? If you have been working with a study group already, is there a Spirit who has already stepped forward as your group Familiar? Be sure to sain the Dolly as you would with other tools. At the saining, you can also wake the Dolly and name her/him. Share pictures with me or the RTA 3 group on the Thread app.

Additional Resources

(archived) original Cornish Witchcraft website (pictures of working tools) — https://web.archive.org/web/20130331112630/http://www.cornishwitchcraft.co.uk/images-tools.html

---

BoS Pages Included

Coven Dolly

7 Circles of Personal Power

Prerequisite Lesson	None specified

Objective

To discuss the Jewels as Circles of Power

To explore the significance of each Jewel

Materials Needed

Cords	Crown
Bone Ring	Pendant
Copper Bracelet	
Amber, Bone, and Jet Necklace	
Garter	

Study Notes

Witches in the Spiral Castle Tradition might wear or carry upon their person several different "Circles of Power" that act as both protections and as marks of achievement and identification.

While we don't forbid Witches from wearing these things before they have earned them (because nobody here is the Witch Police), it isn't our custom to wear them before the milestones they are attached to, as that would be misleading and hollow. Many of these are given as gifts within our Tradition to Witches at specific rituals.

You'll notice that two of them are associated with the Adoption ritual (aka, Dedication). I didn't mention these in the Year 1: Foundations book, because at the time I first made that book available, the only people purchasing and working through it were remote and unconnected to a study group or Coven. That is no longer the case. Many of these Witch Jewels, however, are given as gifts from the Coven as a whole — purchased from operational dues or funds specifically collected for this gifting.

You may, of course, give them to yourself if you are working through the materials on your own. Likewise, you might consider obtaining any that you don't already have.

Copper Bracelet

We associate this reddish metal with the Red Cords and the Adoption Rite. Worn on the left wrist, a copper bracelet cuff was the one Witch Jewel that a Witch might wear outside of Coven gatherings and rituals. As such, it could act as an identifier of Family to others. It is possible to make your own — or there are several reasonably priced options on Etsy. Some jewelers even offer custom engraving or stamping. Since this can be a more public piece, I recommend not having your Craft Name stamped or engraved on it. Rather, you might choose a magickal motto, favorite line from a chant, or some other short phrase. (Mine says, "I am the Light in the Darkness," as a touchstone for Goda.) This cuff is usually purchased or made for oneself following the Adoption Rite.

Amber, Jet, and Bone Necklace

This is a potent talismanic piece, with a long history of Witch-lore. This necklace is the gift we give to fully-raised Witches at their 1st Admission (aka, Initiation). It is a complement to the Triple Cords, and it bears the same three sacred colors we see throughout the Trad. Necklaces of amber and jet are a common Witch Jewel. Necklaces of snake bone are less common, but can be found in the Traditional practices of Cornish Witches (to name just one). We wear amber, jet, and bone (snake vertebral bones, if possible) with a silver triskele as a powerful talisman of the Spiral Castle.

Bone Ring

The Bone Ring is a symbol for us of the 2nd Admission (aka Initiation). The Traditional gift for this ritual is a Bone Ring, which symbolizes the Bone Soul — the Red, Ancestral Soul. I know folks get confused about this, since bone is white. But the core is red with marrow, which produces red blood cells. The Red Soul is carried on the blood, and the blood itself is associated with the Red Thread. This is usually a bone ring in a silver setting, and can be fashioned by wire-wrapping a bone bead. The Home Coven (Coven Caer Sidhe) uses a flat oxbone bead that has been carved into the likeness of a rose.

Cords

We wear cords beginning with our first affiliation with the Coven. In-person groups often utilize Green Cords and a Greening (or orientation) rite and period in order to allow a prospective member to test the waters before commitments and oaths are made. Those cords are cut and burned during the Adoption Rite. (The Adoption is the first formal declaration for solitary RTA students, so there are no cords to cut and burn.) With the Red Cords of Adoption, a formal link is made and blood ties are formed. That Red Cord is the foundation of the Triple Cords that the Witch takes at 1st Admission.

These cords can all be viewed as gifts, though, since it is the Witches of the Coven who prepare and present them to the candidate during these rites, if that candidate works within a Coven. But there is something more to this Circle of Power, since they are a working tool that many Witches have a direct hand in making for themselves. At 1st Admission, the Witch should definitely be involved in braiding their Triple Cords. Our preferred process is for the Witches of 1st Degree and higher to braid the individual black and white cords — three black, three white — prior to the ritual. Then, everyone present including the new Initiate can braid the black cord together, the white cord together, and finally the Triple Cord together. This is still a long process — which is good, actually. It gives an opportunity for a debrief and magickal conversations to happen, and it is a powerful act of magick in its own right. But that bit of prep (braiding six individual cords — ya know, "a bit of prep") can decrease the in-ritual braiding time by a matter of hours.

We also have the Service Cords, which hang from the Triples and indicate our areas of study and service.

Garter

The Garter is the symbol of the 3rd Degree in the Spiral Castle. It is the marker of a Queen, Devil, or Consort. Since we generally perform ritual wearing robes, it ends up being the most private of our Jewels — or circles of power. It isn't a secret, necessarily. You are at liberty to show others within your Coven or the Trad. (There is also no prohibition against nude/skyclad ritual within SCT, in case that is a question. It just isn't our norm, outside of the Link Cutting or Hieros Gamos rituals — one of which you will likely perform annually as a coven, and the other of which you might never perform except in personal, private ritual.)

Our Garters are green, blue, and red and are tied onto the upper calf or upper thigh of the left leg. They can be woven of three strips of dyed leather, braided from colored cording, or embroidered and reinforced fabric. Whatever their manner of construction, they should be sturdy and comfortable enough to wear throughout a ritual — including initiation rituals. A silver buckle can be added for every coven in the Queen's, Devil's, or Consort's line of descendants, beginning with the one they lead, if applicable. (There are a couple types of garter buckles — the ones that fasten the garter together, and the ones that attach to the stocking or sock being held by the garter. We generally fasten our garters to the leg by means of a tie, not a buckle. So the silver buckles we add are the kind that dangle from a cord attached to the garter.) The Garter is made by the Witch and their initiator during the 3rd Admission.

Crown/Circlet

Crowns and circlets are not part of the full Regalia of a Queen, Devil, or Consort within the Spiral Castle, in the sense that a Witch of 3rd Degree wouldn't wear a crown or circlet to a ritual that they were not leading. We wear these more as a mark of office within the ritual. Traditionally, we choose between a crescent moon crown, a horned crown (sometimes called the Grand Array), and a simple unadorned circlet. There are no gender norms within our Tradition that dictate who should wear which type of headdress. This piece is usually presented as a gift at the Rite of 3rd Admission (aka, 3rd Degree Initiation) from the Queen, Devil, or Consort who is leading the ritual.

Pendant

The Pendant is probably the most personal of all the Jewels within this Tradition since it isn't inherently linked to any of our initiations. This is usually a purchase made by the Witch for themselves, and it is often reflective of some symbol or ideal that they value in their on-going journey. That being the case, it is possible for a Coven to develop a tradition or custom around this piece, as well. For instance, in the Clan of the Laughing Dragon (the Trad I was originally trained in), all new Dedicates received the same silver Dragon charm which was worn on a silver necklace/chain. If this is a Tradition you like, you could start the custom of giving all new Adoptees a tektite cabochon, a silver triskele, or a another charm or stone that has special meaning to your Coven.

For all of these pieces, in fact. Coven customs might develop within a group as an expression of group identity. I've shared some of the customs of the Coven Caer Sidhe, for example. Maybe you have the same style of rings. Maybe the garters and crowns are the same for all who achieve 3rd Degree. Or maybe none of them are the same, with each being chosen based on the preferences of the individuals and the means of the one(s) giving the gift.

I would also like to suggest that you consider how these 7 Circles of Power relate to the Dance of the Seven Veils Mystery, because they certainly do.

<u>Assignment</u>

Write a brief reflection regarding these Circles of Power and the Regalia of the Trad. Be sure to include the following:
- Which pieces you already have
- Which pieces you want/need
- Your thoughts on the symbolism and power of these items
- Any research or background information you've encountered on each
- Pictures of pieces you have or would like

Additional Resources	None

BoS Pages Included	SCT Regalia & Gifts
	Cords
	Jewels
	Amber and Jet and Bone
	Garter
	Crown
	Robe, Cloak & Hood
	The Dance of the Seven Veils

Consent Culture in SCT

<u>Prerequisite Lesson</u>	None
<u>Objective</u>	To define "consent" and "consent culture"
	To understand the role of consent culture within the Spiral Castle Tradition
<u>Materials Needed</u>	Note-taking materials

<u>Study Notes</u>

The terms "consent" and "consent culture" are most often used in discussing sex and sexual relationships; however, they have a much broader scope than that.

Consent — the express permission given by a person regarding an action or interaction

Consent Culture — the environment and expectation that personal boundaries will be respected by everyone, every time

This applies to all sorts of interactions between people. Giving a hug, kiss, or other non-sexual touch. Taking a photo. Sharing that photo. Tagging that photo. Giving a gift. Talking about triggering topics. And more.

Essentially, consent culture means that we don't force our Will upon another person, and this is an important part of the autonomy and personal authority that we value within the Spiral Castle Tradition.

We ask before touching someone's hand in sympathy. The person offering the touch might see it as an unobtrusive act of comfort, but the person receiving that touch might be over-stimulated and not want any sort of touch when they are experiencing big emotions.

We ask before we give hugs. Even if we saw one of our Covenmates get hugs from three other people, we still ask — and we take ownership and work on our own emotional reaction if they say no to us. Maybe they were at the end of their tolerance for touch. Maybe it's something else entirely.

A hard topic got brought up in debrief after a ritual. One of our Coveners is crying but doesn't want to talk about it. We offer them space to share, but we don't try to draw it out of them. We let them share and process in the way that makes sense to them.

The Coven is sharing a Dumb Feast with the Ancestors and each other. One Covener has a food allergy. Another has a hypersensitivity about certain textures. We don't require that either of them take or consume those foods.

Features of Consent

There are a few features that we are looking for in our interactions to consider an affirmative response to be consent.

- Explicit — Spoken, nodded, thumbs up, etc. Verbal OR Non-verbal, as long as it is clear.
- Enthusiastic — The "yes" should be all the way. Not "sure." Not "I guess."
- Voluntary / Freely given — It isn't really consent if there are negative consequences for saying no.

Consent Culture and Sex Magick/Sacred Sexuality

In the next three lessons in this unit, we are going to discuss the ways that Sex Magick and Sacred Sexuality are found within Trad Craft — and more specifically, within the Spiral Castle Tradition. Before we do that, though, I want to reiterate and emphasize how unwaveringly vital that explicit, enthusiastic consent is in this context.

Sex Magick and Sacred Sexuality absolutely have their place within TradCraft, which means that they have their place within SCT. However, we recognize the potential for abuse and trauma within acts of intimacy, and so there are some norms within our Trad that are worth stating as plainly as we can.

First, absolutely all of the features of consent that are listed above apply to all acts of sex occurring between Coveners and/or within our magickal spaces. In fact, most of the current discussions around consent were first broached as a reaction to "rape culture" — and the experiences of entitlement and coercion that have existed for far too many people when it comes to sex and physical intimacy. More than that, many of us who have been involved in Magick and Witchcraft for any number of years have seen those abuses play out in Covens and other groups.

So, explicit, enthusiastic, voluntary consent is our first, baseline expectation.

Some other norms for SCT/RTA Witches in terms of Sex Magick and Sacred Sex:

- People who are minors, unconscious, or drunk/drugged are unable to give consent. If you choose to use an entheogen as part of sacred sex rite with a partner, the consent has to be given before the entheogen is used.
- Consent is revocable. A person can decide at any point that they no longer consent, and all sexual activity must immediately stop.
- Sex is never "required" in any setting or as any qualifier for any assignment, degree, or rank within this Tradition. We give our Mastery students and 3rd Degree initiates the opportunity to explore these experiences, in both physical and spiritual realms, but the choice to actively participate is entirely voluntary.
- Queens, Devils, and Consorts are discouraged from starting a new sexual or romantic relationship with their students. Sex Magick, if it is to be explored among initiates, should be reserved for those at 3rd Degree (already initiated, not Year 3 students). This norm is in place as a protection for all, since the power dynamics (perceived or real) can get very confused once sex is introduced.
- Sacred Sex should still be safer sex. Please use reasonable protection against both pregnancy and STD's — unless you are engaged in sex with your own partner(s) and you both (all?) consent to fluid-sharing.

<u>Assignment</u>	Write a brief reflection regarding consent, consent culture, and consent in Sex Magick. Be sure to include the following:

- Questions you would like to explore
- Reactions you have to these ideas
- Experiences that shape your thoughts and feelings on this topic

<u>Additional Resources</u>	"Consent Culture: What Does It Mean?" — https://inbreakthrough.org/consent-culture-what-does-it-mean

<u>BoS Pages Included</u>	None

Sex Magick in Trad Craft

<u>Prerequisite Lesson</u>   10-01 "Consent Culture in SCT"

<u>Objective</u>   To explore reasons for using Sex Magick

To explore methods of Sex Magick that are used within Trad Craft

<u>Materials Needed</u>   Note-taking materials

<u>Study Notes</u>   Many years ago, Sarah Anne Lawless wrote a fantastic article on this very topic for her blog, "The Witch of Forest Grove" (which was eventually changed to an eponymous title). Later, she wrote some scathing (and important) rebukes of a sexual predator in her regional Craft community and the rape culture than enabled them/him to operate without censure. That was during the beginning of the Me Too movement, and she found herself inundated with hateful messages from the Witch-o-sphere calling for her to "sit down and shut up" (essentially). After several months of battling what I'll call the Malandanti, she pulled her personal blogs down and retreated to a more private place, in order to restore and preserve her mental health. She still participates in the community (via her shop — Banefolk), but she cautions others against the pitfalls of sharing personal witchery with the Internet.

I absolutely do not fault her for taking this approach. I've had similar experiences, actually, which I am open to discussing in safe space with folks who are wanting to have real dialogue about creating safe spaces.

As a reader and fellow-Witch, though, I am sad that her remarkable work is no longer available and accessible. (Well, some of it is, if you dig deep enough and wade through the captures of her sites that are stored at the Internet Archive's Wayback Machine.) She was a trailblazer, and her article on "Sex Magick in Traditional Witchcraft" is the first and only treatment I've seen on the subject. If you can find a copy, read it.

At the time that she wrote the article, I was already a fairly accomplished "sex magician" in the sense that I was organizing the "Scarlet Track" at Babalon Rising Festival, a long-standing Priestess of Aphrodite, and a student and teacher within the

Qadishti Movement. I attended workshops and rituals with Don Kraig (who wrote the book *Modern Sex Magick*) — some of which he led, and some of which I led. And my HPS had taught some Witch-specific sex magick within my first coven. But Sarah's article was the first I saw that specifically approached this area of magick and sorcery from the perspective of a folkloric, traditional Witch.

There are lots of resources in the world for information about Sex Magick and Sacred Sexuality, in general. And if this is an area of interest for you, read all you can of those, with an eye toward what comes from folkloric sources, what resonates with your Sense of Arte, etc.

In the meantime, here are a few thoughts of my own on the subject (which I recall being paralleled in Sarah's exquisite article), drawn from observation, experience, and study. All of these reasons and methods are accessible for individuals working alone, for couples/partners, and for groups. They are all offered without reference or alteration based on gender identity or sexual orientation.

Reasons for engaging in Sex Magick:

- *Energy-raising* — Sexual energy is quick and easy to raise, generally speaking. It makes for a great method of raising energy for the charging of talismans or otherwise fueling spellwork.

- *Healing* — Sex magick and sacred sexuality are a good tool to use for engaging in many types of healing work, including healing around psychological wounds and sexual trauma.

- *Energy offerings* — Some Spirits and Deities prefer sexual energy be given to them as part of the regular offerings we might make. You'll generally know if this is the case with a Spirit or Deity you are working with because they will show up in dreams of a sexual nature, come into your fantasies when you masturbate or engage in sex with a partner, or give you "sexy vibes" when you think of them.

- *Altering consciousness for Spirit communication* — Some Spirits and Deities communicate best with a Witch when that Witch is engaged in sexual activity. You'll see images, hear messages, or just have a sense of "knowing" new insights and information.

- *Spirit bonding* — In the same way that we engage in sexual intimacy in order to deepen our bond with a human partner, so too might we build deeper love and trust with a Spirit or Deity.

- *Compacting with Spirits* — Sex is a very effective way to "seal the deal" with a Spirit or Deity. Blood is most commonly mentioned as the seal for compacts — when any bodily fluid is mentioned. But sexual fluids and menstrual blood are both very commonly used, too, since they also carry the life-force of the Witch.

- *Generating the Elixir of Life* — A purpose unto itself is to generate sexual fluids, sometimes mixed with menstrual blood. These elixirs are used to anoint and consecrate magickal tools and are also sometimes consumed — usually mixed into wine or baked into a cake — for a variety of purposes. Sometimes this is a eucharistic act, such as we experience in the Housle. Sometimes it is done for another magickal goal that is specific to the Witch. Sometimes the cake or wine are offered directly to the Spirit as a libation.

- *Initiation* — Sex magick (the Hieros Gamos or Great Rite, in particular) is a pathway to initiation and initiatory experience within many branches of the Craft. Yes, even TradCraft. This is not something that is specific to Wiccan Covens. Moreover, our Spirits and Gods might "initiate" (or "cause to begin") a new stage of our magickal development or experience using sex as a catalyst.

- *Transfer of Virtue* — "Virtue" is a term used within Old Craft (Trad Craft) to signify the power and authority of highest office with a Coven or Clan. (Sometimes it is used simply to mean "power" in the sense of power that is raised in ritual.) When a new Coven or Clannad leader is installed, some groups transfer this Virtue from the out-going Leader to an intermediary "Vessel" and then to the incoming Leader. (It almost always goes from the Old Magister to the Maid, and then from the Maid to the New Magister.) In the Spiral Castle Clannad, we see our Queens, Devils, and Consorts as being instilled with this Virtue directly from one of our three Great Powers at the time of the final initiation. Sex with another person isn't necessary, and would only be the preference in the case of committed partners.

- *Sacraments of ecstasy* — Many practitioners view the pleasure of the sexual act as a sacrament unto itself. The orgasm is "proof that the Godds love us and want us to be happy." (Okay, I know that Ben Franklin aphorism is actually about beer, but … you get my meaning.) Sex doesn't have to have a "purpose" to be sacred. As long as the participants are engaging with consent, sex IS sacred. It IS an act of magick.
- *Gnosis* — We are able to ride the wave of sexual ecstasy into a place of gnosis. We are able to have a higher, deeper, and more complete understanding of ourselves, our partner(s), our Spirits/Godds, and the cosmos.

There are several methods for engaging in Sex Magick, all of which have examples provided to us in folkloric sources:
- *Flight* — We might fly out (or cross the hedge) in order to have dis-corporeal sex with a partner, Spirit, or Godd. Similarly, we might have dis-corporeal sex in Dreamtime or some other non-physical plane.
- *No-Touch* — There are some waking-time partnered and solo practices that can raise sexual energy and create a bond without physically touching. These include eye-gazing and breathwork and are likely to be part of what has been called "fascination."
- *Masturbation* — Moving into physical practices, we can certainly engage in masturbatory sex magick. Again, this can happen alone or with a partner/group.
- *Non-penetrative touch* — Partnered or group touching practices and rituals are far more intense than most people anticipate they will be. The touch doesn't have to involve the genitals to be extremely erotic — nor does it have to include these most overt of erogenous zones in order to be sexual. This is a great way for groups to engage in sex magick together without crossing relationship boundaries or violating oaths and vows made to partners who are not also Coveners.
- *Penetrative sexual intercourse* — Oral, vaginal, and anal intercourse between flesh-and-blood partners are the most obvious methods. They are no better or more preferred than the others we've discussed. Indeed, at the risk of sounding like I am actively discouraging penetrative sex, I would suggest that it can be more difficult to achieve the desired magickal results when you add one or more actual human partners to the mix. After all, everyone needs to share the same intent and consent throughout — not to mention simultaneous climax, according to some philosophies.

There are a couple of notes that are worth making, as you consider all the factors related to sex magick:
- Whole schools of thought and practice revolve around whether or not to orgasm as part of the working. There is no right or wrong on this question, but everyone involved should be on the same page about it before beginning.
- Toys are not forbidden in sex magick. In fact, there is a case to be made for the Gandried as a sex toy, of sorts — which gives the riding of it several layers of double-meanings.

This is an intense, private, and intimate area of magickal study. As such, some cautions should be given:
- *Predatory behavior* — Predators exist in every part of society, at every stage of study and development. I'll even be generous enough to add that some folks don't recognize that they are engaging in predatory behavior — although that caveat doesn't excuse anyone for said predation. We have to take care not to engage in that behavior ourselves and not to give it space to thrive in our Covens. Act swiftly to address these issues if you see them or they are brought to your attention.
- *Pre-occupation/obsession* — Good sex is fun and feels good physically, emotionally, and energetically. Good sex that produces powerful magickal results can be mind-blowing — and a bit addictive. It can certainly lead to a sort of "Sex-Magickal Awakening" and become a pre-occupying element of one's own personal practice. I don't want Covens and solo Witches within the Spiral Castle Clannad to have a prudish sensibility about sex and sex magick. Not as a cultural sort of ideal for our Tradition, at least. As always, there is room for every individual to have their own thoughts and perspectives on the issue. Likewise, I don't want Covens or the Clannad to get the reputation of being a "meat market" where sexy Witches are always looking for sexy Witchy time.

- *Consent, consent, consent* — I cannot stress the need for consent enough. If you are doing sex magick, always be conscious of consent.
- *Pregnancy and STD's* — Being a powerfully-manifesting Witch will not make your sperm, eggs, or any virus comply with your Will. Even if you have every reason to believe it does, show your wisdom, O Witch, by using birth control and barrier-methods of protection.

Assignment

Write a brief reflection regarding sex magick. Be sure to include the following:
- Your experience of sex magick so far
- Your thoughts and feelings about sex magick in your Craft practice
- Your thoughts feelings about sex magick among Coveners
- Your understanding of consent in SCT

Additional Resources

Sex Witch — Sophie Saint Thomas — https://amzn.to/3jcQJHl

Art of Sexual Magic — Margo Anand — https://amzn.to/3PFoEEM

Modern Sex Magick — Donald Michael Kraig — https://amzn.to/3FGNpvq

Sexual Sorcery — Jason Augustus Newcomb — https://amzn.to/3FHaGO5

Sex Magic — Frater U:.D:. — https://amzn.to/3G2lW8T

BoS Pages Included

Sex Magick in Trad Craft
Sacred Touch Ceremony

Spirit Spouse/Lover

Prerequisite Lesson

10-02 "Sex Magick in Traditional Witchcraft"

Objective

To explore the concepts of the Spirit Spouse and Spirit Lover

To explore the concept of Spirit sex within the Craft

Materials Needed

Note-taking materials

Study Notes

When we start talking about Spirit Lovers, Godd Spouses, and sex with Spirits, we actually start to feel a palpable sense of unease, sometimes. These are uncomfortable topics, perhaps for several reasons.

One of those reasons is that we don't typically talk about sex in an open and comfortable way — regardless of who that sex is with. That is considered "private," and many folks feel a lingering sense of shame and embarrassment around sex based on their upbringing or formative experiences. Even if they don't harbor those negative feelings, they still find it uncomfortable or inappropriate to share their thoughts and experiences. With many valid reasons! If you're talking about partnered sex, you aren't just sharing about yourself. You are also sharing on behalf of someone who may find that an invasion of their privacy. Also, a good many folks wouldn't consent to engaging in that talk with you because it is a violation of their boundaries and makes them uncomfortable to hear.

Likewise, Spirit work is often regarded as private and personal, and it often isn't discussed openly. Our experiences within that work are almost entirely in the realms of "Unverified Personal Gnosis" — or UPG. They are true and real for us, but they can seem outlandish and sometimes in opposition to more widely held beliefs and experiences around a Deity or well-known Spirit.

Talking about our UPG can sound delusional to folks who don't know us well enough to know that we are not actually experiencing delusions or hallucinations — or to folks who accept that we might be (experiencing delusions or hallucinations), but don't reject that experience as less mystical or "real." Frankly, it takes a deep level of trust and discernment to share those experiences with folks who are open to hearing about them, because we understand that most folks are going to think we are experiencing a psychotic break.

Not every magickal person engages in Spirit work. Period. Not all Witches do — although I still maintain the argument that Spirit work is a fundamental part of folkloric forms of the Craft. Of the folks who DO work with Spirits, not all of them are drawn into sexual encounters, sexual/romantic relationships, or spousal bonds. On this point, though, I will say that more Witches than you might think ARE engaging in some form of Spirit sex. (They're just not talking about it, for all the reasons stated above.)

Because of all these reasons combined, hardly anybody writes books, blogs, tweets, vlogs, or otherwise shares about this area of magickal experience. That lack of information and discourse adds to the feelings of isolation around these experiences. We think, "It must just be me. I'm the only weirdo having sex with a Familiar Spirit." That perceived isolation traps us in a catch-22-style recursive loop. Nobody's sharing, so we don't share, which means that nobody else wants to share.

Well, my friends, you're in luck. I happen to have the personal philosophy that when I think, "Someone should write about X — or DO X," I take it as a sign that I am "someone" and I should probably start writing about it. So here I am, sharing the secrets.

The terms we use for this experience are fairly new, but the experience is definitely ancient. Our myths and folklore from all over the world demonstrate the propensity of Spirits of all types and degrees (including Godds — who could be described as Spirits with really big PR and broad platforms/audiences) to interact with human lovers, ask for spousal commitments, or sometimes just have a fling.

The logistics of how this works are often dependent on cultural factors, the nature of the Spirit, and the personal preferences and boundaries of the human. Essentially, there is no single right way to have a sexual or romantic relationship with a Spirit, just as there is no single right way to have a sexual or romantic relationship with another human. In fact, the "right way" is entirely unique to that relationship.

I feel like it is also worth noting that Spirits have some very different ideas about what is taboo or inappropriate than humans do. (This might be another reason Witches don't share much about their experience, actually. They may fear themselves or their Spirit-Lover being judged as "deviant" or "perverse" because the flavor of the relationship is too spicy — or even triggering for others to hear about.)

Assignment	Write a brief reflection regarding Spirit-Sex and Spirit-Lovers. For your own benefit, write freely about your thoughts and experiences. If you are sharing with a Mentor or peers, edit your reflection to include only what you feel comfortable sharing.

Additional Resources	"God Spouses and Sex with the Divine" — https://metal-gaia.com/2014/01/07/god-spouses-and-sex-with-the-divine/ *Spirit Marriage: Intimate Relationships with Otherworldly Beings* — Dr. Megan Rose — https://amzn.to/3HUHqpD

BoS Pages Included	The Spirit Spouse

Hieros Gamos

Prerequisite Lesson   10-03 "Spirit Spouse/Lover"

Objective   To consider the purpose and uses of the Hieros Gamos

To consider how the Hieros Gamos fits within the Spiral Castle Tradition

Materials Needed   Note-taking materials

Study Notes   The Hieros Gamos (Greek for "Sacred Marriage") is a ritual of sacred sexuality and sex magick that is found in many traditional cultures and ancient religions. Our earliest records and recollections around this ritual are from Enheduanna — who is arguably the world's first self-described author and poet. She was the En (high priestess) of Nanna, the moon God. She was also a personal devotee of Inanna, the Goddess of Love, Fertility, Sex, War, and Magick.

In the poem called the "Courtship of Inanna and Dumuzi," we see the ritual marriage of the Queen/Priestess/Goddess with the Shepherd/Priest (who becomes King as a result of their union). The following excerpt is just one piece of the ritual:

Inanna spoke:
—*I bathed for the wild bull,*
I bathed for the shepherd Dumuzi,
I perfumed my sides with ointment,
I coated my mouth with sweet-smelling amber,
I painted my eyes with kohl.
He shaped my loins with his fair hands.
The shepherd Dumuzi filled my lap with cream and milk,
He stroked my pubic hair,
He watered my womb.
He laid his hands on my holy vulva,
He smoothed my black boat with cream,
He quickened my narrow boat with milk,

He caressed me on the bed.

Now I will caress my high priest on the bed,

I will caress the faithful shepherd Dumuzi,

I will caress his loins, the shepherdship of the land,

I will decree a sweet fate for him.

We see this same ritual enacted again and again through Greek myth and ritual (the union of Hera and Zeus, the ritual union of the mortal queen with the God Dionysos), as well as in many iterations of Celtic myth and ritual.

In fact, the "Great Rite" is the Wiccan name for this ritual, which is enacted either "in truth" (sexual intercourse between the Coven's High Priest and High Priestess) or "in symbol" (with the insertion of the dagger/phallus into the cup/womb to bless the wine in the eucharist). A very similar symbolic Hieros Gamos is enacted during the Gnostic Mass (Liber XV), which was written by Aleister Crowley for use within the Ecclesiae Gnosticae Catholicae (EGC — the church body associated with the magickal fraternal order of the OTO — Ordo Templi Orientis).

If this sounds purely ceremonial and Wiccan, let me assure you that there is ample folkloric and traditional precedent for the Sacred Marriage Rite in forms of the Craft that consider themselves drawn from pre-modern sources. After all, many of the pre-Christian king-making rites of Europe involved the consummation of this sacred marriage with a representative of the Goddess of the Land. We see this play out in the myths and folklore of continental Europe, Scandinavia, and the British Isles.

Not many Trad Crafters write about their experiences with the Sacred Marriage, though. Not all Traditions within Trad Craft utilize this ceremony, after all, and the ones that do tend to reserve it for the rarest of occasions. Shani Oates describes its place within the Clan of Tubal Cain as the mechanism by which a new Magister is invested with the Virtue of the Clan. A Magister might hold that office for decades. (Evan John Jones held that office for 32 years. And Robin the Dart held it for almost 20.)

Within the Spiral Castle Tradition, we honor and recognize the Hieros Gamos as a beautiful and potent ritual, but we regard it as a deeply personal one. It is tied to our 3rd Degree initiation, but not in a way that demands (or really even encourages) intercourse between the initiator and initiate. In both the in-person initiation and the self-initiation, the initiate-Witch engages directly with one of the three Great Powers, with no audience and no other human participant. Initiates are free to utilize hedge-crossing techniques in order to undertake this ritual in a psychic-spiritual sense, or they are welcome to use masturbation and self-stimulation.

It may seem strange to some folks that we simultaneously embrace sex magick, while eliminating physical intercourse in the one ritual within the Trad where "sex" is always part of the working. The reason for that is the abuse of sex and sex magick within other groups and Covens. It is vitally important that sex and sex magick not be coercive — and that it not be given freedom to reduce a Coven to a swingers party. I have no negative judgments about such parties, by the way. I consider myself a polyamorous person, and I strongly adhere to a philosophy that all enthusiastically consensual sex is a sacrament. I've just had enough experience to know that swinging within one's spiritual community often ends badly for the whole community — unless that community was formed for the purpose of exploring sacred sexuality together. Even then, it takes a tremendous amount of emotional labor to keep the community healthy.

Witches of the 3rd Degree might explore the Hieros Gamos together, if they freely choose to do so. They might also explore it with a magickal partner who is not an active participant in this Tradition, though that might change the texture/flavor or dynamic. If their life partner is a Witch of the Spiral Castle in a different phase of study, they might also explore this magick together.

How to Perform a Heiros Gamos

The execution of this ritual is fairly straightforward, although that doesn't necessarily mean that it is "simple." It can take place between two (or more?) partners of any gender, as long as all of the partners involved are able to successfully invoke a possessory state with a preferred Spirit/Deity. Often, preparatory actions (such as bathing, dressing, adorning with jewelry, applying make-up, inviting the partner to the bedchamber, and disrobing) are ritualized and sometimes involve secondary parties who fulfill roles as a traditional maid or squire — someone who helps their lord or lady get dressed. (These, by the way, are the names I was taught for Queens/Devils/Consorts-in-training. I would add "Page" as a gender-inclusive term for the same role.)

The partners each invoke their respective Spirits/Deities, and they proceed to have sex in this fully-involved state. They might recite invocation chants for each other, or they might each do this for themselves. This can be done simultaneously (if silent invocation processes are used) or one at a time. There are two poems that are used widely among Witches of all sorts for the purpose of calling forth the WitchMother and WitchFather — "The Charge of the Goddess" and "The Invocation of the Horned God." Both were written by Doreen Valiente, who worked closely with both Gardner and Cochrane. Alternatively, you might use a temple hymn associated with the Spirit/Deity, or even write your own.

The purpose for us within the Hieros Gamos isn't fecundity in land and people. It is gnosis. It is enlightenment. It is seeing the Truth of ourselves, of our partners, and of the Spirits we have invoked together.

Assignment

Write a reflection regarding the Hieros Gamos.

Additional Resources

"The Courtship of Inanna and Dumuzi" — D. Wolkenstein translation, accessed at https://web.ics.purdue.edu/~kdickson/inanna.html

"Liber XV: The Gnostic Mass" — https://sabazius.oto-usa.org/gnostic-mass/
— a fantastic annotated version of the ritual as hosted at Sabzius's Invisible Basilica (Sabazius is the national Grand Master of OTO USA)

Tubelo's Green Fire — Shani Oates — https://amzn.to/3HSQknE
— This is the book in which she discusses the Hieros Gamos as it applies to CTC.

BoS Pages Included

Hieros Gamos

Charge of the Goddess

Invocation of the Horned God

Craft Mysteries Reading List

Prerequisite Lesson

None

Objective

To read deeply regarding the Mysteries of Witchcraft

Materials Needed

Complete text of one of the titles below

Study Notes

Here it is again! (It's the list that doesn't quit.)

You may notice that these are titles that were also available to you in both of the last two years. This is a chance to circle back to one that you didn't choose on those occasions. (If you dove right in and read them all, I offer you two options. Either choose one that you didn't analyze before, or re-read one — bringing your years of experience and study within SCT to the material.)

Oates, Shani. *The Taper that Lights the Way: Robert Cochrane's Letters Revealed*. — https://amzn.to/3OXSJ1F

Oates, Shani. *Tubelo's Green Fire*. — https://amzn.to/3gTEuOW

Graves, Robert. *The White Goddess*. — https://amzn.to/3XPF5Sq

1734-witchcraft.org -- This website was originally maintained by Joe Wilson (now an archive, held in trust by a council of 1734 elders from different covens).

Jackson, Nigel. *Call of the Horned Piper*.

Jackson, Nigel. *Masks of Misrule*.

Jackson, Nigel and Michael Howard. *Pillars of Tubal Cain*.

Gary, Gemma. *Black Toad*. — https://amzn.to/3gTEcYm

Black, Laurelei & Natalie. *Liber Qayin*. — https://amzn.to/3B5fzP8

I would highly encourage you to read pretty much anything by Shani Oates, Evan John Jones, Gemma Gary, Michael Howard, Nigel Jackson, Andrew Chumbley, and Daniel Schulke. I also recommend Robin Artisson's work, with the caveat that he promotes some strong opinions about what is "valid" and what isn't. (Just repeat to yourself, "You are not the boss of me," and read with an eye toward inspiration and seeing into the Mysteries. He IS tapped in, and he can point to the path.)

When you're looking for titles to deepen or expand your understanding of the Mysteries, look for ones that are not designed to be how-to books for beginners. (I haven't included a lot of the contemporary Trad Craft writers simply because their work tends toward the prosaic or the instructional. It is good at what it does, but it doesn't elicit the sort of Soul response we're looking for at this stage.)

Also, I recognize that the work by some of the most influential authors for our Trad are no longer being published. (That's why you see price tags of US $150+.) Or they are published by limited-edition, luxury presses. Capall Bann (defunct) and XOANON and Scarlet Imprint (luxury) are three that spring most readily to mind. As an author and indie publisher, I want to let you in on a secret. If the book is out-of-print (and even more so if the publisher is out of business), you are not taking anything away from either the publisher or the author by using non-standard ways of accessing the book. They have received all the money they will ever get in compensation for their work — unless they republish it. Since these aren't books you can find in libraries or other accessible places, I personally do not find it unethical to read a PDF copy, if you can find one. Use your own judgment on that, as you will.

Assignment	Choose one of the titles above* to read in its entirety. Write a book analysis in which you address the following: • Relevance of this work to Traditional Witchcraft — What did you learn from this book that you can apply to your practice? • Accessibility of this work • Three points made by the author which offered clarity or deeper understanding • Four concepts presented by the author that you would like to explore on a deeper level in the future *You may select another title from a well-respected author in the field — such as Andrew Chumbley or Daniel Schulke.

Additional Resources	None

BoS Pages Included	None

Coven Leadership Reading List

Prerequisite Lesson   None

Objective   To read the work of Witch and NeoPagan leaders about managing groups

Materials Needed   Complete text of one of the titles below

Study Notes   You may never seek a Coven Charter. I get that. If you do, though, you need to give some thought to what good leadership looks like. Others have presented a goldmine of information that is worth your time and effort to read.

If you choose not to take a leadership role, reading a title or two on this list will help you be a better Covener by giving you insight into the many forces and considerations that the leaders are balancing.

Each of these titles has insight to share, although some are coming from Traditions that don't particularly look like SCT.

K, Amber. _Coven Craft: Witchcraft for Three or More_. — https://amzn.to/3ixKTjn

Campanelli, Dan and Pauline. _Circles, Sanctuaries, and Groves: Sacred Spaces of Today's Pagans_. — https://amzn.to/3VsJ1XL

Blake, Deborah. _Circle, Coven, and Grove: A Year of Magical Practice_. — https://amzn.to/3VO07PC

West, Kate. _The Real Witches' Coven_. — https://amzn.to/3OTKdkt

Harrow, Judy. _Wicca Covens: How to Start and Organize Your Own_. — https://amzn.to/3gWQ2kA

Harrow, Judy. *Spiritual Mentoring: A Pagan Guide*. — https://amzn.to/3B1gC2z

Knight, Shauna Aura and Taylor Ellwood, eds. *The Pagan Leadership Anthology*. — https://amzn.to/3EXEoOj

Knight, Shauna Aura. *The Leader Within*. — https://amzn.to/3FnEyjy

O'Brien, Lora. *A Practical Guide to Pagan Priesthood: Community Leadership and Vocation*. — https://amzn.to/3irkJP3

S, Taren. *Dedicant's Handbook to Coven Life*. — https://amzn.to/3H4KEXa

Magdalene, Misha. *Outside the Charmed Circle: Exploring Gender & Sexuality in Magical Practice*. — https://amzn.to/3OWtrBa

Williams, Brandy, Crystal Blanton and Taylor Ellwood, eds. *Bringing Race to the Table: Exploring Racism in the Pagan Community*. — https://amzn.to/3OWtrBa

---

Assignment	Choose one of the titles above* to read in its entirety. Write a book analysis in which you address the following:
	• Relevance of this work to Traditional Witchcraft — What did you learn from this book that you can apply to your practice?
	• Accessibility of this work
	• Three points made by the author which offered clarity or deeper understanding
	• Four concepts presented by the author that you would like to explore on a deeper level in the future
	*You may select another title from a well-respected author in the field. Titles don't necessarily need to have a Witchcraft or Magick focus in order to be relevant.

Additional Resources	None

BoS Pages Included	None

Historical/Anthropological Reading

Prerequisite Lesson

None

Objective

To read deeply regarding the history/lore/culture of Witchcraft and Paganism

Materials Needed

Complete text of one of the titles below

Study Notes

As folkloric Witches, we look to the past to inform (but not to dictate) our practice. Studies in history, culture, folklore, and mythology all have a place.

Choose an academically-inclined historical or anthropological text regarding one of the cultures that informs your Craft. (You're looking for a text written by a well-respected historian or anthropologist — or possibly a folklorist. Probably someone with a PhD. Definitely a book with a hearty bibliography.)

The cultures that inform ALL of Spiral Castle Tradition include:
- American (North, Central, and South — including First Peoples)
- British
- Irish
- Scottish
- Welsh
- Continental Celtic
- Germanic
- Scandinavian

I would also encourage you (now or in the future) to dig into titles related to:
- Arthurian Studies
- Templars
- Cathars
- Grimoire Traditions

- Witch Trials

You might also consider Diasporic studies from any culture that informs your practice. These are too numerous to list, but literally nothing is off-limits. If your lived experience and/or magical experience are shaped by a culture, I encourage you to drink deeply from the well of scholarship and study related to it.

Finally, you might consider a scholarly/academic biography of one of the shapers of contemporary magical practice (like Crowley, Gardner, Cochrane, Fortune, Valiente, etc.)

Texts along these lines that you might consider include:

Hutcheson, Cory Thomas. *New World Witchery: A Trove of North American Folk Magic*. — https://amzn.to/3B7W74t

Wilby, Emma. *The Visions of Isobel Gowdie*. — https://amzn.to/3FmnLNC

Wilby, Emma. *Cunning Folk and Familiar Spirits*. — https://amzn.to/3umcMNP

Hutton, Ronald. *Triumph of the Moon: A history of Modern Pagan Witchcraft*. — https://amzn.to/3XMotep

Hutton, Ronald. *Stations of the Sun: A History of the Ritual Year in Britain*. — https://amzn.to/3VuKkVY

(Really, anything by Ronald Hutton or Emma Wilby would be great!)

Jones, Prudence and Nigel Pennick. *A History of Pagan Europe*. —- https://amzn.to/3VKv72X

Ross, Anne. *Pagan Celtic Britain*. — https://amzn.to/3OWj7sN

Kaczynski, Richard. *Perdurabo: The Life of Aleister Crowley*. — https://amzn.to/3gYbPZ8

Heselton, Philip. *Doreen Valiente: Witch*. — https://amzn.to/3XLbYj4

This is a very non-exhaustive list. Use your best judgment regarding titles of particular interest to you.

Assignment

Choose one of the titles above* to read in its entirety. Write a book analysis in which you address the following:

• Relevance of this work to Traditional Witchcraft — What did you learn from this book that you can apply to your practice?

• Accessibility of this work

• Three points made by the author which offered clarity or deeper understanding

• Four concepts presented by the author that you would like to explore on a deeper level in the future

*You may select another title from a well-respected author in the field. Titles don't necessarily need to have a Witchcraft or Magick focus in order to be relevant.

Additional Resources

None

BoS Pages Included

None

Ministerial Reading List

Prerequisite Lesson

None

Objective

To explore training related to the ministerial aspects of serving as a Queen/Devil

Materials Needed

Complete text of one of the titles below

Study Notes

As far as I can tell, there are absolutely zero texts related to the ministerial/pastoral functions of being a leader within Traditional or Folkloric Witchcraft. That is for two major reasons:

1) There are precious few of these titles written for eclectic Witchcraft, Wiccan, and NeoPagan clergy, and we are something of a niche or subset within the sphere of Witchcraft.

2) Many TradCrafters don't view this role as ministerial/pastoral, hence there hasn't been a push to create materials.

Within the culture of the Spiral Castle Tradition, we recognize that leaders and Elders within the Trad are looked to for guidance in times of transition. If we don't prepare ourselves for this role, we find ourselves performing it through trial and error.

The following titles primarily have a Wiccan or NeoPagan slant, which means that we will be adapting a lot of what we find within. (Still, I find this to be an easier starting place for adaptation than the host of Christian texts, which center myths, values, and tenets that we simply don't share.)

Since none of these titles was available when I was being trained in this role, I haven't vetted most of them. (Although, as a funny sidenote, I was the editor for one of them — *The Wiccan Minister's Manual* by Kevin Gardner — shortly after I took my own 3rd Degree.)

As with any text you read, use what is useful, adapt what you can, discard ideas that don't make sense, and generally read with a critical eye. Some of the titles are even quite outdated. Consider this a starting place in your pastoral/ministerial training.

Emore, Holli S. *Constellated Ministry: A Guide for Those Serving Today's Pagans*. — https://amzn.to/3FmyxmZ

O'Brien, Lora. *A Practical Guide to Pagan Priesthood: Community Leadership and Vocation*. — https://amzn.to/3irkJP3

LeVeau, Belladonna. *Awakening Spirit: WISE Seminary, First Year Certification for Wiccan Clergy*. — https://amzn.to/3VIz08w

Gardner, Kevin. *The Wiccan Minister's Manual: A guide for Priests and Priestesses*. — https://amzn.to/3Fjxi89

Gardner, Kevin. *A Handbook for Wiccan Clergy*. — https://amzn.to/3VNIBLf

Savage, David. *Non Religious Pastoral Care* — https://amzn.to/3hb9tGo

Gardner, Kevin. *The Pagan Clergy's Guide for Counseling, Crisis Intervention, and Otherworld Transitions*. — https://amzn.to/3H3Hhj9

Eilers, Dana D. *Pagans and the Law*. — https://amzn.to/3B1m7OL

Campanelli, Pauline. *Rites of Passage*. — https://amzn.to/3gY4t7Y

LaFae, Phoenix and Gwion Raven. *Life Ritualized: A Witch's Guide to Honoring Life's Important Moments*. — https://amzn.to/3H6wRzn

Kaldera, Raven and Tannin Schwartzstein. *Handfasting and Wedding Rituals*. — https://amzn.to/3Vuuivj

Williams, Liz. *Modern Handfasting: A Complete Guide to the Magic of Pagan Weddings*. — https://amzn.to/3H6EpSB

Ferguson, Joy. *Magickal Weddings*. — https://amzn.to/3VtN4TG

Starhawk and M. Macha Nightmare. *The Pagan Book of Living and Dying*. — https://amzn.to/3iA65Fe

West, Carrie and Phillip Wright. *Death & the Pagan: Modern Pagan Funerary Practices*. — https://amzn.to/3EXKUVh

Fenley, Judith Karen and Oberon Zell. *Death Rights and Rites*. — https://amzn.to/3XQ4lYP

Mortellus. *Do I Have to Wear Black?: Rituals, Customs, and Funerary Etiquette for Modern Pagans*. — https://amzn.to/3Fndb9b

Butler, Charles. *Pagan Prison Ministry*. — https://amzn.to/3UB2cgU

Kaldera, Raven. _Candles in the Cave: Northern Tradition Paganism for Prisoners_. — https://amzn.to/3ixWYFg

Spitale, Lennie. _Prison Ministry: Understanding Jail and Prison Culture_. — https://amzn.to/3EUW39r

Hebert, Deirdre A. _Pagans in Recovery: The Twelve Steps from a Pagan Perspective_. — https://amzn.to/3Vuvv5P

Star, Amythest. _The Goddess Way through the Twelve Steps_. — https://amzn.to/3XVPko8

READ THIS (REQUIRED) — "Clergy as Mandatory Reporters of Child Abuse and Neglect" — https://www.childwelfare.gov/pubpdfs/clergymandated.pdf

---

Assignment

Choose one of the titles above* to read in its entirety. Write a book analysis in which you address the following:

• Relevance of this work to Traditional Witchcraft — What did you learn from this book that you can apply to your practice?

• Accessibility of this work

• Three points made by the author which offered clarity or deeper understanding

• Four concepts presented by the author that you would like to explore on a deeper level in the future

*You may select another title from a well-respected author in the field. Titles don't necessarily need to have a Witchcraft or Magick focus in order to be relevant.

Additional Resources

Appalachian Pagan Ministry — https://appalachianpaganministry.com/

The Pagan Federation — https://www.paganfed.org/

"The Limits of Ministry" — https://wildhunt.org/2018/01/the-limits-of-ministry-pagan-clergy-and-serious-situations.html

"Pagan Ministry" — https://www.patheos.com/blogs/paganrestoration/2013/07/pagan-ministry-serving-the-pagan-peoples/

BoS Pages Included

SCT Witching/Baby Blessing
SCT Puberty Rite
SCT Coming of Age
SCT Handfasting/Wedding
SCT Handparting

SCT Wisdom Rite
SCT Crossing Rite

Planning for the Future

Prerequisite Lesson

All previous lessons should be completed to a level of proficiency or mastery

Objective

To reflect on the course work and any insights gained

To pause before moving into whatever the next stage of study or growth might be

To provide feedback to Laurelei/RTA for improving the course content

To prepare for the final exam third degree initiation

Materials Needed

Journaling materials

Study Notes

By this stage in your studies, you have prepared for two other initiations, and you know a bit of what to expect from the preparation and the ritual itself.

This lesson is a pause to gather materials and make preparations for the initiatory process ahead. It is a look back and a look forward. You are on a threshold once again.

This time, however, you have a choice to make. Will you perform a self-initiation, or will you seek in-person initiation with me (or another Magister of the Lineage)? If you are participating within a Coven, the choice is probably much clearer. You will receive the initiation under the direction of a Queen, Devil, or Consort of that Coven — as you have likely done at each step of this process.

Should you choose in-person initiation with me, you can start that process by writing to me at Laurelei@asteriabooks.com — or through the chat feature on the Thread app.

Assignment

For now, I would like you to think about some questions. Please explore them deeply, taking as much time as you need.

- What were your biggest challenges during your 3rd Degree studies?

- What was an insight that you gained about yourself or this path during this course?

- Where do you want to go in your studies or practice from here? What will you explore, now that you are a 3rd Degree?

- Do you anticipate requesting a Coven Charter within the Spiral Castle Trad, now or in the future?

- What sort of worries or concerns do you have about this initiation?

- I'd like you to consider proposing ways in which I might make this class more useful or meaningful to students. I know you still have an exam and initiation to complete, so you might want to reserve critical feedback until those are done. But I am open to hearing suggestions.

Additional Resources

None

BoS Pages Included

None

Year 3 Final Exam

Prerequisite Lesson

All previous lessons should be completed to a level of proficiency or mastery

Objective

To synthesize and assess the year's study

Materials Needed

All of them. Whatever you feel like you need — though you can answer the questions with paper and pen (or in a DOC file).

Study Notes

As it was in the Foundations and Practicum Courses, this exam is an "open book test." I have always been a big believer in "authentic assessment" — which means checking for knowledge and skills within the same context in which they are being needed/used. Since we have access to resources most of the time when practicing our Craft, I feel that this test should be no different.

However, I would challenge you to rely more on yourself than your study materials and previous work. (In other words, don't copy/paste your answers from work you've done for previous assignments — or from things I wrote in the study notes.)

The point of the test is to get at what *you know*, not what you can copy/paste. What have you taken to heart? What has made an impact? I'm hoping that I've designed the test (and that you'll approach it) in such a way that we'll be able to draw those things out together without you regurgitating things I wrote or previous work you did for an assignment.

Assignment	Answer the questions from the next page. Congratulations! You're almost ready for initiation.

You absolutely do NOT have to send them to me, if you plan to self-initiation. I trust that you will be able to discern if you've given a reasonable and accurate answer. (Give these to your Coven Leader, if you are in a Coven.)

If you DO send them to me, please send me a chat message in The Thread app so I get notified right away. I'm sure you'll want my feedback in as timely a manner as possible before your initiation ritual. I get chat notifications faster than emails.

Additional Resources	None

BoS Pages Included	None

Final Exam

Instructions: *Most of the questions are open-ended and will require a few sentences or maybe even a couple of paragraphs. Write as much as you need to say to fully answer the question.*

1. What does it mean to you to walk the path of the Witch? How has this answer changed since you took your 1st Degree?

2. What does it mean to you to be a Queen, Devil, or Consort of the Spiral Castle?

3. Describe the use of a Gandried.

4. Describe the full cosmology of the Spiral Castle Tradition.

5. Write about your understanding of one of the Mysteries you have studied in-depth this year.

6. If you were to lead a Coven, what sort of organizational model would you prefer to adopt?

7. Describe the Hexentanzenplatz.

8. Describe your relationship and what you understand of the three Spirit Allies associated with the month of November in this Tradition.

9. If you were to lead a Coven, how would you view your own role in terms of ministerial and/or pastoral duties?

10. If you needed to perform a banishing spell, which ingredients would you want to include?

11. Describe the role of masks and masking within the Spiral Castle Tradition.

12. What is the Coven Dolly, and how is it used?

13. Write about how your relationship with a Spirit/Godd has changed or grown since your Adoption into this Clannad.

3rd Degree Self-Initiation Ritual

<u>Prerequisite Lesson</u>

All previous lessons (including 12-2 Final Exam) should be completed to a level of proficiency or mastery

<u>Objective</u>

To admit Witch to the level of 3rd Degree within the Spiral Castle Tradition

To claim and acknowledge leadership role within the Craft

To experience the Sacred Marriage with one of the Great Powers of SCT

<u>Materials Needed</u>

Stang, candles, lighter

Cauldron

Anvil, hammer, lancet

Three knives (red, black, white)

Materials for Garter

Bread and Housle bowl

Red wine, cup, mugwort, lemongrass, honey, teaball

Initiation incense, holder, charcoal

Gandreid, flying ointment

Bath sachet, dressed candle, anointing oil

Initiation Gift (crown)

<u>Study Notes</u>

While the initiation into 3rd Degree is different than the ones into 1st and 2nd, the preparations are similar. For that reason, we will be covering similar ground (and using some of the same wording) in our lead-up to the ritual.

Please do no skip sections because you think, "Ah, I have done this before. I already know what to do." I don't want to give you short shrift, and I don't want you to do it, either. Take the time to genuinely prepare for this important step.

Choose Your Ritual

Do not perform BOTH self-initiation AND lineaged-initiation (ie, in-person). You need to decide which one you will undergo. If you choose lineaged-initiation, you will be provided with instructions regarding preparation, which materials to bring, etc.

Mindset

Prior to any initiation is a perfect time, I think, to be asking hard questions of yourself about whether or not you wish and Will to go further. You are under no obligation, after all. All of this study, work, and ritual is for YOU, and if this path doesn't resonate with you, now is a great time to make a change. (If that is the case, though, don't bother with the initiation. Remember: initiations kickstart forces and phases in our lives. If you do the initiation, you are moving forward in the Tradition in the eyes of the Powers, regardless of whether you start a Coven or participate with the other 3rd Degree Initiates.)

This is a time of testing. You have already given yourself a portion of that test -- the intellectual portion via the final exam. There are other ways, though, in which you will test your own readiness to continue into the advanced practice of being a Queen, Devil, or Consort.

This is a time of Mysteries. You are enacting ritual steps that will further open you to the Spiral Castle Tradition Mysteries.

This is a time of bonding. I may not be with you in the flesh for this initiation, nor may any others of our tradition, but you are strengthening bonds with us nevertheless. We are joined by the same oaths, connected by the same Red Thread of blood and fire upon which those oaths have been made, and undergone the same basic training. You still have a secondary bond with other Witches of our Trad who share your Specialty. And now, you also share a bond with the other Queens, Devils, and Consorts.

Under normal circumstances, you wouldn't fully know what to expect at your initiation. There is an air of secrecy around the rite, and I will endeavor to maintain that for the in-person variation of the 3rd Degree initiation. These self-initiations, though, are available to students the moment they purchase the book. The steps and actions of the initiation ritual, therefore, are not mysterious, at all (in the sense of being secret). It is what might transpire within them where the Mysteries can be found.

For this reason, I hope that you will give yourself ample opportunity to experience them by approaching them with love, reverence, and preparation. (This is NOT one of those rituals where you can wipe the cheet-oh dust from your fingers onto your sweatpants and say, "Let's do this.")

Space/Time

This is not a short initiation ritual, and you will need privacy for it. The braiding of the cords (for the Garter) is part of the ritual. (Again.) Trust me, I know better than anyone in our tradition how long this takes. Give yourself time and space for all of it. (These Garter-cords aren't as long as your Triple Cords, so you needn't make part of them ahead of time. They should take roughly the same amount of time as seasonal cords.)

Our home coven always takes time away from our normal routine for initiations. We rent a cabin in the forest together for two nights, performing the ritual the first night after the sun has set and taking as much time as we need for the initiate.

Somehow, give yourself some space and time apart from the people with whom you live — more than just going into another room while they sleep. It is even better if you can get into a different (wilder) space -- like the woods, desert, seashore, etc. Getting away from your own domesticity and daily experience can heighten the experience and help you achieve the liminality of the rite much easier. Rent a cabin. Camp in your backyard. Book a motel/hotel room near a state/national park.

My preference will always be for going to a cabin in the woods because I can get all the amenities I want and need (privacy for duration, bath, toilet, stove, fireplace, private or nearly private access to the forest, campfire outside, comfy beds, etc.). Ultimately, though, you want to make sure that you set-up the surroundings that will allow you to immerse yourself in the experience, feeling safe from outside threat or distraction.

Fasting & Meditation

Fasting and meditation are important acts of preparation leading up to any initiation ceremony. However, we do not have strict guidelines about what this fast should look like or what your meditation practice must entail. Don't let the flexibility here fool you into thinking this step is purely optional. It is not.

Consciously changing your eating habits and sitting in contemplation of the step you are about to take will start to make the shifts of consciousness for you that will help open you up to the initiatory process. Visionary work is often aided by this sort of preparation, and you will be engaging in multiple layers of psychic work during this ritual.

Choose the type of fast that is most appropriate to your health circumstances. Please don't cause yourself a health crisis in pursuit of spiritual revelations. This is completely unnecessary. Altering your food choices a little and eating with mindfulness is truly enough to accomplish the psychic shifts needed, without bottoming out your blood sugar, triggering a migraine, or causing other health problems.

Give yourself a 7-day fast -- so that your initiation day is the 7th day. (**This is different than 1st and 2nd Degrees, which utilize a 3-day and 5-day fast, respectively.**) So if you are performing the rite on Friday, start your fast and meditations on Saturday morning of the previous week. You will not be resuming your normal eating patterns until after the initiation, which will be completed sometime after midnight (or early morning) on Saturday morning.

Definitely cut out sugar, alcohol, and as much caffeine as you can without triggering rebound headaches. (If you are very caffeine-addicted, you may need to have one coffee/soda per day to stave off such a headache/migraine. Do what you gotta do. You can't very well perform an initiation through a migraine, after all.)

As far as what you DO eat, the focus should be on "clean eating" in some capacity. There are a number of ways you could approach that. Whole foods. Vegetarian. Vegan. If your body can handle it, you can certainly do a liquid fast (though I don't recommend that for a 7-day stretch). A "graduated fast" also works well for many folks -- whole foods on Saturday, vegetarian by Tuesday, vegan on Thursday, liquids only on Friday.

The fast that was required by my initiator was a "no-kill" fast. It was inherently vegetarian, but it also meant that we had to be mindful regarding the plant-based foods we consumed. Root veggies (carrots, beets, etc) were out because the entire plant had to die to harvest the root, and so were onions and garlic, which made using almost anything pre-packaged (like sauces) impossible. We really had to read labels, and I learned so much about how various plants grow. At 25 (my age at my 1st Degree initiation), you'd be shocked how clueless I was! (I became quite a "no-kill" chef by my 3rd Degree initiation!)

Potatoes, I learned to my surprise, were a viable option on a "no-kill" fast because you can dig up a single potato from the garden without killing the whole plant. Corn was also okay. Even though modern farmers harvest the whole plant, you can certainly pick a single ear from the stalk without killing the other ear. (Corn, like mammals, usually has two ears.)

This type of fast is still my favorite because it requires mindfulness at every stage -- from menu selection to meal preparation to dining. Well, I bring the mindfulness to the dining; but after 20+ years of developing recipes that I eat almost exclusively during initiation-prep, when I sit down with these dishes, the sense memory is very strong. It helps link me to the initiations I have received, the ones I attended, and the ones I performed for others. Each meal becomes a little Housle.

Ritual Cleansing

It goes without saying that both you and your garments should be clean when you come to the ritual space for ceremonies of this nature. For all initiations that you undergo, attend, or perform, you will go a step further and perform a ritual cleansing in addition to your standard bath/shower. You will have done this for your 1st and 2nd Degree, and the process will be identical.

This step will be undertaken the evening of the ritual. In an ideal scenario, you will shower first to get your body clean, and then you'll fill the tub with water and allow the bath sachet and yourself to soak in it while burning a specially dressed candle.

There are two things you want to happen as part of this cleansing. You want the light of that candle to touch you while it burns. This is a fire cleansing. And you want to immerse yourself in the bath water three times.

If you don't have access to a tub, don't fit in the tub, or have mobility issues that would make this impossible or dangerous for you, get creative. Fill a bucket that you soak the sachet in, and pour this over yourself three whole times. Soak that sachet in the water each time, and get every bit of you wet. (Do this in your shower, obviously.) Or, if even this is genuinely not possible, pour the sachet-infused water over your head three times and use it to wash your hands and heart three times each.

Dressed Candle, Bath Sachet, Ritual Incense, Anointing Oil

I've included the recipes that Spiral Castle Tradition uses as our base recipes for the dressed bath candle, the bath sachet, the incense to be burned during the ritual, and the anointing oil. If you still have incense and oil from your 1st or 2nd Degree, you may use them here (as long as you have enough and they aren't rancid).

As I noted last year, these recipes were specifically designed for use in connecting us with the Powers of the SCT. You may add a personal botanical Ally to the blend, but you may not remove anything. Any personalized blend would be suitable for you alone — at this and any rite where you feel you need the same level of connection.

Don't have access to one or more ingredients? I can help. My Etsy shop doesn't make many apothecary items right now, but I would be delighted to blend these items for you. Just contact me through the app (chat or contact form), and I'll set up a custom order, if you'd like.

Garter

You will make a corded Garter as part of this initiation ritual. It is a simple Garter constructed as a braided and knotted ladder and worn on the left leg — either at the upper calf or the upper thigh. Please choose natural materials for the Garter — leather, cotton, wool, sari silk ribbon, etc. (They can be three different fibers, as well.) As mentioned in Lesson 09-04, our Garters are red, blue, and green.

Third Degree Initiation Gift

It is customary to present a new Initiate with gifts, often ones that are emblematic of their new role. A Crown is the preferred and traditional gift within our Tradition at this stage. The Crown may be a simple circlet, a crescent moon upon a circlet (with the "horns" turned up), a horned animal figure upon a circlet, or a horned headdress. All of these Crown styles are appropriate to persons of any gender within the Spiral Castle Clannad.

I recommend purchasing or fashioning one for yourself as a gift for this momentous occasion, if you are performing the self-initiation. (If you are receiving in-person initiation, you will receive this as a gift from your initiator/team.)

Sabbat Wine

You can make regular mugwort tea (infusion), if you prefer; but it's so bitter that I prefer our full herb-infused sweet red wine blend. Get the sweetest red wine you can find for this -- Oliver's soft red or Manischewitz or something similar. For one person, the ratio should be 1 teaspoon of dried herb to 1 cup of liquid. Heat up the wine in a saucepan over low heat. Put equal parts mugwort and lemongrass in a tea-ball. Steep the herbs in the hot wine for five minutes. (Don't let them over-steep. They get more bitter and much stronger.) If you need to do so, sweeten the brew even further with local, raw honey.

You'll be drinking this early in the ritual, so you could prepare it and bring it before the Compass is raised -- perhaps in a thermal cup.

Secrecy

As I mentioned earlier, initiatory rites are usually cloaked in secrecy. This one, in Spiral Castle style, has been published for the world to see, if they care to look. That has been our way, since we first started the American Folkloric Witchcraft blog.

There is no secret about the structure or nature of this ritual that I could ask you to keep. Even rituals that I don't intend to publish (private, personal rituals or the variation of the 3rd Degree ritual that I offer to witches in-person) aren't necessarily "secret" because the nature of the ritual isn't meant for public consumption.

In some cases, the secrecy is meant to preserve the element of surprise and allow ritual teams to both utilize and subvert expectations during the ritual itself. In most cases, though, the "secrets" are more about the personal experiences of the witches undergoing the rituals and the nature of the Mysteries they uncover. These things are ineffable and inviolate, and it is for these reasons that we speak of them only with those who were present -- and then only in love and trust.

As you undergo your self-initiation, you may experience things that you will never feel comfortable speaking to another living soul. Not because they are horrible or shameful, but because they were for you alone. Or you may find that you can only share them with others who have had similar initiatory experiences and share the Oaths.

Oaths

As someone who has been through two different initiatory lineages (and is the co-creator of a 3rd), I can say that access to oaths isn't always given before the oath is actually being administered. You have the benefit here of previewing the Oath and deciding whether or not you are prepared to make it.

You may add your own additional oaths to the words here, but this is the Oath of a Witch of 3rd Admission in the Spiral Castle Tradition. This is the oath we all take at this level. We share this in common. If you feel you cannot commit to this Oath, then stop here. You would only be setting yourself up for failure and heartache if you proceed in that case.

Again, I repeat that you are under no obligation to move forward. If you have come this far, you have done great work, and you are certainly an adept Witch. I hope I have gotten a chance to know you personally through our social media group, and there is no reason for friendships to end. Indeed, you will always and forever remain a fully raised Witch of this Tradition and a Sibling to us. That is not diminished if you decide that this is your stopping point.

To make an oath is a serious commitment that will follow you, even if you decide to walk away. It is still there, lingering. The Spirits, Godds, and Ancestors who bore witness to it will remind you -- and often exact a price if you don't hold up your end. (Not us. We won't stalk you or guilt trip you, I swear.)

All that being said, I do not believe our Oath is particularly restrictive or terrifying. If you find that it IS too restrictive or scary for you, that is probably a good indication from your Soul or your Spirits that this next step and phase of study is not meant to be under the guidance of the Spiral Castle Tradition. You have our blessing and love as you continue your studies elsewhere — and you will always be welcome in the 2nd Degree gatherings of this Tradition.

Challenges

I have asked several times whether you are ready and whether this is indeed the right choice for you. Consider these my "challenges at the gate" before you proceed. It is right and proper that members of the Tradition and your initiator should ask you again and again if you are sure about this.

I'm not your initiator. You are, and the Godds are if they decide to show up and really put you through your paces. However, I am the co-founder of the Tradition and the vessel or instrument through which this initiation has come. That involves me to the extent that I feel it is important to pose these challenges, to be honest, and to offer my support for your decision to proceed or to walk away.

You can't un-ring a bell, as they say. Once you've taken your initiation, you've *started something*. Things change within you and around you. I say again that this ritual is not an award ceremony for having completed this "year" of study. Among its nested purposes is to initiate sorcerous and mystical changes in you for the work ahead, such that the Mysteries of this Spiral Castle open wider to you.

This is the last challenge I will give you: We can celebrate you for your accomplishment without you having to initiate. Are you sure about this?

Trigger Warnings

There are aspects in most initiation rituals that can be triggering for folks. You may have experienced that with some piece of the Dedication, 1st Degree Initiation, or 2nd Degree Initiation. Initiatory elements that feature sex or death can be especially triggering. However, within this Tradition, we recognize that facing Life and facing Death are not optional, so neither are our participation in these pieces of initiation.

This initiation features Sex — a private Hieros Gamos with one of the Great Powers of the Spiral Castle Tradition (Goda, Kolyo, or Tubelo). We absolutely recognize that this can be triggering for folks who have faced sexual trauma.

Within our Tradition, this Hieros Gamos happens in a private space between you and the Great Power. It need not take shape as a physical consummation. It is intended as an act of powerful intimacy, enlightenment, and ordination between you and the one who Ordains and Coronates you as their Queen, their Devil, or their Consort.

RITUAL

Note: You should begin this ritual after your shower and ritual bath.

Try not to adapt this ritual. If changes must be made, make sure to note them in your debrief (and on your copy of the ritual itself.

Arrange the ritual supplies around the base/holder of the Stang.

Smolder the incense throughout the ritual, starting from the very beginning. Anoint yourself with the oil before beginning the ritual and again after you have taken the Oath.

Before you begin, it's time for you to administer challenges to yourself. Ask yourself again if you are ready to take this step. Weigh your choices and possible consequences carefully before beginning the ritual.

Raise the Stang

Stand with the Stang in the center of your Compass space. The cauldron is placed behind the Stang, and the anvil (or Oath Stone) is placed in front of it, with the hammer on top. Take a moment to energetically connect with the energy of the Forge-fire at the center of the Earth, far below the iron foot of the Stang; and also connect with Star-fire in the heavens, high above but still between the horns of the Stang. Breathe deeply and say, "May the three souls be straight within me." Feel yourself centered.

Lay the Compass

Using your Stang, walk the perimeter of the space, moving in a circle. Mark a circle on the ground by either dragging the Stang or dragging one of your feet. Allow the "lame step" to remind you that you walk between worlds. The Seen and the Unseen are ever present. The Living and the Dead are both here. As one of the Cunning Folk, you lay this compass as a reminder that the hedge is this, and you straddle it.

Open the Gates, Raise the Castles, Call the Realms

I have no way of knowing which Sabbat you are at (or just past) as you perform this initiation. If you are within the tides of Samhain, Imbolc, Beltaine, or Lammas, begin by opening the Gates, starting with the one where you stand on the Year Wheel, and then proceed to Raise the Castles. Start with the Castles first, if you are in the tides of the Equinoxes or Solstices. In either case, finish with the Realms.

Challenges & Trials

•**Challenges** -- Within the ritual space, at the time and place of initiation, ask yourself and answer aloud: "In my _mind_, do I _know_ that I am prepared and do I choose freely to submit to the trials of initiation? In my _heart_, do I _feel_ that I am prepared and do I choose freely to submit to the trials of initiation? In my _spirit_, do I _believe_ that I am prepared and do I choose freely to submit to the trials of initiation?"

•**Sabbat Wine** -- Drink the entire cup (8 oz) of Sabbat Wine or Mugwort Tea. Feel free to drink slowly, mindfully. Be conscious of the properties of mugwort, lemongrass, and wine -- all ingredients known to help relax the borders between the Seen and the Unseen. They are not hallucinogenic, but they are certainly allies for trance work, vision, and divination.

•**Witch Flight** -- After you feel the "opening" of Spirit that comes with the Sabbat Wine, apply a little flying ointment to the back of your neck, under your arms, behind your knees, and the bottoms of your feet. Using your Gandreid, fly out to the Hexentanzenplatz. Explore the Sabbat Grounds and welcome one of the Three Powers of this Tradition to you. You may already know who will come, if you have a deep relationship with one of them. Allow yourself, though, the opportunity to be guided by one of the others, if it is not who you expected to show up.

•**Hieros Gamos** — Welcome this Power (Kolyo, Goda, or Qayin) as your initiator, your crowner, and your lover. If you are not already a Godd-Spouse to a different Spirit, you may find that this ritual **marries** you to the One Who Came. Or you may be lovers for this night only — or for the rest of your days. The bond between you will be powerful, regardless. As you consummate the Hieros Gamos with this Power, allow yourself to be open to communication and gnosis. Allow the Power to fill you. During this consummation, open yourself to a Mystery of the Spiral Castle. When you have found the Mystery and shared climax, you will be invested with the Virtue of that Power and will rise from the sacred bed as a Queen, Devil, or Consort of the Spiral Castle. Your choice of title between these three is your preference. None are reserved for any particular gender — or for the mate of any particular Power.

•**Garter** -- Braid your three threads/strands/leather strips together in the same basic manner that you do with your seasonal cords. Fold them, make a loop and knot on one end (the Goda knot), braid through their full length until you tie the Kolyo knot, leaving a flail, and tie a Qayin knot in the middle. As you braid, consider the Mystery that was revealed to you in the Hieros Gamos, the power (or "virtue") with which you have been invested by the Great Power with whom you joined, and the place you now take as a Queen, a Devil, or a Consort of the Spiral Castle. Tie your Garter in place, either at the top of the left calf or on the upper left thigh. (Tie it tight enough that it stays in place, but not so tightly that you cut off circulation to the leg).

Vows, Oath & Presentation

- **Vows & Oath** -- Move to the Oath Stone and turn your attention to the Vows of 3rd Admission. Ask and answer aloud each question. If you are ready to make your Oath, prick your finger to raise blood, and then grasp the Oath Stone. You will be making your oaths using your full Craft name (that you found in your 1st Degree Initiation).
- **Presentation** -- Stand up, anoint yourself with the initiation oil, and say, "So now do I proclaim myself a true [Queen, Devil, or Consort] of the Spiral Castle. So shall I be recognized among my Folk and Family! I present myself to the Realms, Gates, Towers, Spirits, and Godds of the Spiral Castle. I am, [Complete Craft Name], a full Witch and [Artisan, Bard, Conjurer, Healer, etc], AND [Queen, Devil, or Consort] of the Spiral Castle! So Mote it Be!"
- **Gift** -- Give yourself the gift you have made or purchased for the occasion. Sain it using a bit of the mixture from your Red Meal, wiping it clean, and then putting it on.

Red Meal

Moving counterclockwise, bring the sacrificial meal to the Stang or center of the Compass, while singing the Housle Song, below. Make at least one full circle as you tread the mill. Three is better.

The Housle Song
(To the tune of Greensleeves)

To Housle now we walk the wheel
We kill tonight the blood red meal
A leftward tread of magic's mill
To feed the Godds and work our Will.

Red! Red is the wine we drink!
Red! Red are the cords we wear!
Red! Red is the blood of Godd!
And red is the shade of the Housle.

Say, "For my Ancestors, my Godds, and Myself, I do this."

Bless the bread by saying: "Here is bread, flesh of the Earth, blessed to give us life and strength. I consecrate it in the name of the Old Ones."

Kill the bread by saying: "I take its life and give it to Them." Cut it with the red knife.

Bless the wine by saying: "Here is wine, blood of the Earth, blessed to give us joy and abundance. I consecrate it in the name of the Old Ones."

Kill the wine by saying: "I take its life and give it to Them." Slide the knife over the top of the cup to cut its throat.

Eat and drink of the Meal, making whatever personal offerings you like into the bowl.

The remainder of the wine is poured into the bread bowl. Dip your finger in and anoint yourself. This can also be used for blessing tools, etc.

The Meal is either given to the ground now (if outside) or later (if inside) with the following Declaration:

"By the Red, and Black and White,
Light in Darkness, Dark in Light --
What we take, we freely give.
We all must die. We all must live.
Above, below, and here are One.
All together -- ALL! (And none!)
Here is shown a Mystery. As I Will, so Mote it Be."

Assignment

Perform the ritual included here. Use your judgment, if you need to make minor modifications regarding supplies or peripheral details; but try to keep the major components of this initiation intact. There are deeply interwoven symbol sets at play.

As you have done with other rituals during your studies thus far, take time to write about your experience during and after the initiation. Your debrief should also include:

- any impressions you had or challenges you experienced during the set-up
- a notation of the date and general time you did the ritual
- impressions, insights, and sensations you had throughout the ritual (during the opening portions, the working, or the meal)
- any challenges you experienced while executing the ritual
- ideas that this ritual sparked for you (either for other rituals or for other creative/philosophical endeavors in your world)
- anything else that you feel should be noted

Additional Resources

Blade & Broom shop -- www.bladeandbroom.etsy.com -- Convo me through Etsy to set up a custom order for a dressed chime candle, bath sachet, incense, or anointing oil using the SCT Initiation formulas , if you'd like the ones I make instead of crafting them for yourself.

BoS Pages Included

Laying the Compass

Opening the Gates

Raising the Castles

Calling the Realms

The Housle

Saining of Tools (Year 1 book)

No-Kill Fast Food List

No-Kill Fast Recipes

SCT Initiation Recipes

RTA Third Degree Self-Initiation

SCT 3rd Admission Vows

SCT 3rd Admission Oath

Appendix A
Grimoire Pages

Book

of

Shadows

Chants and Balladry

Eko Eko Chant 1

Eko, eko, azarak. Eko, eko, zomelak.

Bagabi lacha bachabe, Lamac cahi achababe.

Karrellyos.

Lamac lamac bachalyas.

Cabahagy sabalyos. Baryolos.

Lagoz atha cabyolas. Smnahac atha famolas.

Hurrahya.

This version of the Eko Eko chant is often used when summoning the Witch Father or when raising power for trance and spells. The first line(s) of Eko, Eko, seem to be connected to Version 2 of the chant. The remainder, beginning with "Bagabi lacha ..." are very similar to a chant used in a 13th Century French miracle play, and are said to "summon the Devil" – our Folkloric Devil, who is summoned in that play by a sorcerer called Saladin (a famous Islamic military figure from the time of the Crusades who is associated with freemasonry and magick).

Eko Eko Chant 2

Eko! Eko! Azarak! Eko! Eko! Zomelak!

Zod-ru-koz e Zod-ru-koo

Zod-ru-goz e Goo-ru-moo!

Eko! Eko! Hoo...Hoo...Hoo!

This version of the Eko Eko chant is often used when summoning the Witch Father, specifically. This version first appeared in an article by C. Fuller in the Occult Review in 1926, but strikingly similar versions of it were in use by Doreen Valiente and, later, the Farrars.

Eko Eko Chant 3

Eko! Eko! Azarak!

Eko! Eko! Zomelak!

Eko! Eko! Karnayna!

Eko! Eko! Arida!

This version of the Eko Eko chant is often used when summoning the Spirits of the Craft – the Great Powers. The names (particularly the final two names) are often changed for the names of Deities or Spirits specific to a Coven or group.

An example would be:

Eko! Eko! Azarak!

Eko! Eko! Zomelak!

Eko! Eko! Kolayda!

Eko! Eko! Godena!

Invocation of the Horned God

~ Doreen Valiente ~

By the flame that burneth bright,
O Horned One!
We call thy name into the night,
O Horned One!

Thee we invoke by the moon led sea
By the standing stone and the twisted tree
Thee we invoke where gather thine own
By the nameless shrine forgotten and lone

Come where the round of the dance is trod
Horn and hoof of the goat-foot God
By moonlit meadow on dusky hill
When the haunted wood is hushed and still

Come to the charm of the chanted prayer
As the moon bewitches the midnight air
Evoke thy powers, that potent bide
In shining stream and secret tide

In fiery flame by starlight pale
In shadowy host that ride the gale
And by the fern-brakes fairy-haunted
Of forests wild and wood enchanted

Come! O Come!
To the heartbeats drum!

Come to us who gather below
When the broad white moon is climbing slow
Through the stars to the heavens height
We hear thy hoofs on the wind of night
As black tree branches shake and sigh
By joy and terror we know thee nigh

We speak the spell thy power unlocks
At Solstice, Sabbat, and Equinox

Word of virtue the veil to rend
From primal dawn to the wide world's end
Since time began---
The blessing of Pan!

Blessed be all in hearth and hold
Blessed in all worth more than gold
Blessed be in strength and love
Blessed be wher'er we rove

Vision fade not from our eyes
Of the pagan paradise
Past the gates of death and birth
Our inheritance of the earth

From our soul the song of spring
Fade not in our wandering

Our life with all life is one,
By blackest night or noonday sun
Eldest of gods, on thee we call
Blessing be on thy creatures all

Provided by Asteria Books 2022

Charge of the Goddess

~ Doreen Valiente ~

Listen to the words of the Great Mother, who was of old also called Artemis; Astarte; Diana; Melusine; Aphrodite; Cerridwen; Da-na; Arianrhod; Isis; Bride; and by many other names.

Whenever ye have need of anything, once in a month, and better it be when the Moon be full, then ye shall assemble in some secret place and adore the spirit of me, who am Queen of all Witcheries.

There shall ye assemble, ye who are fain to learn all sorcery, yet have not yet won its deepest secrets: to these will I teach things that are yet unknown.

And ye shall be free from slavery; and as a sign that ye are really free, ye shall be naked in your rites; and ye shall dance, sing, feast, make music and love, all in my praise.

For mine is the ecstasy of the spirit and mine also is joy on earth; for my Law is Love unto all Beings.

Keep pure your highest ideal; strive ever to-ward it; let naught stop you or turn you aside.

For mine is the secret door which opens upon the Land of Youth; and mine is the Cup of the Wine of Life, and the Cauldron of Cer-ridwen, which is the Holy Grail of Immortality.

I am the Gracious Goddess, who gives the gift of joy unto the heart. Upon earth, I give the knowledge of the spirit eternal; and beyond death, I give peace, and freedom, and reun-ion with those who have gone before. Nor do I demand sacrifice, for behold I am the Mother of All Living, and my love is poured out upon the earth.

Hear ye the words of the Star Goddess, she in the dust of whose feet are the hosts of heaven; whose body encircleth the Uni-verse; I, who am the beauty of the green earth, and the white Moon among the stars, and the mystery of the waters, and the heart's desire, call unto thy soul. Arise and come unto me.

For I am the Soul of Nature, who giveth life to the universe; from me all things pro-ceed, and unto me must all things return; and before my face, beloved of gods and mortals, thine inmost divine self shall be unfolded in the rapture of infinite joy.

Let my worship be within the heart that rejoiceth, for behold: all acts of love and pleasure are my rituals. And therefore let there be beauty and strength, power and compassion, honour and humility, mirth and reverence within you.

And thou who thinkest to seek for me, know thy seeking and yearning shall avail thee not, unless thou know this mystery: that if that which thou seekest thou findest not within thee, thou wilt never find it without thee.

For behold, I have been with thee from the beginning; and I am that which is attained at the end of desire.

Provided by Asteria Books 2022

Sabbats

Samhain Mysteries

At Samhaintide, it is our custom to explore the Mysteries of:

"Life in Death; Death in Life" — This is a phrase we use to reference something very fundamental to this Tradition. While the WitchMother isn't particularly prominent at this Sabbat, this phrase IS. (And this phrase is very much associated with Her.) This Mystery is also very present with us at Beltaine.

"Rose Beyond the Grave" — Writers from within the Clan of Tubal Cain have written about this Mystery. To contemplate the Rose Beyond (or Within) the Grave is to contemplate what happens to the Souls of the Witch after Death.

"What the Mask Reveals" — The Spiral Castle Tradition associates the West with Samhain. The weapon of the West is the Helm (or Mask). We sometimes work with the Mask in order to better understand both ourselves and That which is represented by a specific mask.

Yule Mysteries

At Yuletide, it is our custom to explore the Mysteries of:

"Robin and Wren"/"Oak King and Holly King" — Here in the darkest time of year is a good time to consider the power of solitude, contemplation, and thriftiness (as well as how these things balance with community, activity, and abundance).

"What is seen by Odin's eye" — The Glass Orb is the vessel associated with the Winter Solstice. It can be thought of as Odin's eye, in addition to its associations with the Adder's Egg or glain. Spend some time with this vessel and consider what it reveals.

Imbolc Mysteries

At Imbolctide, it is our custom to explore the Mysteries of:

"Uneasy Seat Above Caer Ochren" — This is a wonderful time to explore the Mysteries of oracular work. Our Tradition associates Imbolc with invoking Kolyo and asking for Her guidance and wisdom on Her most holy day. She often reveals Her own Mysteries, but the process itself has much to impart, as well.

"The Light in the Darkness, the Darkness in the Light" — Kolyo and Goda share this Mystery, which they teach us using different methods. Starlight in an inky sky. Stark shadows in the brightest sun. Nakedness. Cloaking. Youth. Age. Nothing is as straightforward as it seems. First impressions are often deceiving.

"The Staff" — All of the weapons and vessels of the Spiral Castle carry their own Mysteries. When contemplating the lessons of the Staff, think of its many forms and functions — walking stick, battle-staff/quarter-staff, lantern pole, sounding rod, spear, arrow, wand, hobby horse, tein, distaff.

"Fire and Ice" — Climate change notwithstanding, Imbolc tends to be the coldest and bleakest of the Sabbats in North America. But "far beneath the winter snows, a heart of fire beats and glows." This is a great time to ponder what unseen things are happening during periods of rest.

Spring Equinox Mysteries

AT THE VERNALTIDE, IT IS OUR CUSTOM TO EXPLORE THE MYSTERIES OF:

"The Broom" — In his letters to Joe Wilson, Robert Cochrane discusses what we call "The Mystery of the Broom." He sums it up using the enigmatic phrase "spinning without motion between three elements." The Broom as a transvective tool allows us to MOVE between the Realms — without necessarily moving our bodies at all.

"The Golden Lantern" — All of the vessels and weapons of the Spiral Castle impart their own Mysteries. To better understand the inspiration, poetry, art, and illusion of the Golden Lantern, consider the Sun in alchemy and classical astrology, will o' th' wisps and foxfire in Irish and Appalachian lore, the rays of Awen, and tales of magic lamps.

Beltaine Mysteries

AT BELTAINETIDE, IT IS OUR CUSTOM TO EXPLORE THE MYSTERIES OF:

"Life in Death; Death in Life" — This is a phrase we use to reference something very fundamental to this Tradition. While the WitchMother isn't particular prominent at this Sabbat, this phrase IS. (And this phrase is very much associated with Her.) This Mystery is also very present with us at Samhain.

"The Sword That Cuts Both Ways" — All of the weapons and vessels of the Spiral Castle impart their own lessons and Mysteries. The Sword (weapon of the East Gate) has much to teach. One of the ways it shows up is as the Sword Bridge that we cross into the place of Initiation. As such, we name the Coven Sword as "The Sword That Cuts Both Ways."

Midsummer Mysteries

At Midsummerstide, it is our custom to explore the Mysteries of:

"Robin and Wren"/"Oak King and Holly King" — Here in the lightest time of year is a good time to consider the power of community, activity, and abundance (as well as how these things balance with solitude, contemplation, and thriftiness).

"The Stone Bowl" — All of the vessels and weapons of the Spiral Castle carry their own Mysteries. The Stone Bowl reminds us that "There is no magic without sacrifice" — a phrase which we often paint or carve on the bottom of this dish.

Lammas Mysteries

At Lammastide, it is our custom to explore the Mysteries of:

"What songs the siren sings?" — Goda is Our Lady of Lammas — a time of sacrifice and also joy, abundance, and oaths. This is a great time to contemplate Goda and her associations with love, loss, reunion of the Soul, and song.

"Uneasy Seat Above Caer Ochren" — This is a wonderful time to explore the Mysteries of oracular work. Our Tradition associates Lammas with invoking Goda and asking for Her guidance and wisdom on Her most holy day. She often reveals Her own Mysteries, but the process itself has much to impart, as well.

"The Dance of the Seven Veils" — Goda stands naked, having shed the veils already. What do we find when we strip away our careers, relationships, memories, bodies, desires, etc. Consider Inanna's descent, and the jewelry/garments she relinquishes at each gate. Consider the 7 classical planets, and the 7 most commonly discussed chakras. Consider the process of aging and death, and how we all eventually "stand naked."

"The Shield" — Each of our vessels and weapons unfolds its own Mysteries. Some are better documented than others in the traditions of the Craft and other Mystery Schools. The Shield is one that gets short shrift in most places, but it is still present and powerful. It is related to the Witch's Glove, the

Lammas Mysteries

Pentacle, and even the Cloak (which is a shielding device in myth and literature).

"The Light in the Darkness, the Darkness in the Light" — Kolyo and Goda share this Mystery, which they teach us using different methods. Starlight in an inky sky. Stark shadows in the brightest sun. Nakedness. Cloaking. Youth. Age. Nothing is as straightforward as it seems. First impressions are often deceiving.

Autumn Mysteries

At the Autumnaltide, it is our custom to explore the Mysteries of:

"What the Mask Reveals" — The Spiral Castle Tradition often performs a "Hunt for Mabon" at the Fall Equinox. During this ritual, we usually mask — either as a Hunter or as one of the Five Animals that the hunting party queries. We work with the Mask in order to better understand both ourselves and That which is represented by a specific mask.

"The Mystery of the Cauldron" — Robert Cochrane wrote about the Mys-tery of the Cauldron in his letters to Joe Wilson. He poses a riddle to Wilson, asking him what can't fit within the Cauldron. "Two words: Be Still." The Cauldron holds ALL — all life, all hope, all desire, all abundance, all possibility. It is always moving. Always shifting. Always becoming. There is no still-ness in the Cauldron. (But there can be stillness within us, which we find within this tumult.)

"The Bloody Cup/The Holy Grail" — All of the vessels and weapons of the Spiral Castle impart their own Mysteries. This is probably the most well-known of all the Mysteries we seek. The San Greal — or Sang Real.

"The Five Transformations" — Ceridwen is one of the ladies whom we see most clearly as our Silver Queen. She is the keeper of the Cauldron, and her story of flight, pursuit, and transformation with the young Gwion Bach (who becomes Taliesin) is most revealing.

Spell Bundles

Spell Bundle Instructions

Each of the "spell bundles" in this set were originally designed for sale at Blade & Broom Botanica. Our basic spell bundles have always included:

- an herb mix (used for stuffing poppets, burning as incense, or adding to putzi bag)
- a novena candle (of our own design)
- a candle ladder talisman
- a poppet
- a putzi bag
- a traditional oil or water
- an incense or dirt
- a talisman

Our Spell Bundle Formulary pages include the specific list (and in some cases, the specific formula or design) of the pieces we included. Each page features the complete ingredients list for our herb mix, the gemstones used in our candle ladder talismans, the materials included in our putzi bag, and the symbols we traditionally use on the poppet for that spell intention.

Sadly, there isn't room on the page for the complete ingredients and directions for making each incense, conjure oil, water, or talisman. Fortunately, though, these are included in the complete Formulary set.

We've even included the novena art for you to make your own novena candles with the sale of these pages! All you have to do is trim the graphic and paste it onto a blank candle with a mixture of equal parts school glue and wa-ter.

You can use some of these spell components, or all of them. The choice is yours!

Be Gone

Whether you are trying to rid yourself of a noisome spirit or an unwelcome person in your life, BE GONE is designed with those needs in mind. You can also use this spell set when you need protection against negative energies and emotions. Make or gather one or more of the following spell components to banish spirits, people, or vibrations.

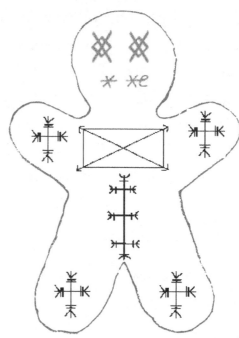

Herb Mix

Sage

Rosemary

Nettle

Wormwood

Gemstones

Lava

Coral

Citrine

Quartz Crystal

Black Tourmaline

Onyx

Putzi Bag

Black or Red cloth

GTFO (HotFoot) Powder

Wasp's Nest

Spent Shotgun Shell

Conjure Formulas

GTFO (HotFoot) Powder

GTFO (HotFoot) Oil

Talismans & Amulets

Hamsa Hand

GTFO

GTFO and Hot Foot Lore

Get the Fuck Out oil/powder is our heavy-duty version of traditional hot foot powder — cayenne, which can be used very effectively to cause an unwanted person to "hot-foot it" out of your life. With crossroads dirt, asafetida, sulfur, sage, salt, AND cayenne blended into castor oil (the base for "command and compel") your nuisance CAN'T stick around. NOTE: Use caution when handling this recipe. The ingredients are caustic and can irritate both the skin and the respiratory system.

GTFO Recipe

Castor Oil base

Cayenne powder

Asafetida powder

Sulfur powder

Sea Salt

Sage leaf, powdered

Crossroads Dirt

* For a GTFO Powder you can sprinkle, omit the oil.

Formula Uses

1. You need something connected to the target person — a photo, lock of hair, item of clothing, etc. Make sure it isn't connected to anyone else or you could make them leave, too. (Nobody else in photo, nobody else's hairs in the comb, etc.)

2. Failing a personal object, you could write as many defining characteristics of that person as possible on a piece of paper — name, description, job, personality, history, birthday, etc.

3. Make 3 X's or +'s (crosses) on the object using the oil with an iron (coffin) nail. Don't get any on your skin, if you can help it.

4. Burn the object.

Black Salt

Black Salt Lore

There are basically three types of Black Salt — Witches' Salt, Black Lava Salt, and Indian Black Salt (or kala namak). The last two are used in cooking, but Witch's Black Salt is a non-edible salt that is used in home and personal protection spells. It is a powerful ingredient in spells and recipes for driving evil away. Black Salt actually comes from Hoodoo practice, but it has become a very popular ingredient in American Witchcraft across a number of Traditions.

Black Salt Recipe

2 parts Sea Salt

2 parts Cast Iron Scrapings

1 part Charcoal, ground

1 part fine ash from burning an equal mix of Lavender, Bay, and Sage

1 part Black Peppercorns

1 part Chicory

Black Salt Uses

Black Salt can be added to any other recipe to add extra power to repulse evil or to banish a negative person or situation. It is often added to War Water, Graveyard Dirt, and Hotfoot blends. You can also sprinkle it around your house to prevent psychic and physical harm to the occupants. If you choose to curse someone (particularly by sending them away), Black Salt will be a great addition to whatever you plan.

Be Still

Haters are gonna hate, but you don't have to let them keep hating on you. Make or gather one or more of the following spell components to silence gossip-mongers, liars, and anyone else who is speaking ill of you.

Herb Mix
Alum

Red Pepper flakes

Devil's Shoestring

Slippery Elm

Lemon Peel

Wormwood

Plantain leaf

Gemstones
Black Tourmaline

Aquamarine

Blue Quartz

Sodalite

Blue Lace Agate

Aqua Aura Quartz

STFU Putzi Bag

Indigo Cloth

Mercury dime
Name paper of target
Herb mix (above)
Coffin nail
Aquamarine stone

Conjure Formulas

STFU (Stop Gossip) Oil

Talismans & Amulets

Psalm 37

Baglamukhi Yantra

STFU

STFU Lore

Shut the Fuck Up oil/powder blend is our go-to formula for stopping gossip, lies, rumors, and other bothersome wagging tongues.

Formula Recipe

Castor Oil base

Alum

Wormwood

Lemon Peel

Devil's Shoestring

- Prepare as an herb-infused oil. Add black tourmaline chips to the bottle when complete.

- For powder only, omit the oil and stones, and grind the botanicals as fine as you can.

Formula Uses

Sprinkle the powder in the path of the one who is speaking ill of you so you know they will walk through it. Dab a little of the oil or sprinkle a little of the powder on their phone, if you can do so without being caught. Anoint prayer candles, petition papers, and putzi/mojo bags with the oil to power a STFU spell.

*By word & will,
by fire & light,
keep your tongue
& lips held tight!*

Watch Over Me

We all need some extra protection now and then. Tough times call for tougher guardians. Call up a "fiery wall" to protect you and yours when baneful energies align themselves against you.

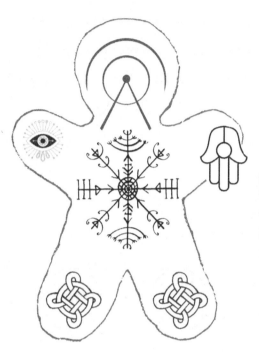

Herb Mix
Cayenne

Rue

Angelica

Cinnamon

Dragon's Blood

Gemstones
Agate

Carnelian

Ruby

Garnet

Citrine

Black Tourmaline

Putzi Bag
Red Cloth

Coffin Nail
Herb Mix (above)
Archangel Michael's Signature
Helm of Awe Talisman

Conjure Formulas
Fiery Wall of Protection Incense

Flying Devil Oil

Talismans & Amulets
Fiery Sword Talisman

Veldismagn Talisman

Fiery Wall of Protection Oil

FIERY WALL OF PROTECTION LORE

This is another traditional formula from Hoodoo practice. It is used to offer very strong protection against "tricks" and psychic attack, as well as from physical harm. You can use it to protect yourself or others, as well as laying down protection over an area. It's scent is spicy and warm, hence the "fire."

FIERY WALL OIL RECIPE

Olive Oil base

Rue leaves

Ginger root

Sandalwood powder

Cinnamon powder

Black Pepper corns

Red Pepper flakes

Dragon's Blood resin

* Prepare the above as an oil infusion, then add essential oils of Cinnamon, Ginger, and Black Pepper.

FIERY WALL OIL USES

Use Fiery Wall of Protection oil to anoint candles for reversing or protection spells. Use it mark wooden furniture and metal fixtures like doorknobs and locks in a place you want protected. Use it to "feed" leather protection talismans or cloth putzi bags. Dilute well if you choose to put the oil on your skin, as the spicy ingredients can be caustic to sensitive skin.

All Is Fair

When you're defending something or someone you love, you're often prepared to go to war. If you find yourself in court battling for what you hold dear, you'll want some magickal aid on your side.

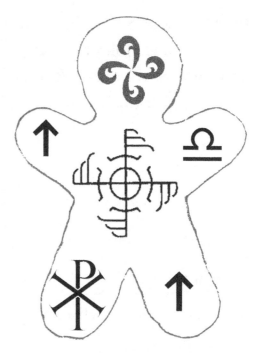

Herb Mix
Calendula

Celandine

Chamomile

High John

Galangal

Gemstones
Bloodstone

Hematite

Lodestone

Garnet

Citrine

Conjure Formulas
Courtcase Oil

Justice Incense

Talismans & Amulets
Scales Talisman

Putzi Bag
Yellow Cloth

Little John Root

Herb Mix (above)

Chi Ro Talisman

Court Case Oil

Court Case Lore

In the Hoodoo tradition, the rhizome Galangal is often called Chewing John (or Little John to Chew) or Court Case Root. Alone and in combination with other botanicals, it is the most potent and active aide in finding a favorable decision in court.

Formula Recipe

Castor Oil base

Galangal, pieces or slices

Calendula flowers

Black Mustard Seeds

Solomon's Seal

Formula Uses

Dress candles, feed putzi bags, and/or anoint yourself with this oil before entering the courtroom.

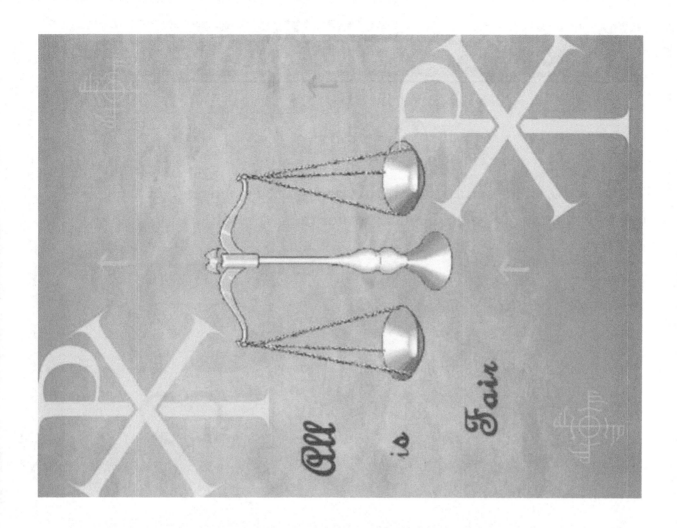

All is Fair

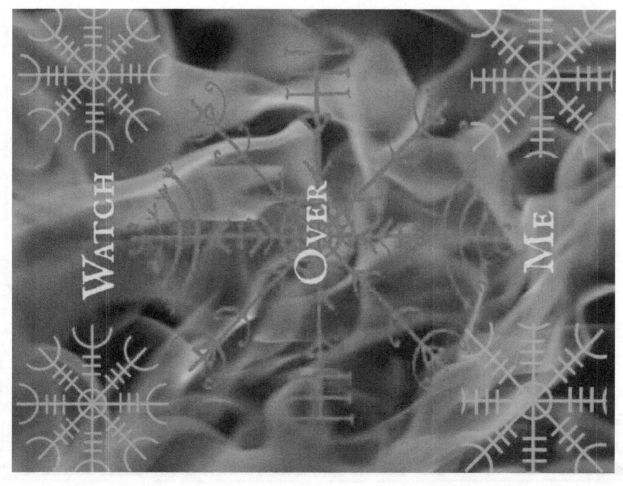

WATCH OVER ME

Domina

Take control of an unruly situation, relationship, or person. Get the upper hand so that you can guide the outcome for the best result.

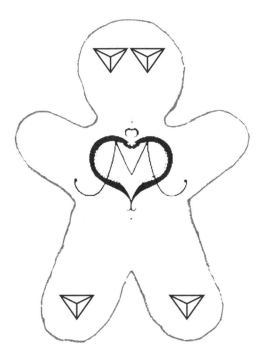

HERB MIX

Gardenia

Clove

Vervain

Calamus root

Tarragon

Hyssop

GEMSTONES

Azurite

Malachite

Opal

Ruby

Clear Quartz

CONJURE FORMULAS

St. Martha Dominator Oil

Bend Over Incense

TALISMANS & AMULETS

Dragon's Eye Talisman

PUTZI BAG

Purple Cloth

Dragon's Blood Resin
Herb Mix (above)
Lock & Key

St. Martha Dominator Oil

St. Martha the Dominator Lore

Saint Martha is the patron saint of servants, and she helps them rise above the bonds of servitude. She is said to have subdued a deadly dragon, using only holy water and a cross. She helps us tap into our Will to subdue and get control of any unruly situation — or person. She brings happiness to the home and returns wayward lovers.

Formula Recipe

Olive Oil base

Gerdenia essential oil

Clove essential oil

Vervain essential oil

Amber oil

Tarragon

Spikenard root

Calamus root

Myrrh

Formula Uses

Use the oil to anoint candles to St. Martha when petitioning her for aid. Anoint a St. Martha prayer book or prayer card with the oil. You can also use the oil to anoint a St. Martha medal to wear for her aid.

Follow Me Boy Oil

FOLLOW ME LORE

The Follow Me Boy line of products are part of a family of coercive, dominating Hoodoo products and spells used to make the target "fall in line" with the petitioner's Will. This oil is used to make the target (a man already known to the petitioner) desire and be faithful to the petitioner. Follow Me Boy is used by straight women and gay men to attract a male lover. It is used to initiate a lusty love affair and also to keep the target faithful. You can also use it to help yourself stand out from the crowd in any competition.

FOLLOW ME BOY RECIPE

Sunflower Oil base

Vanilla bean pieces

Damiana leaves

Catnip leaves

Calamus root pieces

Licorice root pieces

Orris root pieces

Lavender flowers

* Prepare as an infused oil.

FOLLOW ME BOY USES

Anoint a red penis candle with the oil (and some of his semen, if you have access to it). Tie it with a red thread and command him to desire only you. You can also dress the inside of his hat band and the inside of his pants, as well.

"Follow Me" was often inscribed on the soles of courtesans shoes in Ancient Greece, leaving an imprint in the dirt to attract customers. Put this oil on the soles of your pumps to get your man to follow you, too.

Copyright Asteria Books 2017

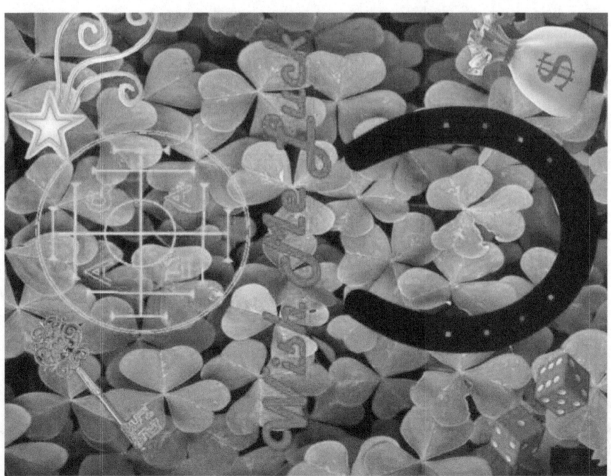

Banishing Spells

GTFO Oil is a heavy-duty version of traditional hot foot powder — cayenne, which can be used very effectively to cause an unwanted person to "hot-foot it" out of your life. With crossroads dirt, asafetida, sulfur, sage AND cayenne blended mixed into castor oil your nuisance CAN'T stick around.

1. You need something connected to the target person — a photo, lock of hair, item of clothing , etc. Make sure it isn't connected to anyone else or you could make them leave, too. (Nobody else in photo, nobody else's hairs in the comb, etc.)
2. Failing a personal object, you could write as many defining characteristics of that person as possible on a piece of paper — name, description, job, personality, history, birthday, etc.
3. Make 3 X's on the object using the oil with an iron nail. Don't get any on your skin, if you can help it.
4. Burn the object.

Banishing ingredients can include cayenne, black pepper, cinnamon, chopped bay laurel leaves, sea salt, sulfur, asafetida, crossroads dirt, dragon's blood powder, gunpowder/shotgun pellets, file powder (ground sassafras root), crushed wasp nest, ground ginger.

Sprinkle your mixture onto your target's shoes, across their doorstep, or into their footprint to compel them to move away. You can also hide/mix it into a gift/item (the soil of a potted plant) that the person will bring into their home!

Bell, Book & Candle
To banish spirits, ring an iron bell 3 or 9 times and chant/read from a text you hold sacred while burning a beeswax candle.

Un-Welcome Mat
Write the names of people who are no longer welcome in your home on individual slips of paper. Cross each with GTFO oil and bury them under your porch or the walkway to your door.

Justice Spells

Hold the Justice card from a Tarot deck (or a drawing/copy/picture of it) in your hands and focus on the situation for which you are calling for justice to be done. Pour into the picture all the ways in which you've been wronged and the specific ways in which the "scales of Justice" can be balanced. When you're ready, place the card/picture on a fireproof plate . Surround the card with a black stone, white stone, and red stone. On top of the card, set and burn a carved and dressed purple taper or chime candle. Light another purple candle every Thursday.

For Justice work that involves the courts, uses galangal root (which is also called courtcase root). You can carry it with you in a putzi bag, or you can chew it and (discreetly) spit it on the floor before the judge enters. Unlikely as it sounds, this will help them favor you in the case.

If you need extra help with Justice – including strength while you fight the good fight – call on the archangel Michael using his traditional invocation. As you say each of the following lines, imagine a flaming sword appearing at each of the locations, close to the body (with the last flaming sword being at the heart energy center).

Angel Michael BEFORE me
Angel Michael BEHIND me
Angel Michael ABOVE me
Angel Michael BENEATH me
Angel Michael at my RIGHT
Angel Michael at my LEFT
Angel Michael WITHIN me

Michael is a powerful being, and has been called upon by magicians outside of the Judeo-Christian context for work involving war and plague, and also protection and healing. He adds a potent punch to Justice work since he will go to any length to do what is right. Just make sure you are on the side of "right" (by his standards) when you call on him.

Ruination Spells

Witch Bottle Hexing

Use a bottle or jar that you can lid, cap, or cork. Fill it with your target's photo, name paper, black ink, War Water, your urine, rusty nails, pins, and botanicals related to your intentions. Seal with wax from a black candle and bury upside down.

Black Candle Spell

Reverse the candle by slicing the top to flatten it, and carving the bottom to expose the wick. Carve and dress the candle using a rusty nail, Flying Devil Oil, and the botanicals of your choice. Chant your intentions while your candle burns.

Coffin Curse

Fashion a wax or cloth poppet of your target. Include their hair, nails, or other items, if you can get them. If not, embed a name paper and photo. Place this doll inside a small wooden coffin. Bury the coffin and place a rock on top.

Curse Tablets

Inscribe sheets of metal or wax with target's name, birthday, etc & your intention for them. Be specific and explicit. Drop it in the sewer (or make your own "sewer jar" with urine and excrement to drop it in, seal it up, and send it to the landfill).

Goofer Dust

This is potent stuff with no single recipe. Variations of it exist outside the African diaspora (under different names & with their own variations). ALL variations are malevolent — with results from effects on sanity all the way to death. The most common ingredients include cemetery dirt, church bell grease, salt, sulfur, gunpowder, and more.

- Toss at target's back
- Sprinkle across target's path or on front steps
- Use it to dress a black candle
- Incorporate it into poppet work

Domination Spells

Sweet Woodruff

Sprinkle the Waldmeister ("Master of the Forest" the German name for this herb) over the path where your target is sure to walk in order to gain dominance over them.

Name Jar

These jars are used to influence people who are either mildly unaware or wildly opposed to you or your goals. Get them in line! Write the name on a slip of paper three times, turning the paper 90-degrees and crossing each with your own name (to make a grid). If you're working on more than one person for the same intention, use a different slip of paper for each person. Fold the papers toward you as tightly as you can. Put the paper(s) into a canning jar with honey, jam, syrup, or sugar. (I prefer raw, natural honey.) Cover the papers completely, saying something like, "[Target] be as sweet to me as this honey is upon my lips." Light a chime candle on top of the jar that matches your intentions. Repeat weekly (on the day associated with your intention) as needed.

Calamus & Licorice

Sweet flag (calamus) & licorice root (not candy) are the basis of traditional "Command & Compel" formulas (along with the castor bean/oil) – dating back to the *Magical Papyri*. Sometimes vetivert (which is also sometimes called calamus) and patchouli are substituted, giving practitioners a few options for mixing and matching. These formulas were used to make both spirits and people obey the commands of the magician. Use calamus & licorice in:

- A ritual bath by making a decoction that you add to the water
- Oils & powders for dressing candles – or simply touch your target after anointing your own hands
- A witch's ladder in which strands of the target's hair have been soaked in a decoction these roots
- A putzi bag that you carry with you to increase your influence and command

Heads, Hands, Feet

These symbols have been used for purposes of control for centuries. Wear a necklace of them strung on red silk cord to control the thoughts and actions of your target. Or carve their name on the sole of your shoe to keep them at heel!

War Water

War Water Lore

War Water (or Water of Mars) is a European addition to the Hoodoo and Voudon practices of New Orleans. It is a nasty blend of rusty iron nails (iron being associated with Mars, God of War) and distressed water (either thunderstorm rain or swamp water). It is very reminiscent of European "witch bottle" formulas in some ways (rust, sharpness, urine), except that the witch bottle was used more as a protective landmine on the witch's property, whereas War Water is used more like a psychic grenade at your enemy's home.

War Water Recipe

Swamp Water or Thunderstorm Rain

Iron nails (can be cut) *

Sulfur

Spanish Moss

* Add baneful focus with:

- Hospital nails = illness

- Courthouse nails = losing in court

- Jailhouse nails = arrest

- Workplace nails = unemployment

- Graveyard nails = death

War Water Uses

Make your War Water in a glass bottle, as it must be broken on your enemy's property to be effective (preferably on their doorstep). You want them to step in the mess to bring chaos, strife, and suffering into their home and family life.

War Water is nasty business.

Witch Cake

Witch Cake Lore

There are two main types of Witch Cakes mentioned in folklore and historical records. One is a cake made from rye meal and the urine of someone under psychic attack. This cake is fed to a dog who, upon biting the cake, causes the attacking witch to cry out in pain. The other type of Witch Cake is found in parts of England as a talisman against harm, serving as a protection for the home. No traditional recipe has been noted for this type, though, so I offer you my own take on the Witch Cake.

Witch Cake Recipe

1/2 cup flour (NOT self-rising)
1/4 cup salt
1/4 cup water (add more as needed)
Rowan berries (dried and ground)
Rosemary (finely ground)
Cinnamon (finely ground)
Honey Locust thorns

Mix the basic salt dough and add in the desire amount of herbs. Form the dough into a ball and then flatten it slightly. Create a hole in the center (big enough for your finger to fit through). Make two rows of spikes around the perimeter of your wheel (6 spikes in each row). Bake this for 2-3 hours or until thoroughly cooked, turning over midway through. Allow to cool.

Witch Cake Uses

Make a new Witch Cake each year during the first week of April. Hang it behind your door with a red ribbon. Before making the Witch Cake the following year, burn the old year's cake.

Ritual, Liturgy, and Spells

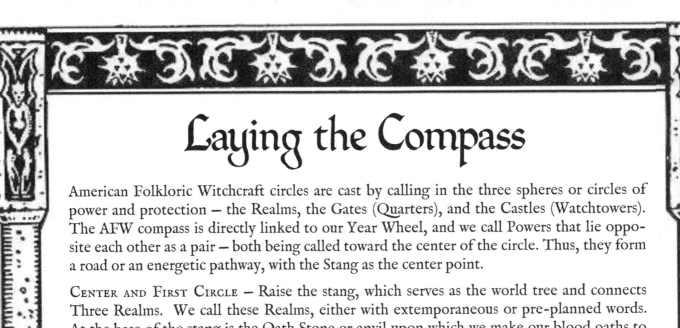

Laying the Compass

American Folkloric Witchcraft circles are cast by calling in the three spheres or circles of power and protection – the Realms, the Gates (Quarters), and the Castles (Watchtowers). The AFW compass is directly linked to our Year Wheel, and we call Powers that lie opposite each other as a pair – both being called toward the center of the circle. Thus, they form a road or an energetic pathway, with the Stang as the center point.

CENTER AND FIRST CIRCLE – Raise the stang, which serves as the world tree and connects Three Realms. We call these Realms, either with extemporaneous or pre-planned words. At the base of the stang is the Oath Stone or anvil upon which we make our blood oaths to the tradition. Near the oath stone are the cauldron and the skull. Also placed at the center of the compass are the personal fetishes of each member of our Clan and the three knives. With the raising of the Stang and the calling of the Realms, the 1st Circle is cast.

SECOND CIRCLE (GATES) – At the North gate are placed the staves of the coven, along with the spear, and the troy stone, or gate stone. Also at this gate are symbols of the Black Goddess, as well as totemic items for Imbolc like an owl's feather, fur from a cat, and a willow switch. Any tools associated with air are kept at this gate, such as the censer if one is used.

The South are symbols of the White Goddess and the shields of the coven. The binding cords and the bread for the red meal are placed at this gate. Horsehair, apples, and swan feathers are all symbols for this gate.

In the East are the tools of fire. Here we place the blacksmith's hammer and tongs and keep a bonfire burning, if we are outdoors. The coven sword is here, as are items related to bull, hawthorn, and bee, such as mead in cow horns.

The West is the gate of water, the quench tank of Tubal Cain. Representations of water are placed here, along with toad and crane. Elder is only brought into the circle for certain dark magics. The weapon of this gate is the helm, and the masks of the Clan are kept here.

THIRD CIRCLE (CASTLES) – At the north-east is the Castle of Revelry. Here we place the lantern of inspiration and the broom, as well as representations of hare, birch, and goose.

In the southwest is the Castle Perilous and the silver chalice, along with the red wine that it will hold. Hawk feathers, vines, and representations of the boar or sow are also placed here.

At the northwest corner is the Glass Castle and its treasure – the glass orb. The totems are goat, holly, and wren. Tools of divination are kept in this castle.

The south-east is the home of the Stone Castle, where we place the stone bowl and the casting stones, along with stag horns, acorns, and oak staves.

Thus is the compass laid. It may be as elaborate or as minimal as your tastes and needs dictate. Although the instructions above explain the placement of all of the gates, treasures, tools, weapons, and totems, simply treading the mill once and acknowledging the four gates and the four castles, along with their rulers, is enough to lay the compass.

Opening the Gates

North Gate

I call to the Winds beyond the North Gate. Open the door from the North, place of Air, Kolyo's domain. By cat, and owl, and willow tree, I call you to open wide the Gate and send forth your road to the center of this, our compass. So mote it be!

South Gate

I call to the Fields beyond the South Gate. Open the door from the South, place of Earth, Goda's domain. By horse, and swan, and apple tree, I call you to open wide the Gate and send forth your road to the center of this, our compass. So mote it be!

East Gate

I call to the Sunrise beyond the East Gate. Open the door from the East, place of Fire, Lucifer's domain. By bull, and bee, and hawthorn tree, I call you to open wide the Gate and send forth your road to the center of this, our compass. So mote it be!

West Gate

I call to the Ocean beyond the West Gate. Open the door from the West, place of Water, Azazel's domain. By toad, and crane, and elder tree, I call you to open wide the Gate and send forth your road to the center of this, our compass. So mote it be!

Calling the Realms

First Realm

My voice reaches high into the etheric Upper World — the Land of Sky, place of thoughts and aspirations and future plans. I call into Ceugent, the Otherworld — place of struggle and enlightenment, the undying realm of birth. First Realm, be the roof of this, our sacred compass. With my breath, I call you to be here now! So mote it be!

Second Realm

My hands reach out into the physical Middle World — the Land of Stone, place of action and progress. I call out to Gwyned, the Green World — place of consensus reality and limitations, the living realm of Earth. Second Realm, be the walls of this, our sacred compass. With my flesh and bone, I call you to be here now! So mote it be!

Third Realm

My roots reach deep into the chthonic Lower World — the Land of Sea, place of emotion and mystery and past memories. I call into Abred, the Underworld — place of preparation and rest, the realm of death. Third Realm, be the floor of this, our sacred compass. With my blood, I call you to be here now! So mote it be!

Raising the Castles

Begin by standing in the center, turn to face the direction associated with the current Sabbat-tide (in this example, Northwest). Hold your arms out in T-shape (if you like).

Glass Castle (northwest – before you)- – "I call to the Castle of Glass, rising up from the Hill of Cloud. Glass Castle! Within your walls, wise ones discern the Truth. Your keeper is the Holly King – Odin, Gwyn ap Nudd, Janicot. The Glass Orb encases its wisdom from the summit of the hall. Castle of Glass, Crystalline Watchtower, be here now! So Mote it Be!"

Stone Castle (southeast – behind you) – "I call to the Castle of Stone, rising up from the Earthen Hill. Stone Castle! Within your walls, warriors train and provisions are prepared. Your keeper is the Oak King – Cernunnos, Herne, Basajaun. The Stone Bowl holds its knowledge at the base of the hall. Castle of Stone, Earthen Watchtower, be here now! So Mote it Be!"

Castle of Revelry (north east – right hand) – "I call to the Castle of Gold, rising up from the Lake of Fire. Castle of Revelry! Within your walls, warriors sing and drink and tell tales of great deeds. Your keeper is the Golden Queen – Freya, Brighid, Aphrodite. The Golden Lantern shines its inspiration from the heart of the hall. Castle of Revelry, Golden Watchtower, be here now! So Mote it Be!"

Castle Perilous (southwest – left hand) – "I call to the Castle of Silver, rising up from the Lake of Blood. Castle Perilous! Within your walls, strong men quake and young girls find their deep power. Your keeper is the Silver Queen – Cerridwen, Morgana, Babalon. The Silver Cup drips its sacrifice from the belly of the hall. Castle of Revelry, Silver Watchtower, be here now! So Mote it Be!"

The Housle

As with many faiths, we partake of a small meal with a spirited drink after our rites. In many witchcraft traditions this is called "Cakes and Ale". We call it the Housle, or Red Meal, and base it in part on a ritual created by fellow walker of the crooked path, Robin Artisson.

THE HOUSLE SONG
To the tune of Greensleeves *To Housle now we walk the wheel We kill tonight the blood red meal A leftward tread of magic's mill To feed the Gods and work our Will. Red, red is the wine we drink Red, red are the cords we wear Red, red is the Blood of God And red is the shade of the Housle.*

When the compass is laid place in the southwest corner: Dark bread in a bowl (or lipped dish) and Red Wine in Silver Quaich or Chalice. In the center, near the stang will be placed the Red Knife.

1. The sacrificial meal is brought from Castle Perilous to the Spiral Castle by an Initiate.
2. Tread the Mill widdershins three times while singing the Housle Song.
3. State: "*For my Ancestors, my Godds, and my Self, I do this.*"
4. Bless the bread saying: "*Here is bread, flesh of the Earth, blessed to give us life and strength. I consecrate it in the name of the Old Ones*"
5. Kill the bread by saying: "*I take its life and give it to Them.*" Cut it with the red knife.
6. Bless the wine saying: "*Here is wine, blood of the Earth, blessed to give us joy and abundance. I consecrate it in the name of the Old Ones.*"
7. Kill the wine by saying: "*I take its life and give it to Them*" Slide the knife over the top of the quaich or chalice.
8. Each person eats and drinks of the Meal, making whatever personal offerings they like. Each person takes the Meal with their left hand, saying "*With my left hand I take it.*"
9. The remainder of the wine is poured into the bread bowl, and each person dips their finger in and anoints themselves. This can also be used for blessing tools, etc.
10. The Meal is either given to the ground now, if outside, or later, if inside, saying the following:

"By the Red, and Black and White,

Light in Darkness, Dark in Light --

What we take, we freely give.

We all must die. We all must live.

Above, below, and here are One.

All together -- ALL! (And none!)

Here is shown a Mystery. As I Will, so Mote

it Be."

Witching Ritual

MATERIALS

- Stang, candle, lighter
- Cauldron, water, lancet
- Anvil, hammer
- Three knives (red, black, white)
- Bread, lipped dish or bowl
- Red wine, cup
- Incense, holder, charcoal
- White Cord for child
- Simple Robe for child
- Drawstring pouch
- Talismans, tokens, and amulets brought by guests
- Extra charms/stones that can be empowered by guests, if needed

RAISE THE STANG

LAY THE COMPASS

WORKING

- NAMING THE CHILD ~ The parents bring the child to the Officiant, who then asks for the child's full and proper name. The Officiant then blesses the child and introduces them to the assembled community by this name, and acknowledges that this child is one of our own.

- CHALLENGES TO PARENTS ~ The Officiant offers three challenges to the parents. Will you love and nurture this child's mind, body, and spirit? Will you respect this child's autonomy as a free, unique, and independent being? Will you guide and teach them all you can so they might find their own way and know their own Souls? After answering yes to all, the Officiant offers a blessing to the parents.

- CHALLENGES TO GODD-PARENTS ~ The Officiant asks the parents to name the child's Godd-Parent(s). The Godd-Parents are offered three challenges. Will you love and respect this child as an autonomous, free, and unique bring? Will you support this child's parents in their obligation to rear and nurture this child? Will you protect and offer succor to this child in times of need? After answering yes to all, the Officiant blesses the Godd-Parents.

- ROBE AND CORDS~ The parents dress the child in a simple robe and tie a white cord at the child's waist. This cord symbolizes the umbilicus that connects each of us to the Family. Whenever the child is present within the Compass, it is fortunate for them to wear this cord — or for the cord to be carried by a parent or Godd-Parent.
- COMMUNITY BLESSINGS ~ The Officiant provides a pouch and asks all those present to give their blessings in the form of tokens, talismans, and amulets. The parents begin, and are followed by the Godd-Parents, and then the remainder of the assembled group. The Officiant is last, and seals the pouch shut before giving it into the care of the child and their parents.

HOUSLE

Puberty Ritual

MATERIALS
- Stang, candle, lighter
- Cauldron, water
- Anvil, hammer
- Three knives (red, black, white)
- Bread, lipped dish or bowl
- Red wine, cup
- Incense, holder, charcoal
- Red candle (taper, pillar, or floating)
- Bowl
- Gifts for the adolescent
- Red and White roses (charms, talisman, embroidery, etc)

RAISE THE STANG

LAY THE COMPASS

WORKING

- PRESENTING THE ADOLESCENT ~ The parents stand with the Adolescent as the Officiant announces: "Today, we celebrate and honor [Name], who has experienced a quickening of the Fire and the Water they carry within. This is a quickening of both the body and the spirit, and it is cause for joy!" (Everyone cheers.)

- WATER ~ The Officiant instructs the Adolescent to use the bowl to dip water from the Cauldron and then set the bowl on the ground. "You now share with us in the watery Mysteries of life and the creation of life. Water flows within us in our tears, our blood, and in our passions."

- FIRE ~ The Officiant instructs the Adolescent to light the red candle. "You now share with us in the fiery Mysteries of life and the creation of life. Fire burns within our hearts, our minds, and in our passions."

- Alchemy of Water and Fire ~ The Officiant instructs the Adolescent to place the candle within the bowl of water, keeping the flame lit. "We all strive to balance the Water and Fire within ourselves. You will experience many trials and

turnings as you work this alchemy for yourself. You will also experience many joys and revelations."

• PRESENTATION OF GIFTS AND ADVICE ~ The Officiant invites the assembled community to offer their gifts (which includes their wisdom) to the Adolescent. Everyone is given the opportunity to speak, if they choose.

• RED AND WHITE ROSES ~ The Officiant presents the Adolescent with the red and white roses (which can be fashioned as a talisman to be worn or carried, or as a talisman to reside on the Adolescent's altar). "Red and White Roses have many meanings among the Wise. One set of those meanings is connected to the quickening you have experienced. There is both beauty and pain in these Mysteries — both are unavoidable, natural, and unique to yourself. I give you this to contemplate as you continue on your journey, along with my blessings and the blessings of our Godds."

HOUSLE

Coming of Age Ritual

MATERIALS
- Stang, candle, lighter
- Cauldron, water
- Anvil, hammer
- Three knives (red, black, white)
- Bread, lipped dish or bowl
- Red wine, cup
- Incense, holder, charcoal
- Blindfold
- Gifts

RAISE THE STANG

LAY THE COMPASS

WORKING

- PREPARING THE YOUNG ADULT ~ The parents walk with the Young Adult away from the group, offering personal advice and reflections on becoming an adult within the community. Before fully returning to the space, they blindfold the young adult and then bring them to the gate of the Compass. During this time, the other adults are divided into two groups — Birthing Parents and Supporting Parents. People will self-select where they wish to be. Birthing Parents will form two parallel lines at ground level (either sitting or kneeling), facing each other. Supporting Parents will stand or sit together as group at the end of this canal or passageway.

- CHALLENGES ~ The Officiant offers three challenges to the Young Adult. "Will you be counted as an Adult within this community? Will you be personally accountable for your words and deeds? Will you support and be supported by this community as you walk the path that is laid at your feet?" After answering Yes, the Young Adult is brought to the beginning of the passageway.

- BIRTHING ~ The Officiant says, "When you were born, it was a struggle. A fight for life. You and your parents worked hard to bring you into this world as an infant. You are now ready to come into the world as an adult, and you and they have worked hard to make that happen, as well." Officiant assists the Young Adult to their hands and knees. "[Name], the Child, kneels here at the passage. [Name], the Adult, is to be found on the other side. Crawl forward, and

make this journey, [Name]." The Birthing Parents squeeze and push against the Young Adult as they crawl. (It should be difficult.) The Supporting Parents call out encouragement and give directions. (The Birthing Parents can also speak words of encouragement and comfort.) When the Young Adult reaches the end, the Supporting Parents help pull them to their feet, remove the blindfold, and give hugs.

• Naming ~ The Officiant says, "When you were born and received within this community, your parents named you [Name]. You may continue to use this name among our People, or you may choose another. Tell us, friend, what is your name?" (Everyone cheers and calls out the name.)

• Presentation of Gifts and Advice ~ The Officiant invites the assembled community to offer their gifts (which includes their wisdom) to the Young Adult. Everyone is given the opportunity to speak, if they choose.

Housle

Handfasting Ritual

MATERIALS

- Stang, candle, lighter
- Cauldron, water
- Anvil, hammer
- Three knives (red, black, white)
- Bread, lipped dish or bowl
- Red wine, cup
- Incense, holder, charcoal
- Handfasting Cord
- Rings
- Lanterns/Torches for each Quarter/Gate
- North: incense and Staff for the couple; South: bread and Coin for the couple; West: Cup of water with cedar asperger; East: candle and Dagger or Sword for the couple

RAISE THE STANG

LAY THE COMPASS

WORKING

- PROCESSIONAL ~ The bridal party enters in this order: One spouse stands with Officiant at Center, North Gate attendant, South Gate attendant, West Gate attendant, East Gate attendant, other spouse (with or without escort). Each enters, makes a full circle, and then takes their place.
- WELCOME ~ The Officiant addresses the assembly. "Beloved Friends and Family, we have come together this evening to witness the sacred profession of Love and Will between NAME and NAME. This act of Magic is a custom from time immemorial, and we are blessed to witness this declaration of matrimony and offer our blessings on the union of these two Souls."
- CHALLENGES AND BLESSINGS AT THE GATES ~ The Officiant says, "NAME and NAME have chosen faithful companions to stand with them on this day to offer challenges, blessings, and talismans as a tribute to their love and commitment to each other. Let us all stand witness to this alchemical union of minds, hearts, bodies, and lives."

North Gate asks: "Marriage is a union of minds. Do you choose to KNOW each

other deeply?" Couple each respond: "I KNOW." North Gate passes incense smoke over the couple and picks up the Staff and says: "With this Staff, I bless you with the shared intellect to overcome obstacles and the wit to defend each other from all foes." Couple respond: "So Mote it Be!"

South Gate asks: "Marriage is a union of lives. Do you choose to speak truthfully to each other in all things?" Couple each respond: "I SPEAK." South Gate offers the couple a bite of bread, then offers them the Coin saying: "With this Coin, I bless you with the sharing of material and social wealth and the ability to build a life together." Couple respond: "So Mote it Be!"

West Gate asks: "Marriage is a union of hearts. Do you DARE to be linked together through times of celebration and also of sorrow?" Couple each respond: "I DARE." West Gate sprinkles Couple with water from the cup, then offers the Cup saying: "With this Cup, I bless you with joy and also with the healing balm that deep partnership offers." Couple respond: "So Mote it Be!"

East Gate asks: "Marriage is a union of passions. WILL you choose daily to commit to each other?" Couple each respond: "I WILL." East Gate says: "With this Blade, I bless you in the forging of your goals and the manifestation of your Will." Couple respond: "So Mote it Be!"

- HANDS-FASTED ~ The Officiant says, "It is a custom among us to signify the joining of lives, minds, passions, and hearts by the symbolic joining of hands. Take the right hand of your Beloved." The couple joins right hands and Officiant ties the cord. "This is what is meant by 'tying the knot.'"
- VOWS ~ Officiant says, "NAME and NAME, you have answered the challenges and accepted the blessings. We now look to you, that you may speak your personal vows to your Beloved, and accept theirs in return." The couple takes turns speaking their personal vows. Officiant says, "These are your promises to each other, and we here stand witness."
- RINGS ~ The Officiant says, "The rings you exchange represent the magick of the circle. They act as a reminder of your Love and Will. Place the ring you have chosen for your Beloved upon their left hand, signifying the commitment you have made to each other."
- KISS ~ Officiant says, "I invite you to seal your vows and consummate your blessings with a kiss." The couple kisses. Officiant says: "And so it is - today and all days to come!"

- PRESENTATION OF THE COUPLE ~ Officiant says, "We have all stood witness to this act of Magic - this bonding under the mighty forces of Will and Love. May we all support you and celebrate with you - today and all days to come." Couple turn to face the guests. Officiant says, "Friends and Family, I present to you, Name and Name, fs the [Last Names]!" (much cheering)

HOUSLE & RECESSIONAL (Couple exits to Feast, followed by bridal party, officiant, and then guests)

Handparting Ritual

MATERIALS

MATERIALS

- Stang, candle, lighter
- Cauldron, water
- Anvil, hammer
- Three knives (red, black, white)
- Bread, lipped dish or bowl
- Red wine, cup
- Incense, holder, charcoal
- Handfasting Cord
- Rings
- Lanterns/Torches for each Quarter/Gate
- North: incense and feather for each individual; South: salt and coin for each individual; West: Cup of water with cedar asperger and holey stones for each individual; East: candles for each individual
- Two small boxes

RAISE THE STANG

LAY THE COMPASS

WORKING

- PROCESSIONAL ~ The couple enters together with attendants for the Gates following them. Each enters, makes a full circle, and then takes their place.
- WELCOME ~ The Officiant addresses the assembly. "Beloved Friends and Family, we have come together this evening to witness and support the dissolution of the union between NAME and NAME. This is an act of Magick — through Love and Will — between these two Souls. We offer them both blessings as they uncouple and lead separate lives."
- CHALLENGES AND BLESSINGS AT THE GATES ~ The Officiant says, "NAME and NAME have chosen faithful companions to stand with them on this day to offer challenges, blessings, and talismans as a tribute to the bond they shared and desire to walk separate paths. Let us all stand witness to this declaration."

North Gate asks: "Marriage is a union of minds. Do you choose to separate from each other's thoughts and deepest confidences?" Individuals each respond: "I choose to know myself." North Gate passes incense smoke over the couple and picks up the two feathers and says: "With these feathers, I bless each of you with hard-earned wisdom and clarity of thought." Individuals respond: "So Mote it Be!"

South Gate asks: "Marriage is a union of lives. Do you choose to keep silent and forfeit your voice and vote in each other's choices?" Individuals each respond: "I choose my own counsel." South Gate offers the couple a grain of salt, then offers them each the Coins saying: "With these Coins, I bless each of you with new potential and individual fortune." Individuals respond: "So Mote it Be!"

West Gate asks: "Marriage is a union of hearts. Do you choose to experience your joys and sorrows separately?" Individuals each respond: "I choose my own heart." West Gate sprinkles individuals with water from the cup, then offers the two Holey Stones saying: "With these Hagstones, I bless you each with rebirth, cleansing, and self-soothing." Individuals respond: "So Mote it Be!"

East Gate asks: "Marriage is a union of passions. WILL you remove your commitment to each other?" Individuals each respond: "I WILL." East Gate says: "With these lights, I bless you in the manifestation of your Wills." Individuals respond: "So Mote it Be!"

- HANDS-PARTED ~ The Officiant says, "Your lives, minds, passions, and hearts were joined by invisible threads, and your hands were bound together in symbolic union. Those hands are now separate, and the cord must be cut." The individuals grasp the cord and Officiant cuts it. "This severing is deep, but we strive for a clean cut." Each individual places their portion of cord in the fire.
- FAREWELLS ~ Officiant says, "NAME and NAME, you have answered the challenges and accepted the blessings as you embark on separate lives. We now look to you, that you may speak a farewell and blessing to the Stranger who was your Spouse, and accept theirs in return." The individuals take turns speaking. Officiant says, "These are your farewells to each other, and we here stand witness."
- RINGS ~ The Officiant says, "The rings you exchanged represented the magick of the circle. They acted as a reminder of your Love and Will. Returning them now to each other is also an act of Love and Will." Individuals remove their rings and give them back to the other.
- BALM ~ Officiant says, "We have witnessed a cutting of ties, a returning of gifts and promises, and many blessings on these two individuals. These conscious divisions are painful, and we offer balm and succor to the raw and ragged places

in each of you." The Officiant anoints each individual's brow, heart, belly, and right hand. Officiant says: "So Mote it Be!"

- PRESENTATION OF THE INDIVIDUALS ~ Officiant says, "We have all stood witness to this act of Magic - this dissolution under the mighty forces of Will and Love. May we all support you both and love you both - today and all days to come." Individuals turn to face the guests. Officiant says, "Friends and Family, I present to you, Full Name and Full Name!" Individuals take separate places in the Compass.

HOUSLE

NOTE: It is preferred that both partners choose to be present to undo the magick of matrimony and cut these links together. However, if that is not possible, this ritual can easily be adapted to fit a single partner.

Wisdom Ritual

MATERIALS

- Stang, candle, lighter
- Cauldron, water
- Anvil, hammer
- Three knives (red, black, white)
- Bread, lipped dish or bowl
- Red wine, cup
- Incense, holder, charcoal
- Red candle (taper, pillar, or floating)
- Cloak
- Staff
- Glass Orb
- High Seat (throne, chair, place of honor)

RAISE THE STANG

LAY THE COMPASS

WORKING

- PRESENTING THE WISE ONE ~ The Wise One stands as the Officiant announces: "Today, we celebrate and honor [Name], whose wisdom and experience have marked them as an Elder among us!" (Everyone cheers.)
- CLOAK ~ The Officiant drapes the Cloak over the shoulders of the Wise One. "Wisdom is often veiled. Wisdom is a shield and a comfort. Wisdom is a mantle of responsibility and honor."
- STAFF ~ The Officiant hands the Staff to the Wise One, who holds it in their right. "Wisdom is a support. Wisdom is a tool. Wisdom is a weapon."
- GLASS ORB ~ The Officiant places the Glass Orb into the left hand of the Wise One. "Wisdom is a clarity. Wisdom is foresight. Wisdom is a dominion."
- HIGH SEAT ~ The Officiant leads the Elder to the High Seat. Before the Elder sits, the Officiant says, "By this robe, this scepter, and this orb, we recognize and honor you as monarch among us — one who rules their own life and domain through Wisdom. We honor you as an Elder of our People — a counselor and regent. Take, now, this place of pride and receive our thanks." The Wise One sits in the throne/chair.
- PRESENTATION OF GIFTS AND ADVICE ~ The Officiant invites the assembled

community to offer their gifts (which includes their service, blessings, and thanks — only other Wise Ones should offer wisdom about this stage of life) to the Wise One. Everyone is given the opportunity to speak, if they choose.

• RED AND WHITE ROSES ~ The Officiant presents the Wise One with the red and white roses (which can be fashioned as a talisman to be worn or carried, or as a talisman to reside on the Elder's altar). "Red and White Roses have many meanings among the Wise. One set of those meanings is connected to the Veiled Queen and the Naked Queen. There is much Wisdom in the Mysteries that run the road between these two. I give you this emblem, which is blazoned on that wagon, to contemplate as you continue on your journey, along with my blessings and the blessings of our Godds."

HOUSLE

Crossing Ritual

MATERIALS

- Stang, candle, lighter
- Cauldron, water
- Anvil, hammer
- Three knives (red, black, white)
- Bread, lipped dish or bowl
- Red wine, cup
- Incense, holder, charcoal
- Kuthun (inheritance)
- Deceased Witch's Cords
- Journals of the Deceased
- Fire/firepit
- Coins, small box/chest
- Cups and drinks

RAISE THE STANG

LAY THE COMPASS

WORKING

- FAREWELLS ~ The Officiant addresses assembled celebrants. "Beloved family and friends, we have come together today to join in both mourning and celebration. We mourn our loss of [Decedent] while celebrating th life they lived among us. I invite any who are so moved to speak their farewells and give voice to their grief." All who wish to speak are given leave to do so.

- CUTTING THE CORDS ~ The Officiant holds up the Cords worn by the Witch. "These Cords have signified the promises, connections, and Mysteries explored by our Sibling. By cutting them, we freely release our Beloved to continue on their journey through the Universe."

- BURNING THE BOOK ~ The Officiant instructs a designee from the kin of the Deceased to bring forward the journal(s). "As a Witch, the records of our Witching are private and personal. In times past, books like these were worth our lives. In deepest respect for our Beloved, we take these private accounts out of the reach of the Living." The designee throws the book(s) into the flames.

•   Kuthun ~ The Officiant brings forward any magickal items that are being passed along to inheritors. "[Name] has noted that these sacred tools should pass into the care of some specific Family members." The Officiant passes along the tool/jewel along with any special notes about its significance.

•   Coins for the Crossing ~ "It has been three (or more) days since our Beloved left this life. The Souls often linger during this time of transition, but they cross fully to the other-side around now. It is an ancient custom to provision the Dead for this journey. Come and place your coins in this box, which represents the tomb and will be buried to aid [Name] on their journey." The box should be open on the altar next to a photo of the Deceased. An attendant can offer coins to anyone who didn't bring one.

•   TOASTS TO LIFE AND DEATH ~ "Mourning and grief are a natural part Death, but we have also come to celebrate the Life of our friend. We choose to remember the joys, the love, and the vitality that they imparted during their time among us. Let us raise a cup and share our stories as a testament to a life well and fully lived." Stories are shared freely. When they come to a natural stopping place, invite the assembly to remain after the Housle for more food, drinks, and sharing.

HOUSLE

Coven Leadership

Under the Rose

To work "Under the Rose" means to work in secrecy, taken from the Latin *subrosa*. Most modern covens assume a level of secrecy for some or all of their meetings and rituals and hold both their membership and meeting place confidential as a matter of precaution. This clandestine air has a two-fold purpose. One is a simple safety measure. The other is an act of guardianship relative to the Mysteries.

While we are no longer hunted openly in Europe, North America, or Australia, it is still not considered entirely safe to be a Witch throughout most of the world (even in places where it is no longer a criminal act). For this reason, the Ardanes (or "laws") of many groups forbid revealing the name of another Witch or the location of the covenstead to a cowan.

Preserving the Mysteries of the Craft (or of the Gods) is another reason for working *subrosa*. Robert Cochrane once said, *"No genuine esoteric truth can be written down or put within an intellectual framework of thought. The truths involved are to be participated in during comprehension of the soul."* This is what is meant by Mystery.

It is said that Eros gave Harpocrates (the Egyptian God of secrets) the rose with which Harpocrates became associated in honor of Eros' own mother Aphrodite. Aphrodite had a long association with the rose — and many delicious (and dangerous) secrets to keep. She kept her own and those of others in many myths.

A rose suspended from a chamber ceiling in the Middle Ages pledged all to secrecy. The Rosicrucians (Order of the Rosy Cross) were a secret society. Many confessionals are decorated with carved roses to reinforce the idea of secrecy.

The Black and White Goddesses of the Craft are both symbolized by the rose, reminding us of the Mystery of life-in-death and death-in-life. — a secret which must be experienced to be understood.

Coven Caer Sidhe - Guidance

Coven Caer Sidhe is the "Home Coven" of the Spiral Castle Clannad. It was the first Coven formed within this Tradition by its original founders, and it is the spiritual home of the Clannad's current Regent.

The policies and procedures of the Home Coven serve as a map or template that other Covens within the Tradition might use to create their own Charters. Each Coven, though, has a unique personality, and their structure and leadership should reflect themselves rather than being a mirror image of any other group.

Norms & Expectations
Coven Caer Sidhe

Coven Caer Sidhe is an egalitarian gathering of like-minded Witches who are connected through the bonds of Family. We honor and recognize the wisdom and experience of the Elders among us and look to them for teaching and counsel.

Participation & Behavior — All persons present are expected to contribute their intellect, skills, care, and labor in meaningful and constructive ways. We complete the tasks for which we volunteer to the best of our ability, and we are accountable to each other for the success of all of our endeavors. All active Coveners are expected to attend the classes, rituals, and meetings of their Degree, if they are reasonably able, and also to complete assignments.

Communication — All members of our Coven communicate as clearly and compassionately as possible, both in-person and via electronic means. Honesty is a deeply held value, though we temper it with our genuine love for each other. Our spaces are "safe spaces," in which members are free to share difficult thoughts, ideas, and experiences without judgment or retalia-tion. They are also "brave spaces" where we understand that challenging assumptions and rationale is a path to personal growth.

Privacy — The names, addresses, professions, family members, likenesses, and experiences of our Siblings are held sacred and are not shared with those outside our Coven, except with the express consent of that Sibling.

Shared Resources — All members are asked to contribute to the resources of the Coven, with-in their means to do so. Financial obligations for supplies will be split between those present, with each "pitching in" what is needed for rituals. Personal tools may be volunteered for group use, either long-term or for a single ritual. Tools may also be purchased or donated for permanent group use. In the event of disbanding of the Coven, tools and supplies will be re-turned to their contributors, if reasonably possible. Any monies collected will be divided evenly among active members. In the case of an individual leaving the Coven, they are enti-tled to reclaim any tool which they had offered (but not _donated_) for group use, so long as they make that claim within three months of their last attendance. *Copyright Asteria Books 2022*

Norms & Expectations, cont.
Coven Caer Sidhe

Set-Up/Clean-Up – The Covenstead shall be kept reasonably clean and tidy by the home-holder so that Coveners are not expected to clean-up or deal with debris, clutter, and soil prior to meetings, classes, or rituals. All Coveners will assist with the set-up of ritual space, according to their physical ability. Any messes that are made as part of the Coven's gathering (including dishes dirtied, supplies and tools displaced, and furniture moved) shall be cleaned, tidied, and restored to their proper places. All Coveners will take part in the clean-up, as well.

Entheogens – Coveners should not be under the influence of any entheogens (alcohol, drugs, psychoactive herbs/fungi, etc) unless such sacraments are appropriate to the ritual or work being undertaken. In these cases, entheogenic use will be explicitly discussed and plans will be made regarding transportation and lodging. (Pain- and anxiety-management concerns should be addressed with the Elders, privately.)

Corrective Measures – Coveners who struggle to meet these expectations will be privately corrected by an Elder and give the opportunity to come into alignment with the Coven. Re-peated abuses or inability to comply could result in a hiatus or leave-taking.

Leadership
Coven Caer Sidhe

Within Coven Caer Sidhe, facilitation of rituals, classes, and meetings is delegated among the Witches active and present. All members of Red Cord and above are encouraged to take on a facilitation role.

Council of Elders — All active Queens, Devils, and Consorts of the Coven are *de facto* Elders, and are members of the Council of Elders. Together, this group guides the policy-making of the Coven and offers advice and mentorship to all Coveners. The Elders rotate the teaching and meeting duties, and all provide Pastoral Care according to their availability and desire.

All facilitation roles within Coven Caer Sidhe are self-selected. The terms are for one calendar year, with a mentoring/transition period of two months (from Samhain to New Year). Not all roles are required to be filled, and it is possible for one Covener to hold two roles. We are also open to adding roles, as needs arise.

The primary roles that are needed within this Coven are:

Scribe — takes detailed notes regarding business issues; concerns and ideas mentioned at meetings and classes; and keeps the minutes of all official gatherings

Pursewarden — provides financial reports at meetings; suggests a budget; maintains account-ing of dues, donations, and expenses

Watcher — provides security at public gatherings and rituals; acts as "vibeswatcher" for all private meetings

Lorekeeper — maintains the Coven scrapbook and/or storybook

Ranger — leads set-up and clean-up activities; delegates tasks as needed within this area; ensures that Covenstead and other gathering places are left better than we found them

Herald — maintains the Coven website; edits Coven publications

Membership
Coven Caer Sidhe

The members of Coven Caer Sidhe are Family with bonds of blood, love, and trust. There is grief and loss when one of our Witches leaves this Family. As such, we take the acceptance of new members very seriously.

Screening and acceptance of new members — Prospective members are first invited to interact with Elders and/or other Coveners in a public venue. We take this opportunity to ask questions, offer access to public materials (like the Coven website/blog), and get to know the person over the course of 1 to 3 months. If all Coveners are in agreement, we invite the pro-spective member to attend classes and rituals with us. They should attend at least two of each before requesting Greening. Greening is a period of orientation that can last another 1 to 3 months. During this time, the Green Cord is given and the new person is included in classes and rituals. If they choose to proceed, they will request Adoption (in writing), and the current active Coveners will come to a consensus to either approve or deny this request. Before Adoption into the Coven, the new Witch should have purchased their own copy of RTA Year 1: Foun-dations and have either a black or white robe with hood or veil (according to the season).

Hiatus/sabbatical of members — It is understood that we all experience cycles during our studies and practice. When a cycle of rest and/or isolation is needed, a Covener need only make their intention known to the Coven's Elders. Hiatus/Sabbatical is taken in quarter-turns of the Year Wheel, with Coveners returning to full participation at Samhain, Beltaine, Lammas, and Imbolc. It is recommended that a Covener not take more than two consecutive "turns" away from Coven life. In cases where Coveners are away for more than 6 consecutive months, the Coven must reach consensus regarding the inactive Covener's re-integration into Coven practice.

Active/inactive members — All Coveners will be considered "active" if they have participated actively and consistently in class, ritual, or other official gatherings in the last month. "Inactive" members in-clude those on hiatus, those with recently lapsed attendance and/or participation, as well as those who have chosen to discontinue their participation or association with the Coven or who have been out of contact with the Elders for more than 6 months. All Coveners, both active and inactive, are members of the Family — bonded by blood and oath.

Decision-Making
Coven Caer Sidhe

The members of Coven Caer Sidhe are Family. As such, all Adopted members are invested with a voice in Coven decisions.

We utilize a consensus model in our decision-making and deliberations. All Adopted Witches (of active status) are included in this consensus-building.

If a situation arises in which the Council of Elders are at odds with the Coven as a whole, the Council will have the final say in the decision, and every effort will continue to be made to bring the whole Coven to a place of consensus.

We recognize that consensus-building can be a time- and energy-consuming way to run a group, but we are committed to the egalitarian principles on which we were founded.

Schedules
Coven Caer Sidhe

As a result of the relocation of some members, and also resulting from the global pandemic, Coven Caer Sidhe is in the process of restructuring its meeting schedules. This is the current schedule that is in place, though it is subject to change.

Red Cord (Foundations) Studies — The Red Cords of the Coven meet every Thursday night to work through the lessons in the Year 1 course manual, as well as to read passages from the current "Book Club" selection. If possible, they meet in person at the Covenstead. Alternatively, Coveners are able to join the class via Zoom. These classes, which include Sabbat celebrations and 4 group lunar workings, are available to all members of the Coven.

Practicum Studies — Coveners engaged in the Year 2: Practicum lessons (and those wishing to add a Specialty Area) meet on the first Friday of the month to share their progress and projects. If possible, they meet in person at the Covenstead. Alternatively, Coveners are able to join the class via Zoom. This is open to all Raised Witches, of any Admission.

Mastery Studies — Coveners engaged in the Year 3: Mastery lessons, as well as those who have been admitted to 3rd Degree, gather once per quarter to fly out, discuss the Mysteries, and perform experimental Witchery together. This gathering is open to Coveners of 2nd and 3rd Admission, only. Attendance is in-person at the Covenstead, and gatherings happen on the 2nd Friday of January, April, July, and November.

Annual Retreat — All Coveners are encouraged to attend an annual weekend camping retreat which happens close to Beltaine.

Titles and Offices

There have been many names for the roles of Coven leadership within folkloric forms of the Craft. The Spiral Castle Tradition does not dictate what names Witches might use for themselves in this or any other capacity, though there are a few titles that are easily recognizable by and among us. These include:

WITCH, PELLAR, CUNNING PERSON/FOLK — These all have slightly different meanings and contexts, but any one of them might be the preferred term for a practitioner of our Artes. These are applicable regardless of gender or level of study, although we say "Witch of the Spiral Castle" to reference a Raised Witch within SCT.

ARTISAN, BARD, CONJURER, HEALER, SEER, VOTARY, WARDEN — Within the Spiral Castle Tradition, Witches of 2nd Admission have studied and practiced a Specialty within the Craft, and they are recognized among us as being at least one of these.

QUEEN, DEVIL, CONSORT — Witches of 3rd Admission are invested with the Virtue of one of our Great Powers and are acknowledged via their relationship to that Power. They may also be a leader of a Coven, or one of the Elders of a Coven.

MAGISTER OF THE LINEAGE — A Queen, Devil, or Consort who was initiated within the founding line (ie, by Laurelei or someone else in her lineage) might additionally use this term. The Grand Coven is the full body of all active Magisters.

MAID, SQUIRE, JACK, VERDOLET, BLACK ROD, PAGE — In Covens with a hierarchical structure, rather than an egalitarian structure, these titles are sometimes given to the understudy(ies) to the leader(s). They facilitate in the absence of the leader(s), and are usu-ally tasked with making sure the people of the Coven know when and where the meeting will take place. Some groups specify that a Witch of a certain degree holds this office. There may be two or three people holding titles such as these, and all should be fully Raised Witches.

REGENT - This title is worn by the Elder who serves as the Head of the Clannad.

Laurelei Black

Dedication in Clan of the Laughing Dragon—Aug. 1999

      by Lady R-M of Dragon Heart Coven

1st Degree in Clan of the Laughing Dragon—Aug. 2000

      as BmTQ

      by Lady R-M of Dragon Heart Coven

2nd Degree in Clan of the Laughing Dragon—Jan. 2002

      by Lady R-M of Dragon Heart Coven

3rd Degree in Clan of the Laughing Dragon — Jan. 2005

      as Lady DnM

      by Lady R-M of Dragon Heart Coven

Foundation of Dragon's Eye Coven — May 2005

Initiation into and Foundation of Spiral Castle Tradition and Coven Caer Sidhe— Jan 2009

      as RTQ alongside LNK

Laurelei is one of the two Founding Mothers of the Spiral castle Tradition, and she currently holds the post of Regent for the Clannad. No lineage documents exist for her initiator, Lady R-M, who studied through 3rd Degree with (what was later revealed as) a "Black Gard" coven in Berkley, CA; up to 1st Degree with one of the daughter covens of the Roebuck; and through 7th Degree with two Welsh Druids.

Laurelei is on the Council of Elders for the "home coven" of the Clannad — Coven Caer Sidhe.

Regalia

Regalia and Gifts

These are the garments, jewels, and other markers worn by Witches of the Spiral Castle Tradition during ritual. A Witch is not compelled to wear anything beyond their robes and cords, unless moved by custom and desire.

GREENING

- Green Cord

ADOPTION

- Red Cord
- Black, hooded Robe
- White, hooded Robe
- Copper Cuff (gifted)
- Black Cloak

Note: Hoods/Veils may be separate from Robes

RAISING

- Triple Cords (Black and White added to Red)
- Amber, Jet, Bone necklace (gifted)
- 3 Knives — on ring belt or Cords
- Witch's Mark — tattoo on ring or index finger (stang or 3 dots)

2ND ADMISSION

- Service Cords — hanging from Triples
- Bone Ring (gifted)
- Crane Bag — on ring belt

QUEEN, DEVIL, CONSORT

- Garter Cords
- Plain, Crescent, or Horned Crown (gifted)
- Red Cloak

ALL

- Seasonal Ladders
- Ritual Talismans
- Star-Stone Ring (any tektites — moldavite, obsidian, Lybian desert glass, etc.)

The Witch Jewels

I have seen the Witch Jewels sometimes referred to as "Rings of Power" — though this can be a misleading (or at least confusing term), since "Ring of Power" is also used to describe the Witch's Compass or the often very complex Circles and inscriptions of the Ceremonial Magician. However, all the Jewels encircle the body and are imbued with Power, so the play on words is clever.

Not every Tradition emphasizes their use or teaches the lore behind all of these Jewels, but many Witches are instinctively drawn to them nonetheless.

The Seven Jewels (which are worn by all genders) include the Necklace, the Pendant, the Bracelet, the Finger Ring, the Girdle/Cord, the Crown, and the Garter.

Necklace — Sometimes called a Circle of Stones, this piece hearkens back in some ways to Freya's *Brisingamen* and Aphrodite's golden *zonai*. Though it is often made of amber and jet (sometimes with bone added, thereby incorporating all three sacred colors of red, black, and white), it is not entirely uncommon for it to be made of acorns (linking it to skulls, life/death, resurrection lore as well as to the Goddesses Macha and Diana, though for different reasons — as well as to the Druids and the woodland Gods and their wisdom).

Pendant — Often used for purposes of fascination and to both cast and turn away the Evil Eye, this jewel is usually made of a semi-precious stone that is dear to the Witch.

Bracelet — Copper or silver cuffs worn on the left wrist and marked with the magical name of the bearer (in Theban or another runic script), along with other mystical symbols, identify the Witch to others, stealthily.

Finger Ring — For some, this is another personal tool of fascination and magic, while some groups use it as a gift upon admission or elevation to a certain rank or degree. Band and stone materials are chosen based on personal or group symbolism. For instance, in the Spiral Castle (AFW) Tradition, the Bone Ring is given at 2nd Admission — symbolizing a Red Soul (aka bone-deep, ancestral) connection to the Craft and each other.

Girdle Cord — The (often-braided) Witch's ladder-style girdle cord serves multiple functions. As a "Jewel," it is a belt that is worn in ritual and spellcasting. But it can also act as a tool to restrict blood-flow, a devotional tool, and a tool for marking the ritual space.

Garter — Within many covens, only Witches of a certain degree wear a garter. In others, all do, but markings embroidered upon the garter indicate rank/degree. It is usually worn above the left knee. Colors and materials vary by group.

Crown — Most groups reserve the crown for either coven leaders or ritual leaders. Some rituals also have crowns or head-wear that is specific to the rite.

Amber, Jet, and Bone

Amber, jet, and bone (which is also called ivory) have been prized jewelry-making components since Antiquity — and especially so by shamans and magic-workers. All three are the result of living organisms, which results in a different sort of energetic experience during ritual use as compared to stones, woods, shells, and metals. Additionally, amber and jet (when rubbed vigorously) produce a natural negative charge, attracting positive ions to it. Finally, these three components collectively represent the three sacred colors of the Celts (and the Craft) — red, black, and white.

Amber

Amber is fossilized tree resin that has been a prized component in jewelry and adornments since the Neolithic era. Its most common color variants range from light yellow to a golden orange-brown, but amber can be almost white in its paleness and nearly black in its sable depths. There are also variations that are cherry red, green, and even blue. Amber gives a soothing, light energy that is both calming and energizing. It can help manifest desires and heighten the intellect, clarity of thought, and wisdom.

Jet

Jet is fossilized and pressurized wood. Like amber, it is warm to the touch (unlike stones and glass, which is useful in distinguishing jet from the black stones many jewelry dealers try to sell under this name). Jet has been found in burial sites as far back at 17,000 BCE, and it was attested in Roman magical records as being capable of averting the "evil eye." It is a powerfully protective stone against all negativity, often crumbling and deteriorating as an alert of the presence of powerful dark forces (such as depression, abuse, and spiritual attack). Jet draws negativity out of the wearer and also aids in alertness and problem-solving.

Bone

Bone is an important material in shamanic ornamentation. The teeth and bones of both humans and every animal imaginable have been found at ancient gravesites in jewelry and ceremonial tools of rulers and priests. Like amber and jet, bone was once a vessel of life, connecting it to the soul itself. American Folkloric Witches wear a bone rose ring to symbolize adoption in the Family of the Craft and the nature of working *subrosa* within the coven. Witch garlands (akin to a rosary, also called a ladder) are made of amber, jet, and snake bone — connecting to the serpent energy of the spine.

The Cords

Cords are seen in both Wiccan and Trad Craft practice.

In Robert Cochrane's writing "On Cords," he describes the use of both devotional and magical cords:

"When worked up properly they should contain many different parts--herbs, feathers and impedimenta of the particular harm. They are generally referred to in the trade as "ladders," or in some cases as "garlands," and have much the same meaning as the three crosses. That is they can contain three blessings, three curses, or three wishes. A witch also possesses a devotional ladder, by which she may climb to meditational heights, knotted to similar pattern as the Catholic rosary."

Above, Cochrane talks first about using the cord for magical operations.

The second use of cords is that of the devotional ladder. While many of us will make and use multiple devotional ladders for trance and meditation work related to a variety of focal objects, a great many Witches receive their first ladder as a cord (or set of braided cords) that marks their admission to a coven.

The cords are usually a length of silk or wool (or other natural fiber) rope, braided yarn, or upholstery cord, whose thickness, length and color vary by tradition. They are versatile, as they are used for cinching ritual robes, indicating rank or degree, measuring the circle, and sometimes for binding blood flow in certain circumstances. When used to control blood flow, they may also be called the *cingulum.*

Cords used as a cingulum help alter consciousness, and they are often employed in initiation rites. There are a few different ways to tie the cords to act in this capacity, but the most common is shown here. However they are used, a cingulum should be administered with care (and training) to avoid causing damage or harm.

Cords can also be used as a meditational or trance tool in much the same way as a Catholic rosary. Because they are usually braided and knotted, often with multi-colored fibers, they bind together symbols and imagery that are important to the Witch who wears them. Meditating on a particular knot, strand, or other element of the cord will produce a focused experience on the symbol set contained therein, while working through all the knots (climbing the ladder) produces a transcendent state.

The AFW Tradition uses a specific progression of cords as markers of admission to the coven. Each length of cording that we use is made of 3 hand-braided strands of cotton yarn.

The Crown

The Crown (Coronet, Circlet, or Headdress) is another of the Jewels of the Witch that can take several styles and has sometimes been entirely abandoned by some practitioners and groups. However, there is ample evidence of its use within folkloric sources, and both mythic and historic material gives us plenty of inspiration if we are drawn to incorporating it within our ritual practice.

The illustrations above show masculine and feminine variations on "horns" — some that are supposed to be intrinsic to the bearer (such as in the case of the black-smithing Devil aided by his helpful Witch Dame); while others are embellishments, such as the up-turned "horns" of the moon born by Hecate (or her triple-horned hat, worn by another of her visages). In the Middle Ages, horned headdresses and hairstyles were very popular among ladies, and sculptural as well as painted art shows us a long history of people donning animal horns and adorning their heads with celestial emblems for spiritual and religious ceremonies.

Horns and antlers have featured most prominently, for all genders, with some cultures or time periods showing a gender preference for certain animals or emblems. Contemporarily, Wiccan crowns tend to assign horns/antlers to those who identify as masculine, with moon crowns (with up-turned points) belonging to feminine practitioners. Ancient myth and art, though, ascribe horns to several Witch Goddesses, including Ishtar, Lilith, and Hecate.

Typically, only the leaders of the coven — the Maid/Dame/Queen/High Priestess and the Magister/Devil/High Priestess — wear a Crown. It is usually seen as an emblem of office or rank. Some groups use specialized crowns or headdresses for specific Sabbats or initiatory practices, in which case, only the indicated ritual role-bearer would wear the Crown. The argument can be made, though, that flower / foliage crowns are traditional and folkloric for ALL coveners, regardless of rank.

When made for ritual, plastic and other synthetic materials should be avoided in its construction. Choose your components carefully — based on what you want activated in your energetic Crown — the seat of the White Soul (the Higher Self, the God Self.)

The Garter

The magical garter has significance dating back to prehistoric times. Cave art in eastern Spain that dates to the Paleolithic period shows a sorcerer performing in a ritual while wearing nothing but a pair of garters just below his knees.

In many traditions the garter is worn only by a Witch Queen, or Queen of the Sabbat. However, the traditional dress of Morris dancers consists of garters, usually red, and "Green Garters" is a traditional Morris Dancer tune.

In the trial record of Margaret Johnson (Lancshsire 1633) the Devil was said to wear: "a suite of black, tyed about with silke pointes (garters)." If we take the position that the "Devil" was the Magister of the coven, then we see that the garter is not the sole province of the Queen of the Sabbat, but was also worn by men.

Red garters were said to be worn by a coven's Summoner, whose job it was to advise members on meeting days and times. The red garters signified to others that s/he was genuine. Gerald Gardner used the red garters as a plot device to this effect in his novel about the witch cult, <u>High Magic's Aid</u>.

In some traditions the garter is prepared with green leather or velvet with a lining made of blue silk. In others the garter is made of red leather or snakeskin. There is usually one large, silver or gold buckle on the garter, representing the Queen's own coven, with additional, smaller silver buckles for each of the other covens under her authority. The garter is worn on the left leg, just above the knee. It may be fastened with the large buckle or with silk ribbons.

Pennethorne Hughes states that when a tortured witch was likely to reveal others, he or she may be murdered in jail by the other witches to avoid further arrests and tortures. To prove that the murder had been done under those circumstances, a garter would be left tied loosely around the victim's throat.

The Witch Garter is found in English history as being linked to the creation of the Order of the Garter. The most widespread story states that the countess of Salisbury was dancing with King Edward III at a court function. As they danced, the countess's garter fell to the ground. The king picked it up and, to save her embarrassment, put it on his own leg with the words, "Honi soit qui mal y pense" (Shame be to him who thinks evil of it.") He went on to found the Order of the Garter, with that phrase as its slogan. The precise date for the founding of the order is not known, since the records have been destroyed, but it is thought to be 1348.

Margaret Alice Murray mentions that it took more than a dropped garter to embarrass a lady in the 14th century, even a lady of the court. However, if the garter dropped was a ritual one, demonstrating that its owner was in fact a leader of the Old Religion, then there would be very real embarrassment, particularly since there were high personages of the Christian Church in attendance at the event. Edward's action, then, was incredibly smart thinking, for in placing the garter on his own leg, he not only saved face for the countess, but also proclaimed himself prepared to be a leader of the Pagan population as well as the Christian. This was a clever move taking into account that a large portion of his subjects were still Pagan at that point in time.

The Robe, Cloak & Hood

There is wide disparity within Craft practice regarding what is required or preferred in regard to vestments. Two of the most vocal and published early proponents of Craft — Gardner (representing Wicca) and Cochrane (representing Traditional Craft) — took very different stances on this.

Gardner advocated for practitioners to be *skyclad* (nude) in their rites, and this is often still the norm in Gardnerian and Alexandrian covens, though some derivations have adopted the use of Tau or T-shaped robes from Ceremonial practice.

The great majority of Craft practitioners wear some form of robe, however. They may use ritual nudity for certain types of magic, but they typically wear special ritual robes. Traditional Crafters are more likely than not to have robes — and even cloaks.

These robes can vary in styles by Tradition, but many groups have specifications regarding the cut, length, fibers (whether synthetics are allowed, for example), colors, etc.

A ritual robe has symbolic connections to the physical body of the practitioner, but a Tradition may also use it to symbolize other metaphysical concepts, as well. While the cloak (an outer garment that is chosen for warmth) may or may not be optional, a black hooded robe can be seen as a woven symbol of the work the WitchMother. It is deeply protective.

Some groups change the color of the robe (or another vestment, like a tabard or sash) throughout the year to indicate change of season. Others use color or style of robe to indicate degree, rank, or office within the group.

Within the Spiral Castle (AFW) Tradition, our members wear either white or black garments of their choosing (depending on the season), so long as they are clean and satisfy their personal sense of Arte. We require a black cloak and a separate deep black hood for specific ritual use.

Having a hood as a separate garment allows for covering the entire head and face during deeply meditative states and certain ritual practices, like hoodwinking.

Practical Craft

Sabbat Wine

"Entheogen" is a Greek-derived word that means "generating the divine within." An entheogen, therefore, is a psychoactive substance that is used in a religious, spiritual or shamanic context. Traditional Witches have used entheogens of several types for centuries, as recorded in the lore of mythology, in the records of the trials and persecutions, and in the regional indigenous shamanic practices that have been assimilated into the Craft in various locales. Among the most commonly used and widely known entheogens in European and American Witchcraft practice are Sabbat Wine and Flying Ointment.

SABBAT WINE

Wine, just as it is, constitutes a powerful entheogen. The Dying and Resurrected God is embodied in the wine in the form of Dionysos -- and in Jesus, for that matter, whose symbolism and mythology associates him with the wine. Dionysos, though, is the "Twice Born" God of the Vine, and his cup is the offering of ecstasy and madness. "I am the vine," he says, and he offers insight into death and rebirth, despair and joy.

Many Witches drink wine -- either a little or a lot -- as a part of their Sabbat rites no matter what. In American Folkloric Witchcraft, we include Sabbat Wine for two separate and distinct purposes -- and the wine is different depending on that purpose.

If we are celebrating the Housle as we usually do within the regular course of ritual, we will sacrifice a cup of red wine. It is the shed blood of the Red Meal that is the Housle. In this instance, we don't add anything to the wine because we don't need any additional entheogenic effect.

If, however, we are doing trance work, flying out, seething, or otherwise seeking an altered state of consciousness, we might prepare our special Sabbat Wine (vinum sabbati). We also prepare this Sabbat Wine for initiations. The vinum sabbati is a sweet red wine in which mugwort and lemongrass have been mulled. After straining the herbs, we add honey to sweeten the mix and cut the bitterness of the mugwort. Both mugwort and lemongrass have gentle psychoactive properties.

It's interesting to note that the term "vinum sabbati" has actually been associated with flying ointment, or the witches' salve, which is the other major entheogen of witchcraft. In fact, Nigel Jackson said flying ointment was "the black wine of owls."

Sabbat Wine

Sabbat Wine Lore

Sabbat Wine is the name of a group of entheogens used by Witches to induce an ecstatic or altered state during rituals. Flying Ointment is sometimes called Sabbat Wine, although many modern Witches make a mulled wine that is sometimes drunk in addition to applying Flying Ointment. This Sabbat Wine blend is suitable for occasional use, such as initiations or special oracle rituals. For more frequent consumption, consider replacing the mugwort with another herb, as it can build up in your liver if drunk too often.

Formula Recipe

2 parts Mugwort

1 part Lemongrass

Steep 1 tsp of the above mixture in 1 cup of warmed sweet red wine. Add raw, local honey to taste.

Formula Uses

The mugwort and lemongrass blend is a very effective, albeit bitter, tea. Blade & Broom Botanica has sold this mix as "Sabbat Night Tea." The bitterness of the herbs works well with a particularly sweet red wine and a little local honey.

Drink a cup or two of the Sabbat Wine before flying out, performing possessory rituals, or holding initiations.

Non-Toxic Flying Ointment

Flying Ointment Lore

Flying ointment is one of the traditional potions of witchcraft. It is the salve used by Witches to induce hallucinations and astral journeying (their method of "flying" to Sabbat). Unfortunately, the recipes for flying ointment in the old grimoires are full of extremely poisonous herbal ingredients. In order to achieve anything but the mildest of psychic "nudges" from those plants, you must literally risk death. This (mostly) non-toxic flying ointment is a witch salve with KICK. It is not a subtle brew! Infused with eight herbs, each of which is known for its psychic/journeying properties, this ointment will "knock you into next Tuesday."

Formula Recipe

4 ounces Olive Oil

1 ounce Beeswax, grated

1 ounce Honey, raw

2 tablespoons Mugwort

2 tablespoons Cinquefoil

2 tablespoons Lemongrass

1 tablespoon Rue

1 tablespoon Dittany of Crete

1 tablespoon Balm of Gilead

1 tablespoon Wormwood

1 tablespoon Calamus root

2 drops Clary Sage essential oil (add after the mixture has been strained)

Formula Uses

Follow the instructions for ointment preparation in the Herbal Crafting section. Pour the salve into airtight containers and store in a cool, dark place. To use, take a three-finger scoop and rub it on until the skin is warm. Apply it to pulse points such as the neck, the wrists, the underarms, the inner thighs & the feet. The scent is intoxicating and smells different on the skin than in the jar. Give it about 15 minutes and begin focusing on 'flying out.' It works well just before bedtime to produce lucid dreams, and (as it was designed) it's ideal for an aid to astral travel, especially visions of flying out on a riding pole. Guided meditations benefit favorably from the use of a smaller dose. It combines well with other entheogens also. We've used it with excellent results with Sabbat wine.

Magical Tools

Personal and Coven Tools

No tools are mandatory within the Spiral Castle Tradition, per se. However, we find these pieces most aligned with our work and encourage individuals and Covens to have and use them, as they choose. Some are naturally acquired and explored during different stages of study, in the period following elevation or admission to that Degree.

AFTER GREENING

- No tools required

AFTER ADOPTION

- Stang
- 3 Knives — Athame, Kerfane, Shelg
- Cauldron
- Small anvil
- Ancestor skull
- 3 Divination tools
- Scrying mirror

AFTER RAISING

- Stone Bowl
- Mazey Stone
- Specialty Area tool(s)
- One of the other Castle Treasures — Glass Orb, Golden Lantern, Silver Cup

AFTER 2ND ADMISSION

- Gandreid (Broom, Staff, Stang)
- Personal Fetich
- Remaining Castle Treasures and Weapons, as desired
- Skull w/ Bones

COVEN

- Dolly
- Sword
- Broom
- Stang
- Cauldron
- Anvil & Hammer
- Housle Bowl
- Censer
- Treasures — Stone Bowl, Glass Orb, Silver Grail, Gold Lantern
- Weapons — Sword, Staff, Shield, Helm
- Spirit Ally symbols

The Gandreid

Gandreið is an Old Norse term that has significant implications for the modern Craft practitioner. It translates most closely to "stick ride" or "spirit ride," and most people take this to mean the Broom or possibly the Stang, as depicted in medieval woodcuts. In the physical sense, it has certainly been applied to a number of "magic sticks" (including the wand and staff throughout Norse, Germanic, and Anglo-Saxon magical practice). Within this particular association, special focus has been made on the tool's use as an implement of spirit-flight — often being interwoven with seething and trancework.

Gandreið is a compound word. *Reid* is a pretty straightforward translation to "ride." But *gandr* references several concepts — spirits, the spiritual realm, magic/ sorcery/witchcraft, monsters, riding animals, and wild animals.

Consider, then, the nursery rhyme about Mother Goose:

Old Mother Goose, when she wanted to wander

Would ride through the air on a very fine gander.

What interesting and exciting implications for the folkloric-based Witch! First, we have to remember that Mother Goose is very often associated with Frau Holda (Dame Hulda, Holle), and it is either she (or later, her male, Anglo-Saxon counterpart, Holt) who is said to lead the Wild Hunt — a flight of spirits and witches across the skies that is alternately said to bless the fields and gather the dead and dying.

Next, though, we want to consider whether Mother Goose is riding a corporeal animal familiar (with "gander" being a male goose), a non-corporeal spirit familiar who (possibly?) takes the shape of this bird, or one of the magic sticks (gandr/gandreid) mentioned above.

In folklore, there are several instances of enchanted sticks or branches acting as "horses" and "birds" to carry their bearers to desired destinations, and also of granting requests when watered with tears, blood, or given other offerings. This would seem to indicate an in-dwelling spirit — a fetch, familiar, or other tutelary spirit, perhaps.

Looking to later staff, wand, broom, and stang lore, we continue to see the threads of the gandreid — the en-spirited branch of Northern European practitioners.

The Broom

In his letters to Joe Wilson, Roy Bowers (aka, Robert Cochrane) says that the Mystery of the Broom is "spinning without motion between three elements." He also relates this Mystery to the Qabbalistic Middle Pillar and the "path to the 7 gates of perception." He is, of course, talking about the practice of trance-work and meditation -- and using a *gandreid* (the Broom, being the most common form within the Craft of the individual gandreid) in order to access ALL THAT IS. The three elements could be said to be represented in the three naturally occurring elements (earth, air, and water — fire having to be ignited by force), which are likewise represented in the traditional materials used in making the Broom (Ash handle, Birch brush, Willow binding).

The Spiral Castle (or the World Tree, if you prefer), the Stang, and the Broom share a certain transvective power with each other. (In truth, the Broom's base stick is a small Stang, as you will see soon.) What the Spiral Castle does for the entire Tradition (accesses ALL wisdom, ALL experience, ALL the realms, gates, and airts), the Stang does for the Coven, and the Broom does for the individual Witch.

The Broom (according to illustrated copies of Cochrane's letters to Wilson) is constructed from a small, forked Ash staff. Between the prongs of the fork, a sacred stone is bound. He calls the stone "balanite," but my research reveals it to be none other than basalt (common black lava stone) — which is excellent for tethering the psyche during spirit-flight.

The Broom can also be used for blessing, blasting, and cleansing magic. For blessing and blasting, carry it over the right or left shoulder, respectively — working deosil or widdershins, as appropriate. For cleansing, sweep the energetic space (above, below, and between). Cleanse the Broom's brush with saltwater after heavy spiritual cleansing work or blasting work.

Skull and Crossed Bones

The Ancestral skulls of the Coveners are placed at the base of the Stang, along with the cauldron and anvil. A pair of crossed leg bones is also placed there with a Coven skull, as well. Sometimes the Coven Skull is hung from the Stang, in which case the two crossed arrows function in a similar capacity as the crossed leg bones.

The bones are crossed when we are not doing necromantic rituals. But if we want to talk to the Dead, we open the leg bones so they make a vertical channel facing out from the skull. This opens the path of communication.

The skull and bones used for this use are from a once-living being, since these are much more effective than stone, paper mache, ceramic, or glass for purposes of communication. But, if you must make a substitution for real bone, use an alternative that feels good to you.

Avoid plastic for any tool that will carry Spirit. A Witch would do better to carve an apple into a crude skull shape and "skin" a couple of sticks to act as the bones, than use plastic ones.

Of the animal bones you might choose, medium to large mammals are best, for practical reasons. The bones are sturdier and less like to break from being held and moved. Horned/antlered animals are the most preferred, due to their association with the Witch Father.

Personal animal Allies are also great candidates for skulls and bones, as long as they're sturdy enough for this use and legal to own.

Coven Dolly

The Dolly is one of the less common bits of folkloric Craft that occasionally shows up in the writings of published Witches. As with many other folkloric pieces, the traditions that have been handed down around the Dolly can vary widely, as do the origin stories or rationales given for her existence.

The Dolly is representative of the Coven Guardian or Familiar. Witches who practice independently might still have one as a House Guardian/Familiar for the home where they live.

The "Hearth Doll" of Old Craft became the "Kitchen Witch Doll" for many Appalachian and Ozark families. These days, they are seen simply as "good luck" — with little awareness of their traditions.

In different parts of the UK, we still see the Hearth Doll (or Chimney Doll) in her place upon the hearth. Gemma Gary's Ros an Bucca Coven used to maintain a website and photo archive of tools that featured just such a doll as this. She is fully decked out with talismans, a beaded and knotted rowan berry necklace, and a hare and is provisioned with a chair, cauldron, and wee blackthorn staff. In essence, she has all the tools she needs to do the work she's been engaged to do.

The Dolly can be simple or elaborate. You can make it according to any number of traditional doll-making methods — or you can purchase a doll (not plastic please) to act as the vessel for the Spirit of your home or Coven. Wooden, corn husk, porcelain, and cloth dolls are all good choices.

The Coven's Dolly is kept at the home where the Coven meets (the Covenstead) and is present for most, if not all rituals. Fashioned as an adult figure (not a child), the Dolly is the vessel of the Coven Familiar and should convey something of that Spirit's nature, if possible.

The Elemental Weapons

Each of the four elemental gates is traditionally associated with a martial weapon. The masculine elements of air and fire are represented by offensive weaponry: the staff (or spear) and the sword. The feminine elements of earth and water are represented by defensive weaponry: the shield and helm. These weapons have antecedents in the four suits of the Tarot: swords, staves, coins (shields), and cups (helms). They are also representative of the four Celtic Hallows of the Tuatha: sword, stone, spear, and cauldron.

The Sword

The sword is the weapon of the east gate, where it has been forged within Tubal Cain's smithy. The sword is a symbol of nobility and initiation. Just as Lancelot crossed the Sword Bridge to enter the country of Melegant, so must we cross step across this threshold to enter the circle of initiation. It is also the Sword That Cuts Both Ways, reminding both initiate and initiator of the nature of Mystery and Oath.

The Staff

The staff is the most versatile, and often the most personal, tool of a witch. It can be a distaff, a blackthorn blasting staff, a battle staff, a spear, or a simple walking stick. The form matters far less than the function of the staff. It is the weapon of the north gate, sacred to the Black Goddess, who, in her crone aspect walks with a staff. In her aspect as the spinner of Fate, she bears a distaff; and in her bloodthirsty warrior aspect, she carries a spear.

The Shield

The shield is both a physical and a metaphysical tool. It can be a literal shield, like a targe, held as a piece of symbolic regalia upon which the symbols of the coven or the witch are emblazoned, or it can be an energetic tool which we cultivate through visualization and discipline. The shield is a symbol of guardianship of the mysteries. It is the weapon of the southern gate of earth.

The Helm

The helm, upturned, is the cup or cauldron of the western gate of water. The helm is symbolic of the mask, which we use in transformational magics and ecstatic ritual. The helm protects the head, which the Celts perceived as the seat of the soul. The western gate is also associated with the land of the Dead.

Helm and Mask

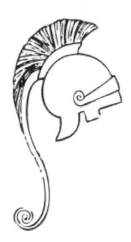

The helm, upturned, is the cup or cauldron of the western gate of water. It is the helkapp that Tubal Cain as the Lord of death wears to grant invisibility. The helm is also symbolic of the mask, which we use in transformational magics, and ecstatic ritual. The helm protects the head, which the Celts perceived as the seat of the soul. Thus, just as the shield protects the physical body from harm, so does the helm, or mask, represent protection of the soul. It is appropriate, then, that the helm be the weapon of the western gate, that place of rest, that realm of the dead, that healer of the soul.

A replica or costume piece (not made of plastic) would work. There are leather helmets of both historical and fantasy origins, as well. It is possible to even construct a leather helm for yourself, if you desire.

Alternatively, you could display a Mask (or multiple masks) in the West. Look to the Dorset Ooser and the Head of ATHO for both inspiration and connection of these symbols.

Shield

The shield is both a physical and a metaphysical tool. It can be a literal shield, like a targe, held as a piece of symbolic regalia upon which the symbols of the coven or the witch are emblazoned, or it can be a magical tool which we cultivate through visualization and discipline. This shield is a semi-permeable barrier of etheric energy that we use for self-defense and cloaking magic. The shield is a symbol of guardianship of the mysteries. It is the weapon of the southern gate of earth, and is sacred to the White Goddess. It is her shining white light which builds the etheric shield, and it is her seelie magic that weaves glamor and cloaking spells that depend on the shield.

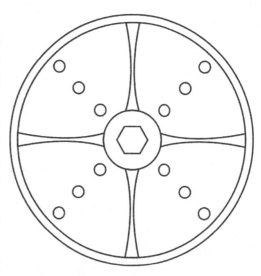

While any style of Shield will do, Witches tend to favor the Targe. A targe is a round shield made of iron or wood that's been plated in iron. It has come to be associated with the Scottish Highlands, though its use was more widespread than that. It is worn on the forearm and has a hand-grip and a strap (usually with a buckle) to secure it to the arm. Shields made for battle were concave, but ours are usually flat.

It is the weapon of ThisWorld. It is a defensive weapon, used to guard against and deflect the dangers and assaults of day-to-day reality. It also represents the ways in which the physical realm affords certain protections and defenses against the slings and attacks of the other magical realities.

A simple shield is very easy to make and really adds to the protective, defensive magic of your home and magical space. Once it is finished, place it in a prominent location to guard your home or altar. When laying the compass for ritual, the Shield would be placed in the South.

To Make a Ritual Shield

Wooden round (like a pre-made table top)
Heavy duty felt
Leather
Furniture tacks
Cabinet handle

Pencil
Scissors
Measuring tape or ruler
Hammer
Staple gun with staples

1. As with any magical crafting project, you should create the targe in sacred space.

2. Place the leather face down on your worktable. Put the wooden round on top of the leather and trace the shape plus 2 inches all the way around. Cut the leather and set it aside.

3. Do the same with the felt, except cut just shy of 2 inches. You'll want the leather to cover the felt completely.

4. Place the leather face down again on the worktable. Put the felt on top of it, followed by the wooden round.

5. Fold the leather and felt over the wooden base at the top-most point of the circle. Staple it in place on the back of the shield. Do the same at the bottom, making sure that the fabric and leather are snug but not too tightly stretched.

6. Repeat the folding and stapling at the two sides, and then work your way around the entire circle. Remember to staple one side and follow it up with its exact opposite. This will keep the leather and fabric even and smooth.

7. You'll end up with staples all around the backside of the shield, holding the leather in place.

8. Next, use the furniture tacks to tack down the leather on the front of the shield. You can make a simple circle of tacks along the outer edge of the flat circle, or tack the outer rim of the shield. Another option is to incorporate a personal design, using the tacks, on the face of the shield. Any of these options will serve the same primary function - keeping your leather snug and secure.

9. Affix your handle onto the back of the shield in a place that will be comfortable when you are holding it.

10. Use a strap of leather (or fur, if you want) to create a strap for your forearm. This will help your shield wear comfortably when you have need to hold it.

11. Finish by placing your sigil and/or bindrune on the back of the shield, if you have one.

12. Dedicate it to magical use after the Shield is complete by saining it. You would be wise to call on Goda, Horse, Swan, Apple Tree, and the Southern Gate to empower this weapon.

The Staff

The staff is one of the most personal tools a Witch will ever create and use. Though an embellished walking stick can be purchased from talented artisans, a much more effective and bonded tool will be gained by the Witch who takes the time to engage in the creation of their own staff. It can be any height, ranging from about hip-height to roughly the full height of the Witch.

CUTTING A STAFF

To make your own staff, start by going into the woods with an offering (silver is traditional, but birdseed is also nice), a handsaw you have blessed to the task, your shelg or lancet, and a small first aid kit. Ask your Spirits to guide you to your staff, and then look for either a straight piece of deadfall that is unmolested by rot and bugs OR a broomstick- to wrist-thick sapling in a healthy stand of the same species. Ask permission of the tree and make an offering of coin/seed and water before cutting or taking the wood. Make a blood bond with the newly-claimed wood, allowing your spirit and that of the staff to meet and mingle. Clean the site where you drew blood. Remove unneeded pieces of wood and leave them for the creatures of the forest, including the bark.

SHODDING A STAFF

Drive an iron nail (such as an old-fashioned "coffin" nail) through the base of your staff, taking care not to split the wood. Alternately, you can fit your staff with a metal butt-cap. This connects the staff to Tubal Cain's forge and prepares it for use in magic.

WIELDING A STAFF

The staff can be used to demarcate the ritual grounds when laying the compass. It is symbolic of the weaver's distaff, the cane of the Crone, the blasting staff, the spear, the battle-staff, the standard-pole, and also the very tree from which it sprung. The staff is also a gandreigh, or riding pole, which means that it can be used in a number of ways to achieve altered states of consciousness — including seething. It is not uncommon to hang the Crane Bag or talismans from the staff.

RETIRING A STAFF

Depending on the uses to which you put your staff, it may deteriorate over time and need to be retired. This is natural. Depending on the level of adornment and embellishment on your staff, you may return it to the earth by using it in the garden as a bean- pole or give it to the fire as kindling. Furthermore, upon the death of a Witch, the staff should not be passed as a kuthun to another Witch because it is so bound to the life and magic of the one who wielded it. Instead, it should be given to the earth, fire, or water as part of the Witch's crossing rite.

Sword

The Sword is a magickal weapon that is common to many traditions of magick and Craft. This is due in no small part to its associations with alchemy and smithing, as well as to its cross-like shape. (Crosses have been important symbols since long before Christianity — having connections to both the Axis Mundi or World Tree and also the Cross of the Elements.)

In the east, the gate of fire, is the forge of Tubal Cain. Created on this primal forge is that most iconic of forged weapons, the sword. The sword is a symbol of nobility and initiation. It is the "sword bridge" we cross to enter the circle of initiation, just as Lancelot had to cross the sword bridge to enter the enchanted country of Melagant. It is also the "sword that cuts both ways," demonstrating that both initiate and initiator are creating a solemn pact. In Arthurian legend the sword Excalibur was drawn from a stone, but in the earliest forms of the myth the sword was drawn from an anvil. In our tradition the "oath stone" of the coven is represented by an anvil in honor of Tubal Cain, Lord of the forge, and the fire of creation.

Within Witchcraft, it is less common for each Witch to have their own Sword — much like this would not have been the norm for our pre-modern forebears. Instead, we often see a single Sword being wielded by the leader of the Coven or leader of a particular ritual.

Double-edged blades are the most common in the Craft. Some blades that might be considered long knives (by blade aficionados) could also work nicely. These might include the Seax, the Arkansas Toothpick, the Gladius, the Tanto, a "hand and a half" dagger, or others along these lines.

The Treasures

Each of the four Castles that act as the Watchtowers of the Spiral Castle Tradition hold within them a Treasure -- a vessel of the Mysteries that can hold and transmute energy, point to Craft secrets, and act as a divinatory device. These four working tools, while referenced in many variations of the lore that we so love, are not necessarily common Craft tools. Assembled together, they are actually somewhat unique to the Spiral Castle Tradition.

Treasures & Weapons

The four Gates (the cardinal points of the Compass) are associated with weapons. Two are usually used in defense (shield and helmet), and two are associated with attack/offense (staff and sword). In reality, ALL of the weapons are both. The Gates, the Weapons, and the Gate-Keepers can be thought of as active (proactive) in their expression.

The four Castles that mark the cross-quarters of our Compass are places of protection that guard us while we work and also protect and preserve the Mysteries. The Treasures held within the Castles are all vessels that hold keys to accessing those Mysteries. All of them have divinatory/oracular uses, and they also hold energy (as opposed to the Weapons, which direct and shape energy). They are the Silver Cup, Golden Lantern, Stone Bowl, and Glass Orb.

Sacrificial Stone Bowl

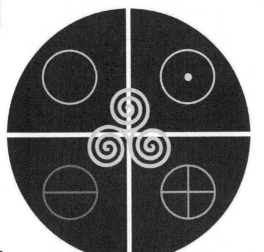

Why to Use the Stone Bowl

There is an ebb and flow to magic. Different traditions have different ways of indicating the way the price for magick will be paid, but nearly all agree that some form of price MUST be paid — whether the witch is aware and willing to pay or not. A cunning person goes into this process with their eyes open and asks up front what the cost will be in order to decide if the prize gained is worth the price to be paid. This bowl is a variation of a tool used in some Trad Craft lines to determine the type and magnitude of that price.

Symbolism & Types of Sacrifice

The design above is painted into a flat-bottoned bowl or lipped dish. The white cross that divides the space represents the crossroads. Starting in the upper right quadrant and moving clockwise, the other symbols represent:

Castle of Revelry (*yellow circle with central point*) ~ sacrifice of abstinence (refraining from sexual stimulation, smoking, alcohol, tobacco, sugar, or other pleasure for a period of time)

Castle of Stone (*green crossed circle*) ~ sacrifice of wealth (giving money to charity, donating items, gifting personal possession to someone, working on a project without compensation)

Castle Perilous (*red halved circle*) ~ sacrifice of blood/pain (submitting to flogging, lifting heavy weights, running an endurance race, shedding your own blood with intent, etc)

Castle of Glass (*blue circle*) ~ sacrifice of comfort (fasting for a period of time, sleeping on the floor, wearing an intentionally irritating garment, walking barefoot on gravel, etc)

Spiral Castle (*silver triskelion*) ~ no sacrifice associated with this Castle

How to Use the Stone Bowl

Cast three stone (one each — black, white red) into the bowl. The stones represent the Black and White Goddesses and the Red God. Whichever stone the red stone is closest to indicates to which Goddess your sacrifice will be made. The circle she has landed on indicates which type of sacrifice. The distance between the black and white stones indicates the magnitude of the sacrifice. So, if the red stone is closest to the white stone, and the white stone is on Castle Revelry, you will make a sacrifice of abstinence to the (any) White Goddess. If the black stone is close to the white stone, that sacrifice would be small. (And if the white stone had landed on the triskelion in this same scenario, there would be no sacrifice required at all.)

Glass Orb

Within Celtic/Druidic lore, we encounter the glain – or Druid's egg, serpent's egg, adderstane, Druid's glass, or snake stone. While Midsummer was the season most attributed to the creation of the glain, Midwinter was also associated with its power. This hard glass bubble (or alternately, glassy stone) awarded its bearer incredible magickal powers, and even Merlin was said to have gone looking for one.

Some of the powers traditionally ascribed to the glain are success in lawsuits, access to kings and high officials, curing diseases at a great distance, seeing into the world of the Unseen, and escaping capture/imprisonment.

In our Tradition, we honor the Glass Orb as having these roots, although it is likely that other influences have shaped our understanding, as well. The Orb is often not a solid, dense glass or crystal ball, but a hollow, clear sphere. It holds the energy of Air.

A simple Glass Orb can be made by perching a hollow glass Christmas bubble atop a glass candle holder (or nestling it inside a lined box – though I like it being out, elevated, and accessible.). Fishing floats, Christmas bubbles, terrarium balls, and garden gazing globes can all make for wonderful Glass Orbs. (Go for clear or translucent white, if possible. Color ... changes things – though this is something you can experiment with, if you like.)

The Glass Orb is a lovely tool for scrying and/or contemplation. It is a superb clarifier of thoughts and ideas.

One of the insights shared and discussed among adept members of our Tradition is that the Glass Orb can be seen as Odin's missing (or glass) eye.

Golden Lantern

The Golden Lantern is the vessel or Treasure of Fire, and it is the Sun, in miniature. In fact, the symbol we use for the this Treasure and the Castle which holds it is the same as the alchemical symbol for the Sun. To us, we see two (main) things within this simple glyph: the fiery star that sits at the center of our solar system circumscribed by the orbit we trace around it, and also, the flame glimmering within the round walls of the lantern.

I could additionally make the case that this glyph is connected to our conception of the Compass in its simplest form. Whereas the symbol for the Stone Castle/Bowl shows the crossroads, the symbol for the Golden Lantern/Castle might be said to depict the Stang and the Moat. There are certainly connections to be made between the fire betwixt the Stang's horns and the light of the Sun/Lantern, as well. If you sit in contemplation of that, do you see the patterns emerging?

Can you see the golden yoke encased in the egg's shell? (Interesting, I think, that the symbol of the egg is so prominent at the Spring Equinox – when the Golden Lantern shines brightest.)

The Golden Lantern acts as a beacon for us, as well as being the light of inspiration, of creation. We often envision myriad markings upon the housing that are illuminated by the radiance within. This is honeyed glow of the poet's gift. The storyteller's art. The creator's talent.

Use your own Golden Lantern to light a signal fire to call out to others, to add hope and charisma to your goal, and to fuel inner growth. Gaze upon its glow when you need a boost of energy and sustenance. Let the symbols upon the housing tell you their stories, sing their songs, and recite their ballads as you watch the flicker and dance of the flame within.

You can find cut glass amber-colored candle holders with hurricane lanterns in antique stores, as well as new release metal lanterns with amber or yellow glass. My own Golden Lantern is a "fairy lamp" style two-piece set made by the Indiana Glass Company in the 1960's (with the pattern name "Stars and Bars"). A very crafty Witch might also consider purchasing a rather plain lantern and then embellish it with glass paints, etching, etc.

Silver Cup

A silvery wine bowl, cup, or quaiche (Celtic cup/bowl with handles) acts as the physical representation of our final Treasure. The Silver Cup is the Holy Grail, and we see it brimming with blood – or wine. It can be linked very intimately with a good deal of uterine symbolism, and also with the cornucopia and/or the Cauldron of Plenty. In fact, it is linked to many of the mystical Celtic cauldrons – Dagda's cauldron of endless food, Bran's cauldron of rebirth, Cerridwen's cauldron of wisdom and transformation, Dyrnwch's cauldron that discerns the brave from the cowardly, the pearl-rimmed cauldron of Pen Annwn.

Where the Stone Bowl is the sacrificial dish (holding the bread, if we like, for the Housle – and also pointing the way to the sacrifice required for magick), the Silver Cup is the sacrificial cup that catches the blood of the slain offering.

There are grim Mysteries within this chalice, but also deep joy, for this is the gift of wine, food, and birth. The Silver Cup is the Treasure that holds precedence at the time of our great Autumnal feast. It is the blot bowl, offering us deep blessing from the blood within.

Any style of silver cup will suffice – coupe, quaiche, compote bowl.

Some of the practical magick of this Treasure includes blessing yourself and saining your tools as part of the Housle. You can also use the Silver Cup to infuse a ritual brew with wisdom, rebirth, bravery, abundance, etc (the qualities attributed to the cauldrons of myth). Scrying into a pool of dark red wine, or reading the herbs that remain after steeping a Sabbat Wine blend are just two ways you might use the Silver Cup in divination.

Mysteries

Life in Death, Death in Life

From   Liber Qayin, The Black Book of Lilith-Sophia:

1)   *In the beginning there was only me.*

2)   *I am the darkness.*

3)   *From the wind in the night I came.*

4)   *I am called Lilith.*

5)   *The Elohim fashioned me from Wind and Blood and dark, rich Earth; for I am the womb of the world, and I am its tomb.*

27) *I am the dark road of death and am called Life-in-Death. Hekate.*

From   Liber Qayin, The White Book of Ishtar-Eve:

4)   *I am the Light in the Darkness, the star-fire of your soul, the hope and joy and pleasure of Gods and men. And I am also Death-in-Life, the little death found in the arms of love.*

5)   *I am all possibility without limit.*

6)   *You see in me the ocean or the vast starry heavens, opening into the fruition of your dreams. And so I am.*

7)   *And if you have Wisdom, you tremble before me.*

8)   *For I am untempered Life come rushing to meet you, unbounded Love poured upon you like the Sea.*

The Rose Beyond the Grave

From *Beyond The Realms Of Death--* by *Robin the Dart*

... For we also celebrate life, having a deep respect for all deserving things around us. More importantly, we believe that life is but a preparation for death. As [Evan] John [Jones] once said to me - "I thought I was learning to live, but I am really learning to die". Blessings be upon him and all past Clan members [always in our thoughts and often with us]. ...

After a substantial preparation, the rite culminates in ritual. Wrapped within the 'Clan' shroud adorned with specific symbols and angelic seals, his spirit finally began its journey with full ceremony. Eventually, the aspirant returned from this complex and involved rite in which success cannot be guaranteed [much depends upon the individual's own egress], a radiant, shining, illuminated soul. When one touches just briefly true Virtue, one brings back a token of that sentience, and as the travelling continues one learns to love life and fear not death, the gateway to eternity.

... Focus is on one's inner self, for out of nothing comes something [ex nihilo]; ... To be the child, the fool, allows us a different perspective. It is this innocence that allows the mask to fall to peer beyond the veil, to be at one with everything, to understand the delusion of illusion. To see beyond the self wherein the heart soars like a bird. The musician tunes his instrument and so must we tune the mind to the frequency of the universe - the music of the spheres.

But there can be no rebirth without the dark night of the soul; we have to feel the pull of the future, not the push of the past. Remember, with writing came the reliance of the appearance of wisdom, instead of the reality of wisdom. ... Rather, the true seeker must look beyond these superficialities to extinguish their Will as subject to True Will. For only then is the bond to material things loosened, only then too of the self to life itself, absolute renunciation, and total freedom from the fear of death. ... the gaze turned inwards engenders something else. This is why real magic is hard work. Zen saying - "show me the face you had before you were born."

... To stand at the setting and the arising, being the living among the dead, as the dead among the living, the quick not the dead. So understand the meaning of the 'Fisher King; where his wound is my wound, his bleeding my bleeding, the cure is to be touched by the same thing, the love of the source the lover and the loved being one [for the hunter and hunted are but one]. To touch the divine, a vibratory rate so high, we as matter, tremble. To experience such an unearthly fear is beyond logic, to explain it denigrates the truth of it. Then comes the pain, the terrible withdrawal whereupon the body becomes an encumbrance.

Yet to have lineage is not to impress with age or authenticity, but simply to have a track to follow our ancestral brethren, distant travellers, guides and guardians of the keys and symbols, into the Void and beyond.

What the Mask Reveals

From ... "The Profane Art of Masking: A Study into the Darker Elements of our Winter Masking and Guising Rituals" [edited extract taken from the entitled article published in 'The White Dragon' Nov. 2008]
--- by Shani Oates

Magically, a mask is understood to represent three characters: the wearer, the personage it represents and the spirit that synthesises the two. ...

Masks are the oldest expression of humanity. They retain the element of mystery, inculcating uncertainty within the onlooker. ... They adopt a public face by hiding the private one; they transform, protect, scare, intimidate, shock, all by inversion! Masks generate transformation in the viewers mind, for the wearer of such a tool, this is immensely empowering. It is also liberating. They are the intercessors between the gods and man, hence all the superstitions accorded to them by onlookers. Masks command attention. ...

To cover ones face is alluring and motivates intrigue, it cultivates curiosity and fear; it arouses suspicion and often engenders unease. ... We cannot know our tormentor, entertainer, anarchist; they remain shadows to our senses. ... There is no full communion between masked and unmasked, interaction is restricted. We are simultaneously seduced and repelled by it. The mask and disguise invites an intimacy that is at once a barrier, paradoxically enforcing separation. ...

Mundanity is vanquished, momentarily banished in this small suspension of reality. We are drawn into an alternative worldview, and we believe it, just for a moment.... For a few brief moments we experience euphoria, elation whilst riding the tide of unease. Friction or fiction? Success depends upon our willingness to engage. Fight or flight. Adrenalin rush either way. This is pure magic and heady stuff. ...

Was it or can it ever be, just harmless fun? Are we drawn inexorably towards aggression, depravity and decadence when immersed in our darker natures? How are such things determined and measured? Is it liberating and edifying or intimidating and oppressive? Surely it all depends from which side of the mask we view the world? And this is precisely where we enter the realms of the sacred use of masking within the Mysteries wherein the individual seeks the companie of the 'other' from both sides of the mask......

"All the world's a stage, and all the men and women merely players........"

The Robin and the Wren

There is much folklore around both the Robin and the Wren, and some bits of folklore and poetry that link them. When sung together, we hear of the love between Cock Robin and Jenny Wren – a love that often ends in tragedy, as one is killed, since they are both birds of sacrifice. We also see them pitted against each other in battles reminiscent of the Oak King and Holly King.

They also have links to the Solstices and to the 3 Realms. Robin is associated with Summer, and Wren with Winter. Robin with the world of the Dead below, and Wren with the path of the Sun in the celestial realm.

THE WREN SONG
The wren, the wren, the king of all birds,
St. Stephen's Day was caught in the furze,
Although he was little his honour was great,
Jump up me lads and give him a treat.

Chorus:
Up with the kettle and down with the pan,
And give us a penny to bury the wren.

THE WREN SHE LIES IN CARE'S BED
The wren lies in her sickbed
In much misery and pining
When in came robin redbreast
With breads in sugared water and wine
Robin says, 'will you sip this?"
And you'll belong to me
No, not a drop, robin
For it has come too late

Oak and Holly King

From Cad Goddeu (The Battle of the Trees):

Holly, it was tinted with green,
He was the hero.

The oak, quickly moving,
Before him, tremble heaven and earth.
A valiant door-keeper against an enemy,
his name is considered.

Robert Graves in *The White Goddess* identifies other legends and archetypes of paired hero-figures as the basis of the Holly/Oak King myth, including:

Lleu Llaw Gyffes and Gronw Pebr
Gwyn and Gwythyr
Lugh and Balor
Balan and Balin
Gawain and the Green Knight
Jesus and John the Baptist

Path of the Kings -- which connects the Horned Lords of Summer and Winter, Basajaun and Janicot — Cernunnos and Odin. They are the Oak King and Holly King, keepers of the Stone Castle and the Glass Castle, guardians of the Stone Bowl and the Glass Orb.

What is Seen by Odin's Eye

Across mythology and folklore, we see tales of figures whose physical sight is sacrificed in order to gain greater wisdom — or even the gift of prophecy. Odin is one of these figures, and he sacrifices one of his eyes at Mimir's Well in order to see into the future.

The Glass Orb of the Spiral Castle Tradition is sometimes called "Odin's Eye" — and also by the names "Glain" and "Adder's Egg."

We recognize the challenges of balancing Sight in other Realms with continuing to see clearly in this Realm. The Glass Castle — or Glastonbury — is a place long associated with both clear-seeing and also illusion.

Upon an Uneasy Seat

In his first letter to Norman Gills, Robert Cochrane writes that a witch *"... invokes the Goddess through 'the dark of night and the evening star meeting together', which as you should know is brought about in the beginning by 'an uneasy chair above Caer Ochren'."* These phrases refer to the Mystery of invocation or possession.

Let's start with 'The dark of night and the evening star meeting together.' This is a reference to possession, which is also called channeling, invocation, aspecting, or being ridden. Later in the same letter, Cochrane says that this process can't be taught in writing.

Perhaps it is easiest to say that the "dark of night" is a reference to the Self – that internal place, the opening, yearning for something greater than what is known and seen. We all have it, this chasm that cries out for spiritual experience, for that which is beyond us.

The "evening star," then, is the Goddess who is being invoked. It could be any Goddess or God. Some covens do possessory work at specific Sabbats or Esbats, and it is often done for the primary purpose of oracular communications from specific Deities. We seek their advice and listen to the wisdom that they share.

Caer Ochren is one of the castles of Grail lore, possibly Caer Sidhe itself. Some of this is just our gut instinct, but a little comes from an interesting linguistic find. "Ochren" means "sides." It could be easy to mistake "sidhe" (which means fairy) as "sides" – or to intentionally muddy the waters by playing language tricks with these words. This is the center point of the witch's compass, opening onto all the sides. A seat above it, poetically speaking, could be the starry point to which the central spire of the castle rises. The North Star, Tubelo's nail star, the iron hook.

It is possibly a reference to the oracle of Delphi sitting upon her tripod stand above the fissure within the temple's floor. The temple at Delphi held the omphalos, the world's navel, the center point. You can use a rocking chair as the tripod, as the "uneasy seat." When a witch sits in the rocking chair at the Sabbat, she begins the process of ascending to the top of the Spiral Castle. It is the seat of wisdom, the seat of vision. By rocking back and forth as she works toward invocation, she is seething, which is a VERY effective way to alter consciousness.

Light out of Darkness, Darkness in Light

The White Goddess rules in the South at Lammas, and the Black Goddess dominates the North at Imbolc. In fact, these are two faces of the SAME Goddess -- the quintessential Witch's Goddess – the Witch Mother. She is both light and darkness.

Through the light half of the year, we mark the influence of the White Goddess whom we call upon as Goda. Hulda is an aspect of the White Goddess, and you will see us later refer to Her as a Queen (for She is the keeper of the Castle of Revelry). The same is true for the Black Goddess (Kolyo), Cerridwen (the Queen of the Castle Perilous), and the dark half of the year.

However, as much as the Black and White Goddesses counterpoint each other on the Year Wheel and within the compass that we lay, we must acknowledge and understand that they work along a continuum. They are not truly separate from each other. One requires the other for full manifestation, and the dynamic balance maintained between the two (within the Year Wheel, the symbolism of the Trad, and the inherent energies They represent) is critical to the practice of the Craft as we know it.

Each holds within Herself the core of the other. Within the darkness of the night, the light of the moon and stars reaches us. During the brightness of the day, shadows lurk. Just as the white knife cuts in the physical realm, and the black in the astral; so, too, do the Goddesses relate respectively to the physical and astral. The two are, in fact, reflections of each other.

From LiberQayin, the Black Book of Lilith-Sophia:

1) *In the beginning there was only me.*

2) *I am the darkness.*

8) *Adam and I lay together, and I conceived a daughter by him. She was Eve, the mother of all races.*

9) *Eve was my treasure, the Light I brought forth from my Darkness.*

10) *But she was also my rival. For I am the Darkness in the Light.*

From Liber Qayin, the White Book of Ishtar-Eve:

Thus spake Ishtar-Eve, consort of Qayin:

2) *I am the Bride, the Queen of Heaven, the joy upon the Earth.*

3) *My names have been many and beloved, as the stars of the heavens, for I am Asherah, Aphrodite, Babalon, the Magdalene, Aradia, Inanna, Astarte.*

4) *I am the Light in the Darkness, the star-fire of your soul, the hope and joy and pleasure of Gods and men. And I am also Death-in-Life, the little death found in the arms of love.*

Fire and Ice

Fire and Ice have been powerful builders and shapers in the world's land-scape. They are both deadly and destructive powerful forces, and they both call to the human Spirit with voices of beauty and allure.

In hard winters, they are both there. Both are threats to survival, and yet both are part of the same life-giving cycle.

At Imbolc, we look to the fires that burn in tiny places under the ground (the metabolic processes awakening in the seeds), the growing light of the Sun, and the fire of the Hearth to stead us through what is often the iciest and harshest parts of the year.

"Far beneath the winter snows / A heart of fire beats and glows"

A deep study of the Runes Nauthiz and Isa (which are present in the holding of the Stav and Tein – or Stang and Arrow) and an exploration of the galdr of these two Runes can be very illuminating.

Whirling Without Motion

In his letters to Joe Wilson, Cochrane says that the Mystery of the Broom is "whirling without motion between three elements." He also relates this Mystery to the Qabbalistic Middle Pillar and the "path to the 7 gates of percep-tion." He is, of course, talking about the practice of trance-work and medita-tion -- and using these tools (the Broom, is the metaphor for the tool) in or-der to access ALL THAT IS.

The Broom (according to the copies of Cochrane's letters that I printed from Joe Wilson's website in 1999, and which actually include illustrations) is con-structed from a small, forked Ash staff. Between the prongs of the fork, a sa-cred stone is bound. The strips used for binding, the broom twigs, and the handle, are each different sacred woods. (A forked Ash staff, Birch bristles, and Willow bindings.) Each of these woods is related to a different element — Earth, Air, and Water. The stone he calls "balanite," we have researched to be none other than basalt — the most common stone on the Earth's surface, which is formed when lava is rapidly cooled in water. In a sense, it is the result of liquid fire meeting water. (Alchemy in action!)

The Mystery of the Broom is an inner alchemy that allows us to enter the trance state — to "spin" (without moving) between the Upper Realm of Air, the Middle Realm of Earth, and the Under Realm of Water.

The Sword That Cuts Both Ways

The English idiom "to cut both ways" is a phrase that refers to the nature of a double-edged sword. It means, in general usage, that an action can have both good and bad effects, and also that it can affect both sides of the arrangement.

Within the Spiral Castle Tradition, our Covens hold a "Sword That Cuts Both Ways" which acts as the "Sword-Bridge" that candidates for initiation must cross at the beginning of the rite. It is across this Sword-Bridge that the threshold guardian gives the challenges and the warnings of the serious nature of the rite.

"For it is better that you rush upon this blade and spill out your life's blood than enter here with fear or falseness in your heart. How do you enter?"

> "In perfect Love and perfect Trust."

This call and response does not represent a threat. Rather, it is a warning. To enter the initiation for the wrong reasons, out of coercion or obligation, with distrust for the initiator or the process, is to invite disaster for both yourself and for the initiator/Coven.

The blade reminds us that the Oaths and Vows impact both those who give them and also those who receive them.

The Fires Under Caer Sidhe

One of the shared visions of the cosmology of the Spiral Castle is that of a Castle on a Hill with the North Star (the "Nail Star" at the topmost spire and Tubelo's forge deep below. With these, we see the Star-fire and Forge-fire that are symbolic of our enlightenment and illumination.

As an extension of this shared vision, one of the Mysteries that we have seen is that of two Dragons below the Castle who blow the fires of the Forge.

Like Vortigern's Dragons, they are Blood Red and Milk White, and also like them, they may represent two (or rather, multiple) influences within our Craft. Unlike Vortigern's Dragons, they are not at odds – slashing each other and shaking our foundations. Instead, they work in tandem, in complement – each fueling the Great Work.

There is undoubtedly a link between these Dragons and the red and white roses we associate with the two faces of the Witch Mother, as well.

Finally, we also know them to be connected to the "sarf ruth" – the "fire in the land" – Dragon-power in the sacred landscape.

There Is No Magic Without Sacrifice

There is an ebb and flow to the Universe, which includes its resources both visible and invisible. We may not be able to see the balance of the scales from our finite perspective, but if we are Wise, we know that a cause over here produces an effect over there.

Magic is any act of Will that produces change. That change can happen within us and then be brought into the world; it can be brought about by logical and practical applications of effort; and it can also happen through triggers and ripples of mechanisms that are unseen by us.

Anytime we seek to produce a change in one area, we set into motion a series of events that changes another area. Perhaps many changes.

In our relationships with both people and Spirits, we understand the nature of reciprocity. A gift for a gift. Whether we always see and understand the mechanisms of the change we have Willed into being, we must always be prepared to give a gift in exchange for the gift we seek.

What Songs the Siren Sings

Excerpted from "Siren Song ---quid Sirenes cantare sint solitae?"
- by Ian Chambers

Robert Graves, that inspired and inspirational poet of the last century, to whom many owe a debt of gratitude, opened his landmark study The White Goddess by reiterating some questions attributed to Dr Thomas Browne, but more correctly from Suetonius(i) "What songs the siren sang?" is one of those questions. Beginning the epic voyage that such a puzzle requires means we must equip ourselves in order to navigate the mythic landscape with a well constructed myth-faring vessel. With a keen ear to the wind, and with the poet cartographer mapping the terrain before us, only then may we set a course to enquire "what songs the siren sang".

...the tone of the siren's song is a sombre lament, although the theme is one of love or desire. The 'siren song' represents something tempting with its allure, while possessing a quality ultimately with mortal consequences. What love song has not contained within it the threat of the lament for the broken heart, just as the gift of life brings with it the inevitable promise of death. The pang of love, while rapturous in our hearts, also causes it to ache at separation and this is the affect of the siren. ...

The song of the sirens, then, is the lament of the soul at being separated from its source, the anima mundi. It is the pine for reunification, the unio mystica where a union of souls occur, an appeal to the heart of the hero who has bound himself to the vessel of the world upon the great sea of the cosmos. Ultimately, to hear the siren song is to feel the irresistible pull of the anima mundi playing the heart strings like the lyre of Orpheus. ...

In answer to the question, then, "What song the sirens sang", we can offer the solution that it was the song of the soul, sung seductively by sirens, calling it back home.

"And Uriel said unto me: 'Here shall stand the angels who have lain with women... and those women whom they seduced shall become sirens."
First Book of Enoch, Chapter 19

The Dance of the Seven Veils

Consider Salome's "Dance of the Seven Veils" as an ecstatic dance to liberate the Soul, an initiatory dance to relinquish the mortal ties to life (if only briefly) and to glimpse the Self — naked and true. It is a re-enactment of the Descent of Inanna, the Descent of Ishtar in which the Goddess of Life and Fertility seeks to know her dark sister and her truest self in order to understand the Mysteries of Death and Rebirth. At each Gate of the city of the dead, she is confronted by a guardian to whom she must surrender the powerful magickal objects that have defined her life.

The First Gate — Sun — Gold — Great Crown — Ego and sense of identity

The Second Gate — Moon — Silver and Moonstones — Earrings — Emotions and intuition

The Third Gate -- Jupiter -- Lapis Lazuli — Beads around her neck — Wealth/Goods and Profession/Vocation

The Fourth Gate -- Venus -- Copper — Toggle Pins at Breast/Heart — Relationships

The Fifth Gate -- Mars -- Iron — Girdle of Birthstones — Reproduction and passions

The Sixth Gate --Mercury — Quicksilver — Bangles on Wrists/Ankles — Memories and thoughts

The Seventh Gate -- Saturn -- Lead/Bone — Robe — Body

The Two Words That Don't Fit in the Cauldron

Robert Cochrane writes on the "two words that do not fit in the cauldron" as a mystery of the Craft. The answer to this riddle is "Be Still" for within the cauldron lies all motion, all potential, and all things. It cannot hold stillness, but this too is a mystery. The cauldron is used not just for the brewing of potions, but also as a vessel for scrying in liquid or flame. To accomplish this we must find stillness within the cauldron, by quieting our own minds.

Cochrane, in his letters to Joe Wilson, mentions a thread of connection between the Goddess of the Cauldron ("one who becomes seven states of Wisdom" and also to the Mystery of the Broom, which he equates with the Middle Pillar exercise and also with the "dance of the seven veils." These are different approaches with similar results.

In an article titled "The Spirals of Existence" written for *The Cauldron* in 1997 (and reprinted in *The Roebuck in the Thicket*), EJ Jones says:

> "In the same guise, she [the Pale-Faced Goddess] is still the keeper of the cauldron, which is now invested with all of the attributes of the Anglo-Saxon wyrd. It is still the same cauldron where past, present, and future are one and the same thing, and it is always in a constant state of flux, always forming and reforming, never still. It holds all of the knowledge of the past and present that combines over and over again to create what is yet to come. It is also the vessel of wisdom and inspiration from which, if we manage to sup from it, we can gain some of that knowledge."

Sangreal

From Liber Qayin, the White Book of Ishtar-Eve:

40) The rose of my love is stained crimson with the blood of his sacrifice.

41) For it is unto me, the Lady of Love and Life and Liberty, that all blood sacrifice must be made and for whom all War must be waged. And so it is that I am She of Love and War, for both are bought with blood.

42) The first thrust of Love and the passage of Birth are marked with my crimson seal, the Rose of Blood, my red flower.

43) You may have neither Life nor Freedom nor Love without paying the price, for these are the deepest magics.

44) My mother Lilith-Sophia is the source, the Fountain, the Sang Real, the Holy Blood.

45) And I am Eve-Babalon, the vessel, the chalice, the San Graal, the Holy Grail.

The power and virtue held within the blood is of particular interest within many Mystery Schools. The term sangreal could mean either "royal blood" or "holy grail," depending upon how this compound word is divided.

The Arthurian Mysteries themselves point the way to many of our Craft Mysteries, and we see the power of blood (both in terms of lineage and of sacrifice) play out in these legends.

We account Witch Blood as coming from the Witch Mother and Witch Father, though we most often discuss the bloodline as the Line of Qayin – a lineage that we share by virtue of our vows and oaths, which are sealed in blood.

Menstruation, sacrifice, and lineage are all tied to this Mystery.

The Five Transformations

Gwion Bach (the "small boy") gives us a peek at the transformations of the Soul through the phases of enlightenment on his own path to becoming the "shining browed" Taliesin.

Awen (inspiration) is the elixir which ignites the shift, and Gwion Bach is chosen by Awen, which he has been diligently stirring for a year's toil at the employment of Ceridwen, keeper of the cauldron and powerful sorceress. Gwion Bach is not Ceridwen's intended recipient of the elixir, but he is chosen by the brew itself — who recognizes him as being the worthy recipient.

In murderous rage, Ceridwen gives chase to the now all-wise child, who knows his doom is at hand.

He transforms into a hare, and she gives chase as a greyhound.

He transforms into a fish, and she gives chase as an otter.

He transforms into a bird, and she gives chase as a hawk.

He transforms into a grain, and she devours him as a hen.

As a woman again, she births the Radiant One.

Their initiatory pursuit leads them through the Realms and beyond — through destruction to rebirth. It tempers the knowledge gained through inspiration into true Wisdom.

Energy and Using Power

The Three Realms

In many cultures where shamanism is practiced spiritual movement takes place in three planes, worlds, or realms. The three realms are the world above (the sky, heaven, land of the gods), the world around (the land, middle-earth, place of the elemental gates, land of the nature spirits), and the world below (the sea, the underworld, land of the dead). In Celtic lore these realms are named *Ceugent* (ky-jent), *Gwyned*, and *Abred*.

Sky, land, and sea,
Three-in-one, one-in-three.
-Celtic prayer

Shamans use certain techniques of trance to access these realms. In many cultures a tree or pole is visualized as standing at the center of all things, reaching up into the sky and down into the underworld. Shamans use this pole to climb or descend to other realms. In our tradition we use the image of the Spiral Castle, Caer Sidhe, spinning around to open its gate to the different points of the wheel of the year. Its spire reaches up to the stars, and its caverns are home to the great forge and the cauldron. The pole is symbolized literally in our circles by the raising of the stang. By its virtue we can "ride" the stang to any place in the realms, though we may also use our own personal riding-pole, or gandreigh, to do so.

First Realm	Second Realm	Third Realm
Ceugent	Gwyned	Abred
Upperworld, Upper Realm, Realm of Sky, Wind	Earth world, Center world, Realm of Land, Middle Earth	Underworld, Realm of the Sea
Otherworld	Consensus reality	Underworld
Birth, beginnings	Middles	Death, endings
The mind	Living bones and flesh	Emotion
Breath	Physicality	Inner self
Metacognition	Consciousness	Subliminal, Unconscious, Subconcious
Perspective	Limits and limitations	Deep mystery
Movement, setting in motion (beginning)	Progress, action, doing	Rest
Struggle and enlightenment	Going through something	Truth beyond substance or thought
Preservation: the undying realm, absence of decay	Day-to-day struggles and concerns	Healing the soul
Expansion/expansiveness	Manipulation of perception/glamory	Empathy
First arm of the Triskle	Second arm of the Triskle	Third arm of the Triskle
Spire of the Spiral Castle	Place of the Doorway of the Spiral Castle	Initiation chamber beneath the the Castle
Entry through flight or climbing	No entry needed (already in this realm)	Entry through caves, wells, barrows, etc.
Black Knife/Athame	White Knife/Kerfane	Red Knife/Shelg

Witch Flight

At its most basic level, Witch Flight is the same as astral projection or soul journeying. (We some-times call it "hedge-crossing" since we are crossing the boundaries between the worlds.) But Witch Flight differs a bit in execution from what is usual-ly called astral travel, etc. Namely, folkloric Witches often make use of a Fetch and a Gandreid (or Gandreigh) when flying.

The Fetch is an etheric "body" that the Black Soul inhabits while traveling in the Unseen Realms. It is anchored to the physical realm through the use of a "fetish" or "fetich" that houses the Fetch when not in use.

The Gandreid is a riding pole that is (in its most essential form) a representation of the World Tree and acts as your "steed" while you travel. It can be a stang, a staff, or a broom. And it is the Witch's hobby horse (or Hob's Horse). Our own Sleipnir with his 8 legs in each of the worlds that are hung within Yggdrasil. It is the Spiral Castle, with its 8 arms reaching to the Castles and Gates.

There are many, many reasons to cross the hedge. At first, our motivations are usually experiential. We want to see and discover what is there. Meet the inhabitants of the Unseen. Encounter the places and objects that are there. Eventually, though, we go "out and about" in search of information, as a way to perform healings (or blastings), or to engage with the Powers or other Witches. All of the reasons that are common to shamanic practitioners for soul journeying apply to us, as well.

There is no single way to fly. We use the term "flight" to encompass any soul journey, even when we don't necessarily picture ourselves flying across the skies. We can follow a guided meditation with the aid of flying ointment or sabbat tea — perhaps with our Gandreid under or between our knees or held lengthwise across our bodies. We can dance with staff or stang in hand, falling to the ground in a trance, and let our Spirits wander free. We can tap out a rhythm with our Stang on the ground and/or tap an arrow against the shaft of the Stang while chanting or intoning the runes (performing galdr). We can seethe while sitting, swaying, and rocking to loosen our Spirits.

The Witches' Dance Floor

One of the "known secrets" of folkloric Witchcraft is that Witches travel to meet each other using Soul journey techniques, and these meetings happen in what some might call "astral temples." That is a very New Age sounding term for what some of our European Craft ancestors would have called the Brocken (or Blocksburg – the highest mountain peak in Northern Germany) or the Hexentanzenplatz (hexen = witches', tanzen = dancing, platz = place).

The Brocken was a specific place that was associated with Witchcraft rituals in the pre-modern era in Europe. Other mountains had similar honors and associations. There are peaks and groves, caves and heaths on every inhabited continent that have come to be known as gathering places for Witches.

Here is what I know of the place: I cross water and fields and stars during my flight. It is in a high place, with a grove of sacred trees encircling it. We know these Tree Allies. It is a broad, open place. Hard-packed earth on a table of rock. Flat. A bonfire is usually set in the center, and stars swim in the dark sky overhead. Witches and Familiars of every ilk revel together here. A huge banquet is laid on a table. The WitchFather and WitchMother preside over the scene – though I can only ever approach one of them at a time. (If I see Him, She is unavailable to me on that flight – and vice versa.)

What do we do there? All manner of magic can be undertaken from here. All manner of journeys can lead out from here. At its most basic level, we can allow our Souls to play, revel, heal, and be inspired here.

The act of meeting in this place is often called "Meeting at the Sabbat." Walpurgis/Beltaine is the Sabbat most strongly associated with this gathering, but since this "astral temple" exists outside of time, we are in the "eternal now" when we arrive there. That means we can access that otherworldly Witches' Sabbat from whatever date and time we find ourselves within the physical world. In other words, you don't have to wait until the first of May to go.

Sex Magick in Trad Craft

Sex Magick is rarely discussed in Traditional forms of Witchcraft, but it is still present (if also private.) All of the purposes and methods shared here are accessible for individuals working alone, for couples/partners, and for groups. They are all offered without reference or altera-tion based on gender identity or sexual orientation.

Reasons for Sex Magick in TradCraft

- <u>Energy-raising</u> — Sexual energy is quick and easy to raise, generally speaking.

- <u>Healing</u> — Sex magick is a good tool to use for engaging in many types of healing work.

- <u>Energy offerings</u> — Some Spirits prefer sexual energy as part of our regular offerings.

- <u>Altering consciousness for Spirit communication</u> — Some Spirits communicate best with a Witch when that Witch is engaged in sexual activity. You'll see images, hear messages, or just have a sense of "knowing" new insights and information.

- <u>Spirit bonding</u> — We build deeper love and trust with a Spirit via "Spirit Sex."

- <u>Compacting with Spirits</u> — Sex is a very effective way to "seal the deal" with a Spirit. Both blood and sexual fluids carry the life-force of the Witch.

- <u>Generating the Elixir of Life</u> — A purpose unto itself is to generate sexual fluids. These elixirs are used to anoint and consecrate magickal tools and are also sometimes mixed into wine or baked into a cake (as a Spirit offering or part of a spell).

- <u>Initiation</u> — Sex magick is a pathway to initiation and initiatory experience within many branches of the Craft. Yes, even TradCraft. Moreover, our Spirits might "initiate" (or "cause to begin") a new stage of our magickal development or experience using sex as a catalyst.

- <u>Transfer of Virtue</u> — "Virtue" is a term used within Old Craft (Trad Craft) to signify the power and authority of highest office with a Coven or Clan. (Sometimes it is used simply to mean "power" in the sense of power that is raised in ritual.)

- <u>Sacraments of ecstasy</u> — Many practitioners view the pleasure of the sexual act as a sacra-ment unto itself. The orgasm is "proof that the Godds love us and want us to be happy."

- <u>Gnosis</u> — We are able to ride the wave of sexual ecstasy into a place of gnosis. We are able to have a higher, deeper, and more complete understanding of ourselves, our partner(s), our Spirits/Godds, and the cosmos.

The Spirit Spouse

Not every magickal person engages in Spirit work. Period. Not all Witches do, either — although one could argue that Spirit work is a fundamental part of folkloric forms of the Craft. Of the folks who DO work with Spirits, not all of them are drawn into sexual encounters, sexual/romantic relationships, or spousal bonds. On this point, though, more Witches than you might think ARE engaging in some form of Spirit sex. (They're just not talking about it -- usually for reasons dealing with privacy and the intensely personal nature of that magick.)

Because of all these reasons combined, hardly anybody writes books, blogs, tweets, vlogs, or otherwise shares about this area of magickal experience. That lack of information and discourse adds to the feelings of isolation around these experiences.

The terms we use for this experience are fairly new, but the experience is definitely ancient. Our myths and folklore from all over the world demonstrate the propensity of Spirits of all types and degrees to interact with human lovers, ask for spousal commitments, or sometimes just have a fling.

The logistics of how this works are often dependent on cultural factors, the nature of the Spirit, and the personal preferences and boundaries of the human. Essentially, there is no single right way to have a sexual or romantic relationship with a Spirit, just as there is no single right way to have a sexual or romantic relationship with another human. In fact, the "right way" is entirely unique to that relationship.

Hieros Gamos

The Hieros Gamos (Greek for "Sacred Marriage") is a ritual of sacred sexuality and sex magick that is found in many traditional cultures and ancient religions. Our earliest rec-ords and recollections around this ritual are from Enhed-uanna. In the poem called the "Courtship of Inanna and Dumuzi," we see the ritual marriage of the Queen/Priestesses/Goddess with the Shepherd/Priest (who be-comes King as a result of their union).

How to Perform a Hieros Gamos

The execution of this ritual is fairly straightforward, although that doesn't necessarily mean that it is "simple." It can take place between two (or more?) partners of any gender, as long as all of the partners involved are able to successfully invoke a possessory state with a preferred Spirit/Deity. Often, preparatory actions (such as bathing, dressing, adorn-ing with jewelry, applying make-up, inviting the partner to the bedchamber, and disrobing) are ritualized and sometimes involve secondary parties who fulfill roles as a traditional maid or squire – someone who helps their lord or lady get dressed.

The partners each invoke their respective Spirits/Deities, and they proceed to have sex in this fully-invoked state. They might recite invocation chants for each other, or they might each do this for themselves. This can be done simultaneously (if silent invocation processes are used) or one at a time. There are two poems that are used widely among Witches of all sorts for the purpose of calling forth the WitchMother and WitchFather – "The Charge of the Goddess" and "The Invocation of the Horned God." Both were written by Doreen Valiente, who worked closely with both Gardner and Cochrane. Alternatively, you might use a temple hymn associated with the Spirit/Deity, or even write your own.

The purpose for Traditional Witches within the Hieros Gamos isn't fecundity in land and people. It is gnosis. It is enlightenment. It is seeing the Truth of ourselves, or our partners, and of the Spirits we have invoked together.

Sacred Touch

The Sacred Touch Ceremony was first developed and taught within the Qadish-ti Movement of sacred sexuality by Michael A. Manor. It is a simple and expandable ritual that offers an egalitarian and accessible approach to sacred sexuality for all participants.

Sacred Space is prepared (laying the compass, etc), and the participants are seated in a circle. Participants are dressed or disrobed to their level of comfort, and they may add or remove clothing at any time. Members of the ceremony take turns occupying a place in the middle of the circle, where they may assume any posture they prefer (sitting, lying prone or supine, etc).

Before any touching begins, the participant in the central space states both their preferences and their boundaries in terms of touch. Sometimes, group boundaries are in place, as well — ie, no touching genitals or breasts, no penetrative sexual acts, etc. Precautions are always taken to prevent fluid exchange and to encourage safer sex (condoms, dental dams, nitrile gloves, etc.), and a safe word is always in place to halt all touch immediately. Those occupying the ring of the circle offer touch up to their own level of comfort and boundaries, after the preferences and boundaries have been stated by the individual whose turn it is to receive. Everyone is offered time in the center to be a receiver of touch.

Participants are given ample time in the center in order to experience loving touch. The group often comes to a natural stopping point together without words being exchanged. Even without penetration or orgasm (or, in some cases, without any nudity at all), participants often experience a climactic and euphoric state of well-being, connection, and intimacy. (These benefits are linked to the neural affects of bilateral, asynchronous touch, which is being studied within psychology for its healing features.)

Initiation

No-Kill Food List

FRUITS & BERRIES
Apples
Apricots
Bananas
Blackberries
Blueberries
Cantaloupe
Cherries
Coconuts
Cranberries
Dates
Figs
Grapes
Grapefruit
Honeydew Melons
Kiwi
Lemons
Limes
Mangoes
Nectarines
Olives
Oranges
Pomegranates
Pears
Plums
Raisins
Raspberries
Strawberries
Watermelon

MANY VEGETABLES
Artichokes
Asparagus
Bell Peppers
Greens (spinach, chard,
collard, kale)
Tomatoes
Avocadoes
Broccoli
Squash (all varieties)
Pumpkin

Zucchini
Brussels Sprouts
Cauliflower
Cucumber

BEANS & SOME LEGUMES
Green Beans
Peas
Peanuts
Black Beans
Kidney Beans
Navy Beans
Pinto Beans
White Beans
Soy Beans, Edamame

MANY HERBS, SPICES & SEASONINGS
Salt
Pepper
Cinnamon
Cardamom
Cocoa (unsweetened)
Allspice
Nutmeg
Curry
Chives
Cilantro
Dill
Oregano
Rosemary
Mint
Basil
Parsley
Sage
Thyme
(All the leafy herbs)
Oil
Vinegar

MOST SEEDS & NUTS
Cashews
Sunflower Seeds
Pepitas
Almonds
Walnuts
Pecans
Pistachios

GRAINS & STARCHES
Corn, Hominy, Grits,
Polenta
Oats, Oatmeal
Quinoa
Barley
Buckwheat
Bulgar wheat
Couscous
Potatoes
Sweet Potatoes
Rice

DAIRY
Butter
Sour Cream
Milk
Cheese
Yogurt
Heavy Cream

UNREFINED SWEETENERS
Agave
Raw Honey
Monk Fruit Sweetener

Copyright Asteria Books 2020

No-Kill No-No List

No-No Vegetables
Beets
Cabbage
Carrots
Celery
Garlic
Leeks
Mushrooms
Onions
Parsnips
Radishes
Turnips

No-No Legumes
Chickpeas
Lentils

No-No Herbs, Spices & Seasonings
Turmeric
Ginger
Most prepared condiments (will have onion, garlic, or turmeric -- or sugar)

No-No Grains & Starches
Pasta (prepared with egg)
Bread (prepared with egg & yeast)

No-No Sweeteners
White sugar
Brown sugar
Corn syrup
Light syrup

No-No Proteins
Animal meat (including fish)
Eggs

As with any type of fast, the No-Kill Fast is intentionally restrictive. However, it's purpose isn't to deprive your body of essential nutrients or create a state of lack or general privation. The purpose is to bring mindfulness, clarity, and purification.

You are free to choose other types of fasts, if you prefer. The Spiral Castle Tradition has always favored this one, however, because it draws such a sharp point of focus while allowing great room for personal choice without leaving any food groups out. With forethought, you should be able to eat balanced meals and snacks during your time of fasting.

Tips: Watch out for pre-packed foods. So many of them have onion or garlic powder or sugar! Read the labels carefully. When in doubt, research "home harvesting" or "is X a perennial" for the ingredient to see if the parent plant would likely be killed in your garden for you to eat this food.

A Few No-Kill Fast Recipes

BREAKFASTS

◇ Quick (or Steel Cut) Oats with honey, cinnamon, cream
◇ Grits with honey and butter
◇ Greek yogurt with berries and toasted oats

Snacks

◇ Cottage cheese with fruit (orange slices, pineapple chunks, or strawberries) and sesame seeds
◇ Parmesan crisps and homemade hummus or guacamole (leaving the garlic out of either dip, of course)
◇ Apple slices with sugar-free peanut butter
◇ Banana with a handful of almonds

Nachos

Corn chips
Freshly chopped tomatoes
Black beans
Shredded cheese (2-3 varieties)
Avocado slices
Sour cream

Three Sisters Bowl

2 cups cubed and peeled squash of choice
1 Tbsp balsamic vinegar
1 Tbsp olive oil
1 pinch salt
Toss these together and roast in the oven for 20-30 minutes (until fork tender).
Meanwhile, sauté the following in a Dutch oven:
2 ears corn
1 1/2 cups pre-cooked or canned beans
1-2 tablespoons olive oil
1 red pepper, diced
2 tablespoons chopped parsley
1 tablespoon chopped sage
1 teaspoon minced rosemary leaves
1 teaspoon thyme leaves
salt and pepper, to taste
Combine. Serve warm as is or over wild rice, quinoa — or even cold with kale/greens as a salad.

Creamy Vegetable Soup

I start with the most basic potato soup ever — peeled cubed white potatoes, water, butter, a little salt, and heavy cream. To this I add BARLEY and whatever chopped vegetables I like and can find from our list, preferring ones that are in season. Favorites include okra and squash. I really don't measure anything, as you really can't "mess it up."

Initiation Recipes

INCENSE

2 tbsp Red rose petals (Kolyo)
2 tbps Jasmine blossoms (Koda)
1/2 tsp Forge scale for Tubal Cain
1 tsp Dittany of Crete
1 tsp White copal resin
1 tsp Rowan berries
1 tsp Sandalwood
10 drops Amber oil

Anointing Oil

1 oz Base oil (Jojoba, Grapeseed)
10 drops Rose oil
10 drops Jasmine oil
5 drops Amber oil
3 drops Clary Sage oil

Dressed Candle

Dress a white chime candle using a small amount of your anointing oil and incense. This is the candle you will burn during your preparatory bath.

Bath Sachet

Place the following in a muslin drawstring bag or cotton/linen hankie tied with a string:
2 tbsp Crushed rose petals
2 tbsp Crushed jasmine blossoms
1 tbsp Mugwort
Pinch of Sandalwood
Pinch of Sea Salt

Add 1/4 cup Apple Cider Vinegar directly to water

Sabbat Wine

Warm 1-2 cups of a VERY sweet red wine (like Oliver soft red or Manischewitz Concord grape) in a saucepan.

For every cup of wine, steep the following herbal mix in equal parts (using a teaball):

Mugwort
Lemon Balm

Steep for 5 minutes, then remove the teaball. Add raw honey to sweeten.

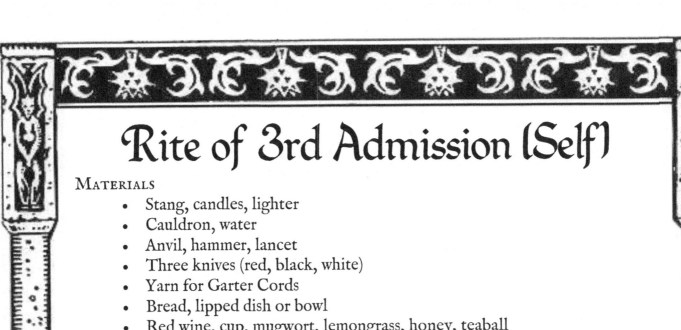

Rite of 3rd Admission (Self)

MATERIALS

- Stang, candles, lighter
- Cauldron, water
- Anvil, hammer, lancet
- Three knives (red, black, white)
- Yarn for Garter Cords
- Bread, lipped dish or bowl
- Red wine, cup, mugwort, lemongrass, honey, teaball
- Initiation incense, holder, charcoal
- Bath sachet, dressed candle, anointing oil
- Gandreid
- Initiation Gift (crown)

RAISE THE STANG

LAY THE COMPASS

OPEN THE GATES & RAISE THE CASTLES & CALL THE REALMS

CHALLENGES & TRIALS

- CHALLENGES -- Within the ritual space, challenge and query yourself by Mind, Heart, and Spirit.

- SABBAT WINE -- Drink the Sabbat Wine or Mugwort Tea.
- WITCH FLIGHT -- Fly to the Brocken and meet your Initiating-Power.
- GARTER -- Braid your Garter Cords while contemplating the Virtue and Mys-tery you have received, and your place as a Queen, Devil, or Consort in the Clannad.

VOWS, OATH & PRESENTATION

- VOWS & OATH -- Before the Oath Stone, ask and answer aloud each Vow. Then make your Oath in blood upon the Stone, using your full known Craft name.
- PRESENTATION -- Anoint yourself with the oil, and say, "So now do I proclaim myself a true [Queen, Devil, Consort] of the Spiral Castle. So shall I be recognized among my Folk and Family! I present myself to the Realms, Gates, Towers, Spirits, and Godds of the Spiral Castle. I am, [Complete Craft Name], a full Witch and [Artisan, Bard, etc] and [Queen, Devil, Consort] of the Spiral Castle! So Mote it Be!"
- GIFT -- Give yourself the Crown (or other gift)

HOUSLE

Vows of 3rd Admission

I have come to this place as a Raised Witch and a [Specialty] of the Spiral Castle, to offer myself in service and study -- to the Powers whose Kindred this is, to the Family, and to MySelf. Having passed the Trials of Initiation - tests of mind, heart, and spirit -- I move forward. I have danced among the Mysteries, planned and prepared for leadership, and have received the Virtue of one of our Great Powers. I have proven myself worthy of the name [Queen, Devil, or Consort] in partnership to the Powers, the Family and MySelf, but I am not bound to serve. I am free in all things. I remain a Raised Witch -- a full member of the Family who can never be cast out of the tradition, even if the cords are burned, the Mark is cut from the flesh, and the blood withdrawn from the stone. The bond of the Secret Name exists between the Initiate and the Mighty Ones and can be broken by no one.

Do I choose with my own free will to take a place as an Elder in the Spiral Castle?

I have passed an examination of my knowledge of the Craft. Am I ready to fulfill my intellectual responsibilities as a Witch of 3rd Admission?

I have ventured to the Brocken. Am I willing to fly-out in search of ecstasy, union, and Truth?

Am I prepared to continue seeking the face of the Mysteries, all the days along my Path?

I have received the Virtue of [Goda, Kolyo, or Qayin]. Am I ready to manifest that Virtue within the Clannad?

I have sought the balance of practical magick and esoteric gnosis. Am I able to continue seeking this balance as I walk my Crooked Path?

I say plain: I would be sworn a Witch of 3rd Admission and a [Q,D,C].
I say again: I would be sworn a Witch of 3rd Admission and a [Q,D,C].
By Thrice-three I lay my claim: I will be sworn a Witch of 3rd Admission and a [Queen, Devil, Consort] in the Spiral Castle Tradition. So mote it be!

Oath of 3rd Admission

Turn to the Oath Stone.

Kneel and grasp the Stone with your blooded hand, both to give and receive the Oath of 3rd Admission.

I, _____, do take this solemn Oath of 3rd Admission. I will serve and study as Elder member of this Family and Tradition from this day forward. I vow to serve Tubal Qayin, Kolyo, and Goda who have made this Path their own, through my skill, knowledge, and experience. I will continue to seek the Mysteries – among them the Light, Shadows, and Contours of my Souls. By taking these vows, I freely begin the work of the Elders of the Spiral Castle. I promise to speak honestly and behave with integrity. I will serve the Spiral Castle to the very best of my ability. [Additional vows may be added here.] So swear I, _____. As I will it, so mote it be. So mote it be! So mote it be!

So now am I proclaimed a Witch of 3rd Admission and a [Queen, Devil, or Consort] of the Spiral Castle!

Appendix B

Year 3: Mastery
Complete Resource List

I thought it might be handy to have a link-list to ALL of the books recommended in this year's course manual. These are live links, so they should take you right to the target (from the PDF and in the app).

Two notes:
- Links change over time. That can even happen quickly, in some cases. I've done my best here, but if you come across a "dead link" you may need to use your own Google Magick to track down the reference. (That was, after all, how I found it.)
- Links to books are through my Amazon Associates (affiliate) account. It doesn't cost you anything extra, but it helps me out a little if you choose to buy through this link. As in all things, do your Will.

Mysteries and Esoterica

Oates, Shani and Robert Cochrane. *The Taper that Lights the Way: Robert Cochrane's Letters Revealed.* — https://amzn.to/36Lezni

Oates, Shani. *Tubelo's Green Fire.* — https://amzn.to/3qtZ0aE

Graves, Robert. *The White Goddess: An Historical Grammar of Poetic Myth.* — https://amzn.to/3qzETb4

Howard, Michael. *The Book of Fallen Angels* — https://amzn.to/3NmlFzw

Jackson, Nigel Aldcraft. *Call of the Horned Piper.* — https://amzn.to/36Olyfi

Jackson, Nigel. *Masks of Misrule: The Horned God & His Cult in Europe.* — https://amzn.to/3qU1Ohx

Jackson, Nigel and Michael Howard. *Pillars of Tubal Cain.* — https://amzn.to/3tyLX9K

Gary, Gemma. *Black Toad: West Country Witchcraft and Magic.* — https://amzn.to/3L64QXo

Faerywolf, Storm. *Forbidden Mysteries of Faery Witchcraft.* — https://amzn.to/3j37Xna

Grimassi, Raven. *Wiccan Mysteries: Ancient Origins and Teachings.* — https://amzn.to/36LRyB3

Farrar, Janet and Gavin Bone. *The Inner Mysteries: Progressive Witchcraft and Connection to the Divine.* — https://amzn.to/3J5ehoA

Mankey, Jason. *Transformative Witchcraft: The Greater Mysteries.* — https://amzn.to/37ckUbk

Finnin, Ann. *The Forge of Tubal Cain.* — https://amzn.to/3j7n5jb

Telyndru , Jhenah. *Avalon Within* — https://amzn.to/3OZ0EMs

1734 website — www.1734-witchcraft.org

CTC website — http://www.clanoftubalcain.org.uk/

Ruebsaat, S. (2013). What Does a Mythopoetic Inquiry Look Like?. *SFU Educational Review, 6.* https://doi.org/10.21810/sfuer.v6i.372

"Beyond the Realms of Death" by Robin the Dart — http://www.clanoftubalcain.org.uk/beyond.html

Liber Qayin — http://afwcraft.blogspot.com/2015/03/liber-qayin-complete-text.html

"The Profane Art of Masking" by Shani Oates — http://www.clanoftubalcain.org.uk/masks.html

"Siren Song" by Ian Chambers — http://www.clanoftubalcain.org.uk/sirensong.html

Sabbat Studies

"The Jaw-Dropping History of Jack O'Lanterns: A Tale or Turnips, Samhain, and Severed Heads" — https://irishmyths.com/2021/09/19/jack-o-lantern-history/

Witch-Flight and Hedge-Crossing

"Aphantasia and Astral Travel" — https://www.thedragonslibrary.net/blog/aphantasia-and-astral-travel

Shamanic Drumming track — https://www.youtube.com/watch?v=ivCOrc1HWxI

"Was the Eko Eko Chant Originally and Arabic Chant to the Devil?" — https://witchesandpagans.com/pagan-culture-blogs/paganistan/was-eko-eko-azarak-originally-an-arabic-chant-to-the-devil.html

"Vcror and Gandr" Helping Spirits in Norse Magic" — https://journals.lub.lu.se/anf/article/download/11542/10231/26582 (This is a PDF download)

Spirit Work

Black, LM. *The Witches' Key to the Legion: A Guide to Solomonic Sorcery* (Expanded and Revised Edition). — https://amzn.to/3NiDAXv

Duvendack, Bill. *Spirit Relations: Your User-Friendly Guide to the Spirit World, Mediumship and Energy.* — https://amzn.to/3wz0O5O

Ellwood, Taylor. *Walking with Spirits: How to Work with Spirits and Get Consistent Results.* — https://amzn.to/3uoln2m

Grimassi, Raven. *Communing with the Ancestors: Your Spirit Guides, Bloodline Allies, and the Cycle of Reincarnation.* — https://amzn.to/3NieXKv

Vaudoise, Mallorie. *Honoring Your Ancestors: A Guide to Ancestral Veneration.* — https://amzn.to/3iu5vpv

Day, Christian. *The Witches' Book of the Dead* (10th Anniversary Revised and Expanded edition). — https://amzn.to/3uolzyC

Paxson, Diana. *The Way of the Oracle: Recovering the Practices of the Past to Find Answers for Today.* — https://amzn.to/3qzphEl

Paxson, Diana. *Trance-Portation: Learning to Navigate the Inner World.* Weiser, 2008. — https://amzn.to/3D9rsDR

Wilby, Emma. *Cunning-Folk and Familiar Spirits: Shamanistic Visionary Traditions in Early Modern British Witchcraft and Magic.* — https://amzn.to/3wDukaC

Illes, Judika. *Encyclopedia of Spirits: The Ultimate Guide to the Magic of Saints, Angels, Fairies, Demons, and Ghosts.* — https://amzn.to/3D7sMH0

Miller, Jason. *Consorting with Spirits: Your Guide to Working with Invisible Allies.* — https://amzn.to/3wuWp3X

Lecoutuex, Clade. *The Tradition of Household Spirits: Ancestral Lore and Practices.* — https://amzn.to/3D57NEZ

LaFae, Phoenix. *What Is Remembered Lives: Developing Relationships with Deities, Ancestors & the Fae.* — https://amzn.to/3NtcD3I

Dempsey, Corinne. *Bridges Between Worlds: Spirits and Spirit Work in Northern Iceland.* — *https://amzn.to/3NiEuTT*

Internet Sacred Text Archive — https://www.sacred-texts.com/

Theoi Greek Mythology — https://www.theoi.com/

Norse Mythology — https://norse-mythology.org/

Journals for Folklore Studies (Ohio State University) — https://cfs.osu.edu/about/resources/journals

Mythology, Fair Tales, and Folklore Journals (NYU) — https://guides.nyu.edu/fairytales/journals

Tools

Left-Hand Rabbit — https://www.etsy.com/shop/Lefthandrabbit

(archived) original Cornish Witchcraft website (pictures of working tools) — https://web.archive.org/web/20130331112630/http://www.cornishwitchcraft.co.uk/images-tools.html

Sex Magick

Sophie Saint Thomas. *Sex Witch* — https://amzn.to/3jcQJHl

Margo Anand *.Art of Sexual Magic* — https://amzn.to/3PFoEEM

Donald Michael Kraig. *Modern Sex Magick* — https://amzn.to/3FGNpvq

Jason Augustus Newcomb. *Sexual Sorcery* — https://amzn.to/3FHaGO5

Frater U:.D:. *Sex Magic* — https://amzn.to/3G2lW8T

Dr. Megan Rose. *Spirit Marriage: Intimate Relationships with Otherworldly Beings* — https://amzn.to/3HUHqpD

"God Spouses and Sex with the Divine" — https://metal-gaia.com/2014/01/07/god-spouses-and-sex-with-the-divine/

"Consent Culture: What Does It Mean?" — https://inbreakthrough.org/consent-culture-what-does-it-mean

Pastoral Care & Ministerial Studies

Kaldera, Raven and Tannin Schwartzstein. *Handfasting and Wedding Rituals.* — https://amzn.to/3Vuuivj

Williams, Liz. *Modern Handfasting: A Complete Guide to the Magic of Pagan Weddings.* — https://amzn.to/3H6EpSB

Ferguson, Joy. *Magickal Weddings.* — https://amzn.to/3VtN4TG

MacDowell, Katherine. *Ethics & Professional Practice for Neopagan Clergy.* — https://amzn.to/36jiBn3

Starhawk and M. Macha Nightmare. *The Pagan Book of Living and Dying.* — https://amzn.to/3iA65Fe

West, Carrie and Phillip Wright. *Death & the Pagan: Modern Pagan Funerary Practices.* — https://amzn.to/3EXKUVh

Fenley, Judith Karen and Oberon Zell. *Death Rights and Rites.* — https://amzn.to/3XQ4lYP

Mortellus. *Do I Have to Wear Black?: Rituals, Customs, and Funerary Etiquette for Modern Pagans.* — https://amzn.to/3Fndb9b

Butler, Charles. *Pagan Prison Ministry.* — https://amzn.to/3UB2cgU

Kaldera, Raven. *Candles in the Cave: Northern Tradition Paganism for Prisoners.* — https://amzn.to/3ixWYFg

Emore, Holli S. *Constellated Ministry: A Guide for Those Serving Today's Pagans.* — https://amzn.to/3FmyxmZ

O'Brien, Lora. *A Practical Guide to Pagan Priesthood: Community Leadership and Vocation.* — https://amzn.to/3irkJP3

LeVeau, Belladonna. *Awakening Spirit: WISE Seminary, First Year Certification for Wiccan Clergy.* — https://amzn.to/3VIz08w

Gardner, Kevin. *The Wiccan Minister's Manual: A guide for Priests and Priestesses.* — https://amzn.to/3Fjxi89

Gardner, Kevin. *A Handbook for Wiccan Clergy.* — https://amzn.to/3VNIBLf

Savage, David. *Non Religious Pastoral Care* — https://amzn.to/3hb9tGo

Gardner, Kevin. *The Pagan Clergy's Guide for Counseling, Crisis Intervention, and Otherworld Transitions.* — https://amzn.to/3H3Hhj9

Eilers, Dana D. *Pagans and the Law.* — https://amzn.to/3B1m7OL

Campanelli, Pauline. *Rites of Passage.* — https://amzn.to/3gY4t7Y

LaFae, Phoenix and Gwion Raven. *Life Ritualized: A Witch's Guide to Honoring Life's Important Moments.* — https://amzn.to/3H6wRzn

Spitale, Lennie. *Prison Ministry: Understanding Jail and Prison Culture.* — https://amzn.to/3EUW39r

Hebert, Deirdre A. *Pagans in Recovery: The Twelve Steps from a Pagan Perspective.* — https://amzn.to/3Vuvv5P

Star, Amythest. *The Goddess Way through the Twelve Steps.* — https://amzn.to/3XVPko8

Appalachian Pagan Ministry — https://appalachianpaganministry.com/

The Pagan Federation — https://www.paganfed.org/

"The Limits of Ministry" — https://wildhunt.org/2018/01/the-limits-of-ministry-pagan-clergy-and-serious-situations.html

"Pagan Ministry" — https://www.patheos.com/blogs/paganrestoration/2013/07/pagan-ministry-serving-the-pagan-peoples/

"10 Simple Steps to Ensure Legal Ordination" — https://www.startchurch.com/blog/view/name/10-simple-steps-to-ensure-legal-ordination

Jones v. Jones case — https://law.justia.com/cases/indiana/court-of-appeals/2005/49a02-0501-cv-64-0.html

"Why Satanic Panic Never Ended" — https://www.vox.com/culture/22358153/satanic-panic-ritual-abuse-history-conspiracy-theories-explained

"Clergy as Mandatory Reporters of Child Abuse and Neglect" — https://www.childwelfare.gov/pubpdfs/clergymandated.pdf

Coven Leadership

K, Amber. *Coven Craft: Witchcraft for Three or More.* — https://amzn.to/3ixKTjn

Campanelli, Dan and Pauline. *Circles, Sanctuaries, and Groves: Sacred Spaces of Today's Pagans.* — https://amzn.to/3VsJ1XL

Blake, Deborah. *Circle, Coven, and Grove: A Year of Magical Practice*. — https://amzn.to/3VO07PC

West, Kate. *The Real Witches' Coven*. — https://amzn.to/3OTKdkt

Harrow, Judy. *Wicca Covens: How to Start and Organize Your Own*. — https://amzn.to/3gWQ2kA

White, Ethan Doyle. *Wicca: History, Belief, and Community in Modern Pagan Witchcraft* — https://amzn.to/3HnvInf

Harrow, Judy. *Spiritual Mentoring: A Pagan Guide*. — https://amzn.to/3B1gC2z

Knight, Shauna Aura and Taylor Ellwood, eds. The Pagan Leadership Anthology. — https://amzn.to/3EXEoOj

Knight, Shauna Aura. *The Leader Within*. — https://amzn.to/3FnEyjy

O'Brien, Lora. *A Practical Guide to Pagan Priesthood: Community Leadership and Vocation*. — https://amzn.to/3irkJP3

S, Taren. *Dedicant's Handbook to Coven Life*. — https://amzn.to/3H4KEXa

Magdalene, Misha. *Outside the Charmed Circle: Exploring Gender & Sexuality in Magical Practice*. — https://amzn.to/3OWtrBa

Williams, Brandy, Crystal Blanton and Taylor Ellwood, eds. *Bringing Race to the Table: Exploring Racism in the Pagan Community*. — https://amzn.to/3OWtrBa

Hauck, Kenneth. *Antagonists in the Church: How to Identify and Deal with Destructive Conflict* — — https://amzn.to/3FE9cnN

Communication Coach Alex Lyon — https://www.youtube.com/@alexanderlyon

Organizational Communication Channel — https://www.youtube.com/@orgcomm

(This is also Alex Lyons)

Historical/Anthropological Studies

Hutcheson, Cory Thomas. *New World Witchery: A Trove of North American Folk Magic*. — https://amzn.to/3B7W74t

Wilby, Emma. *The Visions of Isobel Gowdie*. — https://amzn.to/3FmnLNC

Wilby, Emma. *Cunning Folk and Familiar Spirits*. — https://amzn.to/3umcMNP

Hutton, Ronald. *Triumph of the Moon: A history of Modern Pagan Witchcraft*. — https://amzn.to/3XMotep

Hutton, Ronald. *Stations of the Sun: A History of the Ritual Year in Britain*. — https://amzn.to/3VuKkVY

(Really, anything by Ronald Hutton or Emma Wilby would be great!)

Jones, Prudence and Nigel Pennick. *A History of the Pagan Europe*. —- https://amzn.to/3VKv72X

Ross, Anne. *Pagan Celtic Britain*. — https://amzn.to/3OWj7sN

Kaczynski, Richard. *Perdurabo: The Life of Aleister Crowley*. — https://amzn.to/3gYbPZ8

Heselton, Philip. *Doreen Valiente: Witch*. — https://amzn.to/3XLbYj4

Appendix C

Personal Mentoring with Laurelei

Some students need to form a more in-depth relationship with their teacher during their studies. Others need more personal guidance to make sense of the lessons. Yet others want to deepen their understanding and really dig into the work.

Whatever your goals, I am offering my RTA students an incredibly special opportunity to connect with my coaching services at a reduced amount. You are eligible to receive monthly 1-hour coaching sessions with me (via Zoom, Google Chat, Messenger, etc) -- for as many or as few sessions as you need. The best way to make arrangements for Mentoring is to become a "Mentorship" Patron at patreon.com/laureleiblack.

These sessions are a great way to tackle areas of challenge in both your personal life and magical practice. They will help you dive deeper into the material and have a great depth and breadth of understanding. This coaching experience is entirely customized to your needs, goals, concerns, and achievements.

What makes you a good Magical Life Coach, Laurelei?
- I am a teacher. -- Bachelor degree in Secondary Education with several years of classroom experience

- I am a Witch. -- 1st degree, August 2000, Clan of the Laughing Dragon tradition

- I am an ordained Priestess. -- 2nd degree, January 2002, Clan of the Laughing Dragon tradition

- I am a Queen. -- 3rd degree, January 2005, Clan of the Laughing Dragon tradition; co-founder of the Spiral Castle (American Folkloric Witchcraft) tradition, January 2009

- I am a public speaker. -- Presenting classes, rituals, and temple experiences at Babalon Rising Pan-Thelemic Festival, Chrysalis Moon Festival, Starwood, ConVocation, and most events at Camp Midian (from 2013 - 2021)

- I am a psychic intuitive. -- Offering professional readings online, in shops, and at festivals since 2010

- I am a Pagan community leader. -- Co-founder of Midian Festivals and Events in 2014, lead event organizer until 2022; former area coordinator for Indianapolis Pagan Pride Day, 2005-2011; co-founder of Indy CUUPS, 2005; organizer and co-director of Babalon Rising Pan-Thelemic Festival since 2009; director of the Women's Goddess Retreat since 2009

These are my credentials, but they aren't necessarily what makes me good at what I do. If anything, they are evidence that I am dedicated to serving my community and my Gods through teaching, advising, and practicing Witchcraft.

What makes me good at this is the fact that I love it and that I have a natural skill-set that I have honed through years of study and service.

I am called to teach. That is my work in this lifetime; maybe in all my lifetimes.

My greatest desire is to lead an authentic, meaningful, and passionate life and to help others do the same. I believe that the principles of Witchcraft are inherently tied to these goals, for me and for my students.

What are the goals of the coaching relationship?
That depends entirely on you. The goals are YOURS, not mine. What do you want and need to deepen your practice, broaden your understanding, or live a more magic-filled life?

Our monthly sessions can be focused on goals related to your Witchcraft studies:
- Get in-person, in-depth feedback on your assignments

- Practice your divination skills with me

- Explore Craft concepts in a personalized way

- Seek advice regarding specialties within the Craft

- Discuss personal experiences in ritual, meditation, and magic

- Get assistance with problematic projects or concepts

Or, our sessions can be focused on goals related to other areas of your life:
- Find your life's purpose (your Great Work)

- Untangle and decode the symbols in your own personal myth

- Create wealth and abundance

- Find your soul's mate(s)

- Implement new magical techniques and information

- Create healing for your mind, body, and spirit

I can help you achieve the goals that are important to you, whatever they are. Your sessions will include traditional coaching techniques, blended with divination, magic, meditation, and symbol exploration.

What You Need to Know

* As part of our coaching sessions, you will receive a 60-minute video-call each month, a personalized plan for reaching the goals you have set for yourself, the possibility of additional "homework" assignments and activities to help you achieve those goals, psychic reading services included within your call to support your efforts, and email communications throughout the month to check-in with your progress.

* Because of the deep discount on my coaching services for this special student offer, payment is required before each session, and refunds are not an option.

* A coach (even a psychic, witchy one) is not a counselor, but more of an advisor. My role in your life is different than a therapist or a doctor; and I am telling you unequivocally that I am neither of those things. I am here to help you reach your goals, and I will do that in a no-nonsense, plain-speak sort of way. I will be gently honest with you at every step of the way.

* I can't do the work for you. You have to take responsibility for your progress.

If you want to get started with your personalized coaching sessions, email me at laurelei@asteriabooks.com.

Appendix D

SCT Retreats

Coming Soon!

I love organizing and hosting weekend-long getaways with like-minded folks. It's one of my favorite things.

Starting in 2023, I plan to start hosting an annual Spiral Castle retreat close to my home in the Midwestern United States.

Here is a little of what we can expect from such a retreat:
- A recurring event happening each summer
- Open to all "corded" members of the Tradition
- Multiple group rituals
- Opportunity to witness and practice ritual and magickal techniques
- Engaging group discussions for SCT-ers at every level of study
- Special sessions for Initiates at each level
- Bewitching bonfires for dancing, drumming, magick, and more

Please make sure that you download the Thread up so you can stay up-to-date with Spiral Castle Tradition news and events.

Appendix E

In-Person Initiation (3rd Degree)

Some students have asked for an in-person initiatory experience, and I am so ecstatic to be able to offer this amazing weekend-long retreat as a capstone for the full 3 years of study to those who are interested.

<u>Why do an in-person initiation?</u>
The benefits of an initiatory experience under the leadership of an experienced initiator (or initiatory team) include:

- Preservation of the Mysteries of Initiation. This initiation ritual is, by necessity, different from the one offered as a self-initiation at the end of the independent study course. As with all true initiatory experiences, you won't know the exact format or symbols included in the initiation until you undergo the ritual, which preserves the anticipation and heightened awareness that usually accompanies the initiation.

- Symbolically-Rich Ceremony. The language, actions, altar dressings, etc all work together to add many layers of meaning, which provides excellent fodder for reflection and gnosis.

- Safety. Not only am I an experienced ritualist and initiator, I am also CPR certified through the American Red Cross, and I have received training for crisis prevention, management, and intervention.

- Passing of Craft Lineage. We will have worked together (albeit, at a distance) for three years or more. This in-person initiation allows me the opportunity to formally create the bond of mentor and initiator with you. That is an energetic reality that has some potent magical benefits, as attested by magical traditions worldwide.

- Confidence in Your Skills. All initiation has some level of ordeal or trial built into it. You must prove yourself worthy to move into the next stage of spiritual development, to join the group or society. It's difficult to fully and fairly test oneself. In our initiation ritual, though, it is me who is testing you (and the Godds through me). When you have passed those tests, you will never doubt that you really did pass.

- Bonding Within the Tradition. Because there is ordeal (uncertainty, testing, stress) within an initiation, you feel much more connected to your initiator and to any others involved in the process. You are truly part of the Family, and you will know at least a few siblings with whom you have a deep bond.

<u>What is the process?</u>
Our Initiation Weekend will be scheduled in advance. You should start the dialogue with me about 2 months before you would like to take advantage of this opportunity. I'll need to verify your assignments have been satisfactorily completed, and then we'll choose a weekend that is convenient for us both. I'll reserve the cabin

and make arrangements for meals, as well as coordinate with the other members of the initiation team.

I'll provide you with a list of things you need to bring with you. Getting yourself and these few items to the initiation location will be your own responsibility. (I can pick you up from the airport or bus/train station, if you travel from afar. Or I'll give you the address of the cabin, if you are driving.)

We will either be renting a cabin in Southern Indiana or Central Kentucky, depending on availability and your preference. The address and phone number will be provided to you once the arrangements are made.

The experience is a retreat, so we suggest limited phone and social media usage, but the only time we will be incommunicado will be during the prep, ritual, and debrief. No photos or video of the initial ritual will be permitted, of course.

I'll also be getting information from you regarding medications, medical concerns, allergies, etc., as well as providing you with instructions for the preparatory actions you will need to take as we approach the initiation date.

We will be together for 3 days and 2 nights -- Friday afternoon to Sunday afternoon. The team will consist of me and at least one other person. If you wish, you may bring someone with you, but we will need to make arrangements for their meals (at an additional cost), and they will need to vacate the premises for the duration of the initiation ritual (several hours during the night and early morning), unless they are also a Spiral Castle Tradition initiate of at least the same degree.

What is included in the cost?
Due to economic fluctuations, it is no longer possibly to quote the specific fee for the initiation package. (As of Jan. 2023, that cost is $1000, but you will be provided with a more accurate fee when you make arrangements.) The following are included in the package fee:

- Fasting-compliant meals on Friday (lunch and dinner) and Saturday (breakfast and lunch)

- Celebratory feast on Saturday night

- Non-fasting meals on Sunday (breakfast and lunch)

- Vacation-style cabin accommodations -- 2 bedrooms (bedding provided), at least 1 bathroom (linens provided), full kitchen (basic cookware provided), and possibly a hot-tub

- Private (and possibly group) coaching sessions -- at least one each day

- Psychic readings -- at least 2 (one before, one after initiation)

- Initiation cords, regalia, and other items

- Lineage binder

- Framed, signed certificate of initiatory degree

To schedule your initiation weekend, email me at laurelei@asteriabooks.com.

Wait! I changed my mind!

Most RTA students who want to pursue in-person initiation arrange for a mentoring relationship in Year 1, and we start assignment feedback and relationship-building early in their studies. That isn't the only way, though.

If you've come to the end of Year 3 and decided, "I want in-person initiation, after all!" it's not too late to make that happen.

You can compile all your work and send it to me for review, along with the initiation application/request, whenever you're ready. Just be aware that it will take me longer to review that many assignments and make a decision, and also, we'll need a few VOIP (Zoom, Google Meet, Skype, etc) sessions. I need to know you before I spend a weekend with you — before I share with you something so vital in our practice, in our Tradition.

You can share this large group of lessons with me in one of three ways:
- Zip the files together as one large .zip file and email it
- Convert all the files to PDF, merge and compress them into a single file of the smallest size you can manage — and then email them
- Upload all the files into a single folder (see below) and share it with me at laureleiblack@gmail.com on Google Drive

Also, please organize your files so that they appear in numerical order when I open the file/Drive. If you're sharing to Google Drive, use the following org conventions:
1. Create a single folder called RTA Homework—[Your name]
2. Within that folder, create 3 folders titled RTA1 [Your Name], RTA2 [Your Name], RTA3 [Your Name]
3. Place ALL assignments in their correct folder
4. Name the lessons according to their unit number: 01-01 [Your Name], 01-02 [Your Name], etc
5. If a lesson has multiple files (for instance, picture files that aren't embedded into a document, or multiple sections), use the same naming convention above to force Drive to group the pieces together in the order they should be viewed. For example: 01-02 pic 1 [Your Name}, 01-02 pic 2 [Your Name], etc.

If I get confused because one or two pieces are out of place, I will reach out for clarification. If the whole lot is jumbled, though, I'll ask for your to spend a little time cleaning it up so I can find all the pieces. Remember, you need me to see everything.

When I receive your application, I will reach out to start making arrangements. You can contact me through the Thread app or via email at Laurelei@asteriabooks.com if you have questions along the way.

Appendix F

Queen, Devil, or Consort
And
Magister of the Lineage

The Spiral Castle Tradition recognizes that not every Witch sees Witchcraft as a religion. We do not require a Statement of Faith or other adherence to a doctrine of belief in order to be recognized as a Witch of the Spiral Castle.

Simultaneously, we acknowledge that the Spiral Castle Tradition has all the hallmarks of a religious body — including relationship with supernatural forces, shared mythos, sacramental rites, and holy days.

We believe in the power and authority of the individual Witch to perform ALL of the rites and rituals of our Tradition on their own behalf on behalf of their own Family (including their Craft Family), with the exception of those rituals reserved for Queens/Devils/Consorts of the 3rd Degree. Rituals and functions that are open to all Spiral Castle Witches include: Self-Dedication, Self-Initiation, Study Group formation, the Housle, Link-Cutting, private or public Sabbat and Esbat rituals, Rites of Passage (Witching, Puberty, Coming of Age, Handfasting, Handparting, Wisdom, and Crossing rites), as well as the rituals and functions associated with their Services Area(s) as undertaken in the 2nd Degree.

Additionally, Queens/Devils/Consorts (Witches of the 3rd Degree) are invested the power to Dedicate and Initiate others, Charter a Coven, and perform all of our Rites of Passage on behalf of members of the community or general public. We recognize these as the functions and powers of a Queen/Devil/Consort — a teacher, leader, and clergyperson of our Tradition. Those rights and powers are granted by the Witch Mother and Witch Father at the time of the 3rd Degree Initiation — whether administered as a self-initiation or administered by a Magister of the Lineage.

A Witch of the 3rd Degree (a Queen, Devil, or Consort) is considered a "Magister of the Lineage" if they have been initiated to the 3rd Degree directly and in-person by me (Laurelei Black) — or directly and in-person by someone I have initiated as a Queen, Devil, or Consort of the Spiral Castle.

Why does this distinction matter? Well, it honestly doesn't matter to many people. It matters, though, to the members of the "home coven," Coven Caer Sidhe. It matters to me (Laurelei). And it will matter to some of the Witches seeking initiation within this Tradition for reasons that are unique, varied, and personal. From my perspective, there is a bond and sharing of power that happens in the initiation. There is a recognition. There is an intimacy, of sorts. There is also a community or Family "spirit" that is nurtured. And finally, there is a sort of verification that work has been done well and fully. (No shortcuts, no preferential treatment, no shrinking away from the hard places in the path.)

A Magister of the Lineage (or simply "Magister") is provided with the following:
- Lineage documents
- The scripts/outlines of the Rites of Passage and Rites of Admission used by the Home Coven. (These are somewhat different than what has been made available for self-initiation, for both practical and energetic reasons.)
- Admission to the Grand Coven, which is comprised only of Magisters of the Lineage and who meet together for certain workings and also to discuss spiritual and magical issues or questions that arise within the

Tradition.

No Queen, Devil, Consort, or Magister will ever be obligated to form and Charter a Coven. A Magister may practice independently or within a Coven, as they freely choose.

All Queens, Devils, Consorts, and Magisters are considered "ordained" within this Tradition — irrespective of the method of their initiation to the 3rd Degree. Those wishing to solemnize marriages will need to consult the laws and regulations of their State or Territory for details related to this issue. To receive certificates relative to your Degree(s), please contact Laurelei directly.

Appendix G

Coven Charter

In order to run a **recognized** Coven within the Spiral Castle Tradition, you need to receive a Charter from the Grand Coven. This Council is comprised of all of the Magisters of Lineage of the Spiral Castle.

The issuing of Charters isn't based on ideas of control or oversight. We encourage Covens within the Spiral Castle Tradition to operate as they see fit, under their own authority, with the guidance of their Queen/Devil, Consort. We simply want to know and be connected to the People of this Family — this Clannad. (The application form is somewhat involved in order for us to be familiar with structure and culture of your local group.)

In order to be granted a Coven Charter, all of the following requirements must be met:
- File application
- One member of 3rd Degree — Devil/Queen/Consort or Magister
- At least one other chartering member — 1st Degree or higher
- Sign Charter Agreement

The Application for Coven Charter is submitted online at : https://forms.gle/xn8pBEquc42MY2CQ6

It includes the following questions:
- Name and contact info of Queen/Devil/Consort/Magister
- Names and contact info of Chartering Members
- Proposed name of the Coven
- List of Coven officers, their duties, their selection procedure, and their term of office — or other description of Coven organization and administration.
- Description of meeting location(s) for classes, business meetings, rituals, and initiations.
- Description of financial plan for Coven — including dues paid by members, budgeting of monies, planned fundraising activities, and accounting procedures.
- Listing of Coven-procured assets (Coven-owned tools, subscriptions, supplies, etc) and their disposal/distribution in the event of dissolution of the group. (This list should be updated regularly as part of Coven business meetings and included in the minutes of those meetings.)
- Initial/Intended meeting schedule (including special groups or committees — ie, Greening/Orientation, 3rd Degree group, Focus Area groups, etc).
- Process for screening and accepting new Coveners.
- Process for removing Coveners.
- Process for mediating conflicts between Coveners.

- Other notes to describe the nature and character of the Coven, as deemed necessary by the Chartering Members.

Answers can be clarified or revised during the submission and review process.

Upon acceptance of the application by the Grand Coven, the new Coven's Queen/Devil/Consort and Chartering Members will sign the Chartering Agreement and return a copy to the Grand Coven. Upon acknowledged receipt of this signed document by the Grand Coven, the Coven will be fully chartered and recognized as a Coven of the Spiral Castle Tradition.

Coven Charter Agreement

The Charter Agreement that the Founding Queen/Devil/Consort and Chartering Members of each Coven will sign states the following:

- The Coven will always have a Queen/Devil/Consort/Magister as one of its Officers/Organizers.
- Coven will provide an Annual Report to the Grand Coven (membership and activity).
- Coven will notify Grand Coven of changes in Coven leadership right away.
- Coveners must purchase their own copies of the course guides for their study.
- Coveners are encouraged (but not required) to participate with the entire Tradition via SCT online forums and online/in-person gatherings.

Additionally, it states that the Grand Coven will:

- Provide counsel, comfort, and aid to the Coven's leaders and members, when requested.
- Provide opportunities for interaction and fellowship with others in the Clannad.
- Provide an annual epistle regarding the Clannad and its activities, contact details, and changes or updates to the rituals, teachings, and texts of the Tradition.

It is our intention foster healthy, free-flowing communication and the strengthening of Family bonds within the Clannad, while maintaining the autonomy and unique character of each Witch and Coven.

Also by Laurelei Black

Aphrodite's Priestess
Cult of Aphrodite: Rites and Festivals of the Golden One
Temple of Love (fiction)
Crown of Violets: Words and Images Inspired by Aphrodite
Wisdom of Love: Cowrie Divination System

Writing as LM Black

Red Thread Academy — Year 1: Foundations (Course Manual)
Red Thread Academy — Year 2: Practicum (Course Manual)
Red Thread Academy — Year 3: Mastery (Course Manual)
The Witches' Key to the Legion: A Guide to Solomonic Sorcery
Asteria Books' Complete Herbal Grimoire

Writing as Delilah Temple

To Call Ye Forth (Witches' Rune series, Book 1)

Coming Soon

Darksome Night and Shining Moon (Witches' Rune series, Book 2) — Delilah Temple
The Witches' Key to the Unseen World: A Comprehensive Guide to Spirit Work — LM Black
Asteria Events' Guide to Pagan Festival Planning — Laurelei Black
Asteria Mystery School's Digital Lesson Library — LM Black
The Hierodule Handbook (College of the Doves course manual) — Laurelei Black

Thank you for purchasing this book and taking part in the RTA Courses!

Your feedback matters.

Scan the QR code or follow this link to go to the Etsy listing and leave a review. (Or access your Purchases & Reviews in the "Your Account" tab.)

https://www.etsy.com/listing/1380239875/3rd-year-online-interactive-traditional

Reviews on Etsy, Amazon, and even on your own social media accounts help others know if courses like this are the right fit for them.

Please take a moment to let folks know what you have valued about the Red Thread Academy.

Made in the USA
Las Vegas, NV
16 February 2023